PRAISE FOR *TRANS*

"*Transformed* is a truly inspiring story of an abrupt transition to a new land, survival, and perseverance—the definition of the SEAL creed of *never quit*. A descendant of warriors and chieftains from Africa, Remi Adeleke became a warrior and a leader here. America needs to understand why he became the patriot he is and learn from his amazing journey."

—Scott McEwen, #1 *New York Times* bestselling
coauthor, *American Sniper*

"Remi Adeleke is a miraculous mountain of a man. His story is a living testimony to the unfailing love of his Lord and Savior. He is truly transformed in the deepest sense of the word, and his book will have a lasting impact on many souls."

—Kathie Lee Gifford, *Today* cohost, *New York
Times* bestselling author, and friend

"I'm incredibly fortunate to know Remi Adeleke. Proud to say I understand him even more now after reading this book. To know Remi is to know a man of true purpose. It's sometimes easy to fall victim to the false narrative that we can't rise above our station. And yet Remi takes that premise to task in this powerful memoir. It is akin to having an amazingly candid conversation with one of the most formidable and honest human beings you will ever know. He takes the soldier's story and turns it inside out by looking at how his incredible past gave way to his present.

"*Transformed* is a uniquely familiar story. I laughed, cried, and celebrated Remi's successes as if they were my own. From the streets to a Navy SEAL, his raw and harrowing journey of hope and inspiration left me absolutely speechless!"

—Corey Hawkins, lead actor, *Straight Outta Compton,
Kong Skull Island*, and *6 Underground*

"This book is more powerful than I could have imagined! *Transformed* is less about invincible, somewhat mysterious supersoldiers and more about very flawed, vulnerable, yet courageous men, a strong story about the trial and error of the human spirit. Remi Adeleke has written a personal timeline of redemption and faith, and I am truly blown away and humbled by his story."

—Neil Brown Jr., lead actor, *SEAL Team*, CBS, and *Insecure*, HBO

"Remi and I developed a unique bond while working overseas together. As I mentored him in his career as a SEAL, his faith, and his pursuit to be a dedicated husband and father, I was blessed to hear his story of transformation firsthand and be a part of his continued transformation. *Transformed* is a masterful display of the good, bad, and ugly that life tends to throw our way. In this book you see how overcoming adversity became a normal way of life for Remi and, equally important, how you can mimic Remi's attributes to overcome the odds in your life."

—Joe Kuhns, Navy SEAL Senior Chief, retired

"From riches to rags to *true* riches, *Transformed* is the epitome of perseverance and triumph. We may all navigate life's journey differently, but if you look closely, you just may find a Common Denominator."

—Gene "No Malice" Thornton

"Stripped of his birthright in Nigeria and thrust into the Bronx, fatherless and without a penny to his name, it's not hyperbole to call Remi Adeleke the product of one miracle after another. Aptly titled, *Transformed* is the incredible true story of a warrior's brokenness and long road to redemption—the kid from the Bronx who couldn't swim who became a sailor, the sailor who became a Navy SEAL. It is one of my greatest joys to call this man my friend."

—Cody Gifford

"I met Remi Adeleke at the Lee Strasberg Theatre and Film Institute as a student in my acting class. Remi has a quality that no one can teach. Star quality. He is a profoundly gifted actor. His work is riveting. His depth of understanding character and bringing it to life is breathtaking.

"I did not anticipate that Remi's gift as an actor would translate into writing his life story, which is equally riveting. There are many heroes in his story; most of them are women, including his wonderful mother, grandmother, Aunt Dokey, Navy recruiter Petty Officer Reyes, HM2 Brown, Cecilia, Nia, and his wife. It took these strong women to bring this extraordinary man to where he is today.

"I loved this book. Remi's life and personal triumphs are gripping. I could not put it down. If you want to learn what it means to never give up under any circumstances, you must read *Transformed*. Remi scaled the highest mountains. See how he did it."

—M. J. Karmi, Lee Strasberg Theatre and Film Institute

"In *Transformed* Remi Adeleke lays out the entire mosaic of his life and doing just what the title promises: showing true transformation. This book is great!"

—Nate Bobbett, LD Entertainment

"Want to learn from the best? Someone with a wealth of experience and who is always committed to using his life to help others? Then this book about Remi Adeleke's journey through life is a must-read."

—Ivica J. Hudika, Navy SEAL Senior Chief, retired

"Remi Adeleke's ability to explore the *why* then focus on the *what* is riveting as *Transformed* screams out, 'A failure is only a failure if you don't learn from it.' At Saint Mary's our program has been transformed, thanks to Remi for his ability to reshape and define exactly what it takes to be the best you can possibly be at all times."

—Tim O'Brien, Hall of Famer and head rugby coach, Saint Mary's College of California

"Remi Adeleke's transformation story is awe inspiring for anyone who has a dream. His remarkable achievement of goals set throughout his life—when most people would have given up or never would have dared to dream—is what makes *Transformed* different from other books. From a young boy in Africa to a troubled teen in the Bronx, Remi moves through each phase of life with great difficulty, but he *never quits*. Between his never-quit attitude and his strong family and spiritual bonds, he figures out his life. I recommend you go on this journey with Remi by reading this book and getting to know what makes him special among a group of special operators: the Navy SEALs."

—Stew Smith, Navy SEAL veteran, fitness trainer, and author

"Remi Adeleke is the real deal. His story will humble you, inspire you, and compel you to be better today than you were yesterday. I was blessed to have gone through SEAL training with Remi and to have struggled with the same aspects of training. His support, upbeat attitude, and unwavering commitment to lift up others was invaluable to me in some of the most challenging moments of my life. Watching him grow into the man he is today has been an absolute joy. If you have been knocked down by life, *Transformed* will teach you how to get back up."

—Nick Hays, former Navy SEAL, Harvard Business School alumnus, author, and speaker

TRANSFORMED

TRANSFORMED

A NAVY SEAL'S UNLIKELY JOURNEY FROM
THE THRONE OF AFRICA, TO THE STREETS
OF THE BRONX, TO DEFYING ALL ODDS

REMI ADELEKE

W PUBLISHING GROUP

AN IMPRINT OF THOMAS NELSON

Published in Nashville, Tennessee, by W Publishing Group, an imprint of Thomas Nelson.

Thomas Nelson titles may be purchased in bulk for educational, business, fund-raising, or sales promotional use. For information, please e-mail SpecialMarkets@ThomasNelson.com.

ISBN 978-0-7852-4166-9 (TP)

Library of Congress Cataloging-in-Publication Data

Names: Adeleke, Remi, 1982-
Title: Transformed: a Navy SEAL's unlikely journey from the throne of Africa, to the streets of the Bronx, to defying all odds / Remi Adeleke.
Other titles: Transformed: a Navy SEAL's unlikely journey from the throne of Africa, to the streets of the Bronx, to defying all odds | A Navy SEAL's unlikely journey from the throne of Africa, to the streets of the Bronx, to defying all odds
Description: Nashville, Tennessee: W Publishing Group, [2019] | Includes bibliographical references. |
Identifiers: LCCN 2018032873 (print) | LCCN 2018038967 (ebook) | ISBN 9780785219743 (E-book) | ISBN 9780785219767 (hardcover)
Subjects: LCSH: United States. Navy. SEALs—Biography. | United States. Navy. SEALs—Military life. | United States. Navy—African Americans—Biography. Special operations (Military science)—United States. | Nigerian Americans—Biography. | Yoruba (African people)—Nigeria—Lagos—Kings and rulers—Biography. | Lagos (Nigeria)—Biography. | Coming of age. | Bronx (New York, N.Y.)—Biography.
Classification: LCC UA34.S64 (ebook) | LCC UA34.S64 A34 2019 (print) | DDC 359.9/84 [B] —dc23
LC record available at https://lccn.loc.gov/2018032873

Printed in the United States of America

21 22 23 24 25 26 LSC 8 7 6 5 4 3 2 1

I dedicate this book to my sons, Cayden, Caleb, and Carter; my daughter, Ciana; my nephews, Seth, Sebastian, John, and Muhammed-Ali; my niece, Zainab; and to all future Adeleke generations. May you take all my mistakes and use them as lessons. May you learn from my achievements and know that because of the faith of your ancestors and the DNA that runs through your veins, you have the ability to achieve even greater things than I have.

CONTENTS

CONTENTS

CHAPTER ONE

FALSE KINGDOM

*It's easy to do the wrong thing; it's
hard to do the right thing.*

I *need a lot of money fast if I'm going to bring my dream to fruition*, I thought to myself as I made my way to my office cubicle and started making cold calls. The year was 2001, and I was in my second month at WCT, a mobile phone sales company. I knew I was in the right business. I was confident in my abilities and determined to make it. Yet the road to success and fortune started out very slow.

"No, *fool*, I don't need a phone; I'm on one now!" a potential client yelled at me.

"Yes, ma'am, I understand," I replied with a slight hint of agitation. "But you gotta hear me out. I'm talking about a *mobile flip phone*, the Motorola StarTAC. You can take it anywhere with you. And check this out: it's small enough to fit in your wallet. Not just your purse, your *wallet*."

"Ooooh, are you talking about that Tic Tac–looking phone that's in all the new music videos?" she replied.

"Yeaaahhh—um, excuse me, *yes, ma'am*. Think about it: You want to go on a date with that dude in your building. You don't want to bring that big purse, but you do have a hot pink Baby Phat wallet that would look nice with your dress—"

She cut me off. "I don't like hot pink, but you're right, I do have a Baby Phat wallet that would look good with—"

"Exactly!" I saw that I might have her sold. "Yes. *That* phone will fit in *that* wallet, which will go with that dress you like. So we can start the process right now, and I can have your phone to you by the end of the day. How's that sound?"

Her tone changed. "Hold up! Isn't that phone five hundred dollars? I can't afford that!"

"You're right; it is. But if you're willing to make the purchase right now—because I like you—I'll waive the cost of the phone. But only if you sign up for a two-year contract."

I was lying. Even if she did have the money, the phone would be free with a two-year activation. I just needed the golden three—full name, Social Security number, and date of birth—and then I could make her believe her dream phone would be hers for free. This tactic almost always worked.

"You would do that for me?" she asked.

"Only if you purchase now," I said.

"Okay, I'll take it. Sign me up."

"Great. I'll need your Social Security number, date of birth, full name, address, and current phone number. I'll also need a copy of your driver's license. Let me give you my fax number."

"Why do you need all that? I'm just signing up for a phone, not the CIA!"

Laughing through my reply, I said, "I understand, but I need it so I can run your credit. To activate your account, a line of credit must be open, and in order for a line of credit to be open, you gotta have good credit." I added cautiously and slowly, "Which I'm sure you do?"

"Why would you get all my hopes up only to tell me I can't get the phone I want!" she yelled.

"Um, miss, I never said you can't get the—"

"My credit is jacked up!" She hung up.

Ahhhhhh, I wasted so much time on that damn call. I'm not gonna make my quota again this month! I said to myself. I stared at my call list in dejection while slowly rubbing the top of my head, trying to figure out my next steps.

Unbeknownst to me, Frank, one of the office's top salesmen, had been across the hall in his cubicle, paying attention to the entire exchange.

"Hey, Remi, come here," Frank said.

I got up, frustrated, but made my way over as if nothing bad had just happened.

He got straight to the point. "Look, man, I'm going to help you out . . . but you gotta keep your mouth shut and just follow the program."

The man had my attention. "No problem. You have my word," I told him, and he proceeded to give me the keys to his success.

Frank explained to me how he used illegally acquired personal information (full name, date of birth, Social Security number) from previous clients and other sources to activate phones. I was shocked, and clueless as to why he trusted me enough to tell me about his scheme. I guess he figured I was so desperate for a sale that I wouldn't snitch. Desperation does tend to make one overlook protocol.

"With one person's personal information—and depending on their credit score—you can activate up to three cell phone lines. As you know, the phones are either free upon activation or charged to their line of credit, depending on the phone model."

I whispered, "Yes, I know all that. So you're telling me you're stealing people's credit and then activating phones?" I had carried out illegal activities in the past, but this was a stretch even for me. "Damn, that's cold-blooded."

Frank gestured to keep my voice down. "Cold-blooded pays my bills, puts food on the table for my kids, and keeps my wife happy. This company doesn't care about you, and it doesn't care about me, so yes, I'm cold blooded. Now, you have a choice: you can keep struggling through cold calls, or you can be the same."

His point struck a nerve. "Sorry. I don't mean any disrespect, but this is just crazy to me." Still in shock I said, "Okay, so what do you do after you activate the phones?"

"Over the years of being here, I've developed a network of people I sell to—"

"So let me get this straight. You activate phones, get a sales commission for the activation, then sell it for a profit on the streets?"

"Yes," he replied.

"Wow!" I said, still in a state of disbelief.

"I started out with family and friends I trust and know. I don't sell to anyone unless they come highly recommended by a known and trusted client. And even then, I sell the phones through the trusted client to them. If the new client snitches, I'm unidentifiable. And I only deal in cash!"

The more he explained, the more the wheels began to turn in my head. I could sell phones for cash on the street, make a commission from the company for selling those phones, and not have to make any more cold calls. The amount of time I spent trying to find sales could be spent on my music and the music company I was trying to establish. I'd make hundreds—no, thousands—of dollars! My shock began to turn into curiosity.

"After three months, WCT will cut off the phones because payments haven't been made by the 'client,'" Frank continued. "The account will be sent into delinquency, then collections. My clients don't have to deal with any of the fallout because the phones aren't in their names. So after the phones are cut off, they simply throw them in the trash, then come running back to me for a new three-hundred-dollar phone with unlimited calls for three months."

"And you've never been caught?" I asked.

"Nope. As long as I have a copy of their photo ID and a 'signature,' that's enough to deny that I activated the phone illegally. I can just shift the blame to an anonymous family member who stole their poor uncle's credit because they wanted a phone. We're totally protected."

Frank had created an enterprise within an enterprise.

I got up to return to my cubicle, my mind racing.

"Fed time," Frank said. He leveled a grave stare at me.

"What?"

"You get caught, you're going straight to federal prison. *Be smart* and keep your mouth shut about this. This conversation never happened."

That would be the only time Frank and I ever discussed what I would later call "my hustle."

I walked slowly back to my desk in complete disbelief and deep contemplation. The idea was crazy but would solve all my financial problems. I could move out of my mom's apartment, get a car, invest in my record company, and be somebody. No more struggling! And once I achieved all my goals, I'd go straight. This solution would be temporary.

Imma do it!

I immediately started my enterprise, using personal information from previous clients, which I had easy access to, and selling to friends I trusted. It was amazing, kinda like magic! One minute I was cold-calling and struggling to make a sale, and the next minute I was getting calls from friends and associates of friends, all asking for multiple phones. In the first week I rang up $4,000 in illegal sales and their commissions. I had never seen that much money in my life. It was like I couldn't stop the cash from coming in. Yes, at times my conscience bothered me, but I buried the guilt deep within me and kept my eyes on my goal: get out of the Bronx and *be somebody*.

• • •

One day a client reached out to me and said he had a friend who wanted to purchase some phones. We set the meeting location at the White Castle parking lot off Fordham Road, across the street from Fordham University. I pulled up in my Silver 2001 Lincoln LS, which I had recently purchased with funds from my hustle.

When I stepped out of the car, the new client immediately recognized me. "Yo, Remi!" He pointed to me and said to his friend, "I went to high school with this cat!"

As soon as the guy said "high school," I remembered who he was. Taj. We had a few classes together.

I was relieved. Why? Because I knew he was too young to be an undercover cop and too street to join the NYPD. He embraced me with a hand slap and a hug, joked around for a bit, and then we got down to business. I handed him four boxes, three containing a phone with its accessories. "New StarTACs, Tic Tac phones. These are legit."

"Yessir!" I replied.

Referring to the fourth box, he asked, "What's this? Timeport? This is the new two-way that Jay-Z rapped about!"

The Timeport was a new flip-up texting device. It resembled a mini laptop with a keypad and multidirectional control, and it came in two colors: black and the unforgettable Space Grey. The device also served as a pager and organizer. Thanks to the hip-hop community, which featured the device in a host of music videos, *everyone* wanted one, especially the Space Grey. This coveted device would triple my profits.

Inspecting the box with delight, he said, "I didn't ask for it."

"I know you didn't. I just brought it to let you know I'm carrying them. Everyone is buying them up, so I figured—"

"How much?"

"Since you're buying the three phones, I'll throw the pager in for two fifty."

"If everything checks out, I'll take it." He turned on the four devices to test them, went through all the functions, made calls and sent texts, then slipped me the cash.

After our transaction he said, "It's good seeing you. If you ever need anything, hit me up."

An idea struck me. I had come to the realization that using previous clients' personal information could backfire because my activation credentials were attached to it. Frank said I was protected, but my street smarts led me to realize I needed another layer of protection.

I said, "Actually, if you ever come across someone that has access to Socials, dates of birth, full names, and copies of driver's licenses, let me know."

"Do I! My girlfriend works at a hospice nursing clinic. I can get you an unlimited supply of that information. People are always rotating in and out. I mean . . . dying."

"How much?"

"Hundred dollars a sheet. Each sheet contains information on five patients," Taj said.

"Done deal! Let's connect later this week. I'll bring the cash, you bring the documents."

Before the week was up, we were off and running. It was just what I needed. Each ID activated three phones, and each phone sold for $300, which meant each sheet netted me $4,400! And that didn't include the commission I got for activating the phones. To me, drug money wasn't anything compared to this. And because of the weak monitoring of the industry, the risk was extremely low.

Soon I was competing with Frank for salesman of the month. My confidence increased, my commissions grew, and I was in a position to buy whatever I wanted. I was selling the illegal phones, which I started calling "blow-up phones," and the Timeport pagers for $200 to $400 apiece, depending on the model. The price was steep, but with the high cost of cell phone service, and the then nonexistent unlimited plans, it was a great bargain for three months of unlimited service. But despite all the cash I was bringing in, my thirst for more money, power, and respect was insatiable.

Now that I had a new and unlimited supply of personal information, I needed to expand my client base. I couldn't risk selling the blow-ups to random people who could possibly snitch or potentially be undercover. I needed a stable pool.

Through my network, I eventually met a couple of drug dealers from the east side of the Bronx. Because of their illegal activity, drug dealers were always trying to stay one step ahead of the police. And having participated in the same activity in the past, I knew they would be the perfect clients to partner with. The popularity of cell phones for drug dealers was enormous at that time. Compared to current cell phones, the technology was archaic, and the dealers' activities were not as traceable as they are today. I was able to build up a favorable following and reputation with them.

One particular dealer named Devan loved my product. I can't remember how we met, but we struck up a partnership immediately.

"Remi!" Devan said as he knocked on my passenger-side window. Per our arrangement, I'd parked on Holland Avenue.

I unlocked my doors, and he scurried in to escape the winter cold.

"What up?" I said.

"What you got for me?"

"The usual: six phones, two pagers, no boxes." I handed him the blow-ups, and he handed me the cash. Our meetings were always brief and to the point, so I expected him to leave, but he didn't.

Devan hit the automatic lock switch and said, "I think we can do some good business together and make some serious money."

"We're already doing business. What more can I do for you?" I replied.

"Buying a couple here and a couple there isn't enough. I need bigger orders. If I were to place bigger orders, could you fill them for me?"

"How big?" I asked.

"Say, twenty to twenty-five," Devan replied.

I had been trying to sell no more than twenty a week just to be safe. I could have sold more, but I was trying to be smart about it. I had a process that was working and had proven to be safe. If I sold that many phones to one person, I'd have to stop selling to other individuals.

I sighed, then said, "That's a lot that you're asking for. It would change a lot on my end." He didn't respond or give me any expression of disappointment. It was as though he knew I was open to it and was just waiting for me to say yes. I thought further. I hadn't been caught, and it wasn't like I'd be supplying him with twenty to twenty-five every week. I decided I could work it out.

"Let's do it. I'm in it to win it! When do you want to start?" I asked.

A smile crept across his face. "I'll shoot you a call next week with the exact number I need. This is going to be good!"

As Devan got out of the car, I immediately regretted my decision. My strategy had been working, and I let him change my strategy. As I drove away I said to myself, *You done went off and messed everything up, Remi!*

I knew two things: one, Devan didn't care about me, and two, he wanted those phones so that he could—like most of the other hustlers I sold to—flip them for a greater profit. But the weeks passed, and the cash poured in for both of us.

Late one evening, after about two months of mutually satisfying business transactions, I received a call from Devan. He cursed me in his native Jamaican dialect without telling me what was wrong. Devan ended the call by saying, "I'm on my way to your apartment."

I knew this wasn't good. Devan never talked to me like that, and he usually gave me a two- to three-day notice before meeting. Something must have happened. I paced around my mom's apartment, wondering what it could be. After about thirty minutes I stood in front of the living room window, watching for his white Chrysler to pull up. As I stared out the window, I could see the Christmas lights that decorated the other apartments in the complex. For the past few months I had been living like every day was Christmas, and now I worried my end might potentially come during the time of Christmas.

About an hour later Devan's Chrysler pulled up to my building. The five-foot-six Jamaican stepped out of his vehicle in the big North Face bubble jacket he always wore. As he walked toward the building, I thought back to that day when I agreed to sell him blow-ups in bulk: *Why did I agree to it? I'm such a fool.*

Two minutes later the doorbell rang. As I walked slowly to the door, I thought two things: something wasn't right with this dude, and, whatever it was, I hoped it wasn't *too* wrong because my mom was asleep in the other room. Whatever I did, I wasn't going to let him into the apartment.

I got to the door, looked through the peephole to make sure he didn't have a gun ready to drill me, took a deep breath, then turned the knob. As the door passed from right to left, his perturbed face slowly appeared. He was wearing his typical baggy blue jeans. His dark blue bubble jacket was big enough to conceal a weapon. His demeanor in person matched his demeanor on the phone. I had never seen him stare at me with such disdain and anger. There was an uncharacteristic iciness to his eyes and aggressiveness in his posture. I brushed off my instincts and tried to play it cool.

"Yo, what's the deal . . . you need some more phones? It's kind of late, but I can have some for you by tomorrow afternoon." My voice echoed in the third-floor hallway.

In his strong Jamaican accent, he said, "The phones that you sold me, all of them cut off."

This was a huge problem because I had just sold him that last batch two weeks earlier. I was also worried because this meant that someone at WCT might have caught on to my hustle. And if that was the case, like Frank told me, I was looking at fed time! With all those thoughts going through my mind, I almost wanted the dude to put me out of my misery.

He spoke briefly and more calmly than I expected. "I like you, and because I like you, I'm going to do you a favor. I'm going to give you one week, and if you don't have my money by next week, things are not going to go well for you." I believe that was his nice way of saying, "I'm going to kill you."

After Devan's brief monologue, he turned around and walked to the elevator. I kept the door open, just waiting to hear him say something else, something that would ease my mind, but he didn't. All I heard was the elevator door open, then close, and a slight buzzing from the hallway light above me.

I knew Devan would see his threat through. What made the situation even worse was the fact that he had threatened me in my mom's house, a few feet from where she slept. I was confronted with a huge wake-up call.

The next day I did what I had to do to get Devan his money. I had some cash from previous sales, so between that and a few sales that day, I had the total payoff in less than twenty-four hours. I gave Devan a call to set a meeting time. We decided to meet at the intersection of Fordham Road and University Avenue at eight that night.

Because we were meeting in my neighborhood, there was a lot less stress on my end. As I waited on the corner, I said to myself, *This is it. I'm done with this dude for the rest of my life, and I'm done with this hustle. I don't know what I'm going to do, but I'm not doing this.*

His car pulled up behind mine right at eight. Looking through my rear-view mirror, I could see he was alone, which was good. We both got out of our cars at the same time. As I approached, I noticed he looked as happy and jubilant as he did during our usual transactions.

"Remi, what up, man? That was quick," Devan said.

I handed him the money. "Yeah, it's no big deal. I sold you a product, it didn't work, and here's your money. You shouldn't have to wait for it."

As he counted out the seventy-five hundred, he said, "You the man. That's why I like working with you."

"I'm done, man," I said.

"What? Don't let how I was yesterday stop what we got going."

"Nah. It's not that. Your phones cut off early. That shouldn't have happened. If they cut off early, someone may be on to me. And if they're on to me, I can't guarantee the phones will stay on for ninety days anymore. It's a wrap. You got your money. I'm done."

I could tell he wasn't happy that it was the end, but being who he was, he probably knew it was the right decision to shut down the operation.

"Peace, Remi. You're a stand-up dude."

But I knew I wasn't. I was a cold-blooded dude who might get what he deserved. That was the last time I ever saw Devan.

In my naive mind I figured that if I resigned before my scheme was revealed, the company couldn't touch me. But if I was caught and fired, they'd be able to charge me with fraud. I don't know how I came up with that notion, but resignation seemed like my only way out of the mess. My mom wondered why I was quitting, and I just told her, "It's too much drama going on there that I don't want to get involved with. I think it's best that I leave." She was baffled, partly because she had no clue what was going on, but she helped me write a professional resignation and thank-you letter anyway. After the letter was complete, I put on my slacks, white collared shirt, and tie, and headed to my car to make the drive from the Bronx to Midtown Manhattan.

The first time I walked into that big building on the East Side, I took a packed 4 train from Fordham Road to Grand Central Station. This time I was riding up Park Avenue in my Lincoln LS. On my first train ride I was excited about the opportunity to make clean money, enough to invest in my music company. This time I was dejected and wondering if I would walk in a free man and walk out in handcuffs.

I pulled into the building's parking lot as usual.

"Twenty dollars an hour," the parking attendant said as I pulled in.

"Damn, man, twenty dollars? I'll just be parked here for fifteen minutes," I replied.

"Fifteen minutes or an hour, it's still twenty dollars."

Before that day I'd never questioned the parking attendant. But now it finally set in that my cash flow had been cut off. Once the remainder of my money was gone, it was gone.

Full of trepidation, I walked into the big building with the Sam Cooke song "A Change Is Gonna Come" playing in my head. I stared at everyone with suspicion. *Is that dude FBI? What about her: is she an undercover? Will there be a bunch of undercovers waiting outside the elevator when I arrive on the twenty-eighth floor?* My palms were sweaty, and my heart was pounding as I passed the first security guard. I swiped my key pass and proceeded to the elevator. No one had stopped me yet, but I figured it was coming. I stepped into the elevator, turned around, and faced my vague reflection in the elevator door, as I had done many times in the past. I was about to fix my tie but decided, *Who cares? When I get thrown to the ground and patted down, nobody's going to care what my tie looks like.*

Ding. The elevator door opened to the twenty-eighth floor. As I stepped out of the elevator, I paused and looked around. No feds, no undercovers, at least from what I could see. Still, my heart was pounding out of my chest as I anticipated a group of twenty feds jumping out and shouting, "We got ya!"

I walked past my cubicle and Frank's. He wasn't there, but I had a good idea of what he was doing. I made it to my manager's office and knocked on her door.

"Hey, Remi! There's my young star sales rep!" she said. "What can I do for you?" Again, I was a bit relieved.

"I'm sorry, Ms. Green, but I'm resigning." I handed her my resignation letter.

"What? Why? You're doing so well here. You're making so much money! *Why?*"

Because I wasn't expecting that type of welcome, it hadn't crossed my mind to think of an excuse as to why I was resigning, so I had to come up with something fast! To stall, I acted as if I was ashamed, then said, "I got a better offer for a higher commission and salary from a cell phone company in New Jersey. It's a better opportunity for my mom and me. I don't want to leave, but the extra pay will help us out tremendously. As I stated in the letter, I appreciate you for hiring me and giving me the opportunity. I've learned so much here."

With watery eyes, Ms. Green said, "Remi, I totally understand. You have to do what's best for you and your family. We're definitely going to miss you around here."

"I'm going to miss it around here too," I replied.

We exchanged hugs; then I made my way back to the elevator with the thought still in my mind. *Here it comes. She's in on the whole thing; she was just acting like she doesn't know. She was probably wearing a wire. As soon as you get downstairs, they're all going to be waiting to wrap you up.* But when I got down to the lobby, it was as calm as it had always been. I ran to my car, paid the parking attendant the twenty bucks, and raced away as if a hundred people were chasing me.

When I was a child, spankings for me were almost a daily occurrence. That negative, gut-wrenching experience with Devan and WCT was a proverbial spanking. Though the money was intoxicating, the scare was all I needed to give it up. I got a glimpse of the potential consequences of my actions—death or imprisonment. I had jeopardized the life of my mother as well as myself. My world could have been completely shattered.

Yes, I was relieved when my resignation was accepted by WCT without a lot of questions, but a constant cloud of fear hovered over me after that. Would I get tracked down from my illegal use of personal information? Would the FBI knock on my mother's door at any hour and arrest me? What lie could I pull out of my hat to explain my actions to my mother? Though I wasn't locked up physically, I was locked up psychologically.

For the next six months I sat at home and did nothing but wonder how my life had gotten to where it was.

CHAPTER TWO

ROYAL SON

My priority is my people.
—JOHN ADEBAYO ADELEKE

As I lay in bed, I heard what sounded like multiple instruments playing downstairs. I picked up my head and turned to my right to see if my older brother, Bayo, was still asleep; he was. After slowly creeping out of bed, I made my way into a small room connected to ours. It was our live-in nanny, Jane's, room.

"Jane . . . Jane," I whispered. There was no answer. She was fast asleep. I saw my chance. Almost every weekend my parents would host lavish parties on our Victoria Island estate in Nigeria.

Located on the west coast of Africa, V.I., as Nigerians call it, was and is one of the most expensive places to live in Nigeria, comparable to New York's Hamptons. At my parents' parties, expatriates from France, Bulgaria, Lebanon, India, Italy, Canada, and the UK would socialize, talk about hot topics, and dance the night away as a live jazz band played.

I, being five and the more mischievous brother, made it a habit to try to sneak down to the party every weekend. My goal was to get to my dad as fast as I could. He didn't mind me hanging out for a bit; he found it funny. My mother and Jane, on the other hand, weren't too fond of my game.

I crept down the hallway in my one-piece pajama suit, stopping and hugging the wall at any sound I thought I heard coming from the second floor. The music and laughter got louder as I got closer to the staircase. I went by my parents' master suite and approached the room I always dreaded passing at night. I called it the Skeletor Room. My dad loved art so much that he had amassed a vast collection. The Skeletor Room was filled with Nigerian and Beninese art, such as Ibeji sculptures, carved ivory masks, copper masks, Benin Bronzes, beaded Yoruba crowns, Gelede masks, and sixteenth-century Yoruba armlets. The masks and life-size head statues scared me. It was almost as though they were staring into my soul, and at times I could swear I saw them move.

I closed my eyes and ran past the open room. When I was sure I was safe, I opened my eyes and found myself by the first landing of the U-shaped floating staircase.

I knelt to peek down into the oversize living room. My eyes grew large. There had to be at least twenty people in my view. A band was positioned around our baby grand piano, and our manservant, Fredrick; maid, Fehin; and driver, Felix, walked around with platters of drinks and hors d'oeuvres.

I scanned the crowd, looking for my mom. I couldn't let her see me first.

"Mum," I whispered when I spotted her. She was mingling with a group of women by the floor-to-ceiling bookcase.

Now that I knew my mom's position, I had to find my dad so I could beeline to him. I looked and looked but couldn't find him. Then I heard his unforgettable laugh, followed by his thick British accent. I looked straight down, and there he was, right below the second platform of the staircase, talking with a group of men.

I ran down the steps, hoping my mom wouldn't see me before I got to him. I must have run too fast, and the color of my pj's must have been too bright, because before I got to my dad, I heard, "Remi! Remi!" My mom started to make her way toward the staircase. I kept running down the steps, and when I got to the bottom, I clutched my father's leg and wouldn't let go.

"Remi," my father said enthusiastically. I didn't respond. I just held on tight with my eyes closed.

A European man asked, "I take it that this is your son, Chief?"

My father was Chief Adebayo Adeleke of the Yoruba tribe. He was the first son born to my grandfather, who, devout in his Muslim faith and customary to the time, had many wives. Being the firstborn son of a chief, my father was marked as special, but he lived up to his given status at an early age.

Dad had an uncanny gift of memorization. Whatever was put in front of him, whether the Koran at his Islamic elementary school, or a language, or a common book, he would quickly memorize it. Before the age of ten, he spoke and read fluently in both English and his tribal language, Yoruba. He also spoke and wrote fluently in two other prominent Nigerian languages, Hausa and Igbo. The guy was a savant.

My grandfather died when my father was twelve, so he and my grandmother moved to the southwestern region of Nigeria to be close to her family. The move would change the trajectory of Chief's educational path.

At the time, Christian missionaries permeated the southern region of Nigeria and provided free education. Muslim clerics and Islamic-centric studies were replaced with Christian missionaries, biblical studies, English literature, world history, math, and science. My father's intellectual gifts became evident as he easily recited chapters of the Bible with an encyclopedic memory and dazzled his teachers by excelling in all subjects, especially mathematics and science. In gratitude to the missionaries for the education they provided him, Dad legally adopted a new first name, John.

After completing the US equivalent of high school, Dad received a full-ride scholarship to the University of London, where he obtained his degree in civil engineering (MICE). He also earned degrees in architecture and business.

When he returned to Lagos, years after completing his studies abroad and attaining great success in the West, he was endowed with the title of Chief, a hereditary title for descendants of Yoruba royal lineage.

As the seventies approached, my father had created a vast enterprise that operated out of the Western House building in Lagos. His businesses consisted of an insurance company, a civil engineering company called City Property Development Ltd., and two car dealerships. His office also served as the headquarters for the World Trade Center of Nigeria (of which Chief was president), as well as the base of operations for one of his most passionate endeavors, the Lagoon Development Project.

Chief wielded enormous power and wealth, not just nationally but internationally. In the 1970s he served on the board of the World Teleport Association in London. That feat was historic for a black man at that time. Equally if not more historic was the fact that he also served on the New York World Trade Center board for many years—a man from "the bush" on a board with the elite of the elite. As one family friend would put it, "Chief was never restricted by where he came from."

As I clutched Chief's leg, my dad looked at the European man and said proudly with a smile, "This is my son Remi!" Then he turned his attention to my mother, who was quickly approaching, and said, "And this is his . . . perhaps . . . not so happy mum."

"Dad, I want to stay," I said.

He looked down and said, "I'll see what I can do."

My mom, who was a born-and-raised New Yorker, approached Chief and gave a courteous smile to the European guy, which prompted him to walk away. She pointed down to me as she looked at Chief and said, "John."

He replied with a smile, "Madam."

"Remi knows what he's doing," she said.

Chief switched from his British accent to a Nigerian-English pidgin dialect and said, "It is okay. Let the boy enjoy the festivities with us."

Fighting back a smile, Mom said again, "John."

Dad continued, "I will give him five minutes amongst our friends. Then I will send him up."

Mom couldn't help but chuckle and then capitulate. "Five minutes, Remi."

Chief paraded me around the party for a whole five minutes. In that time Mom must have awakened Jane because she was on the second landing of the stairs, waiting for me when my time was up. I could tell she wasn't happy, not just because this wasn't the first time I had snuck down but because she was in her nightgown with no makeup around a group of rather dapper individuals. Jane took me by the hand, marched me right back to my room, and watched me until she was certain that I had fallen asleep.

• • •

May 1, 1981

We feel grateful to His Excellency for allocating the Lagoon development and can assure him that our plans will bring credit not only to us, but to Lagos and to His Excellency. We also feel honoured by this allocation because it is one of the rarest opportunities ever afforded to private enterprise in Nigeria. Needless to say, we feel that this is a challenge worthy of our organization and we will strive our utmost to live up to the trust placed in us.

Chief Adebayo Adeleke

This excerpt is from a letter Chief wrote to the Lagos State Government after he won a land dispute case. Years earlier, Chief had spent millions of dollars of his own money to buy a large area of V.I. called Maroko. His plan was to build a residential and commercial complex. He had a vision of Nigeria rising above the stereotype of a third-world country and being a beacon of innovation to the rest of Africa and the world.

Unfortunately the Lagos State military regime led by Lateef Jakande decided no one man should have so much power. They stripped Maroko from my father without returning a penny, and a court battle ensued. In 1981, four years after his money and land were stolen, the courts decided to settle, hence the above excerpt.

The settlement was simple. The Lagosian government asked my father what he wanted for compensation: land or money? Equipped with a stellar intelligence and an engineering background, his answer was short.

"I want the part of Lagos Lagoon that sits at the northeast corner of Ikoyi."

They thought he was mad! "What will this man do with a body of wata?" they said in pidgin. "He is a fool! The man wants wata!"

Even Chief's close friends respectfully questioned his decision. "You're giving up millions of dollars for *what*? It's wata! How are you going to build on wata? Who does that? It's 1981, not 2050!"

But the government didn't know my father, and his friends probably didn't know how far he was willing to go to make Nigeria what he knew it could be. You must understand, among the many gifts Chief possessed, he also had this ability to see a way in matters when everyone else said, "There is absolutely no way!" And in the case of the "wata," he saw a way as clear as day. He named his vision the Lagoon Development Project.

Chief spent another few million to hire the Westminster Dredging Company. Westminster was known for constructing man-made islands, using massive amounts of sand to form land. It was similar to the process used to build part of Ellis Island in New York and hundreds of other locations around the world. At the time, the Dutch were masters of the technique. Their sole responsibility for the next few years would be to dredge the Ikoyi foreshore and create six interlinked and symmetrical islands in the space that was allocated to Chief.

While the islands were being created, Chief signed joint ventures with fast-food restaurants (including McDonald's), London's Marks & Spencer retail shop, the Waterfront restaurant chain, and Disney. He hired his good friend Minoru Yamasaki, the architect of New York City's World Trade Center, to work alongside him in designing the Lagoon City Twin Towers. And he supported and befriended Nigerian artists, assuring them that their artistic contributions would be highlighted in a spectacular museum that would be built on the islands. This is one man, mind you, in the 1980s. And he spent a good chunk of money on this before 1982, the year I was born.

My mom will tell you that she and my dad rarely had a disagreement. I personally never witnessed one, but the enormous spending became a great concern for her and led to their biggest point of contention. Her inclinations were quite understandable. Chief had been dumping everything he had into the Lagoon development. My mom would beg him, "Why don't you direct some of those finances into the States so we can have a financial cushion there, just in case something happens again with the government? You're putting too much into this, and if the government pulls the carpet out from under you again, we'll be left with nothing. . . . Your children will have nothing!"

Chief responded with the same patriotic speech he gave her anytime she asked: "My first priority is to my country. Once we get the Lagoon Development Project off the ground and we're selling plots of land, leasing out commercial space, and forming it into the vision that I have . . . I promise, that's when we'll redirect funds to the States. But I cannot abandon Nigeria, even in the smallest way."

My father could have easily been a success anywhere he chose, but his heart was in Nigeria. And his focus was not on bringing attention to himself, but to his beloved country. He knew Nigeria's potential, and he personally befriended the most celebrated citizens of the country: writers, artists, musicians, engineers, politicians, doctors, and lawyers. He knew that his vision had the power to unite all Nigerians into one powerful force. After all, the country possesses one of the richest commodities in the world—oil—and the petroleum industry in Nigeria is the largest on the African continent.

Surely the country was in a position to be looked upon as a shining lighthouse of development not only for itself but for the continent as well. All it needed was a spark. Being the innovator that he was, Chief saw the Lagoon Development Project as that spark.

• • •

Every weekend Chief would take my mom, brother, and me out on a boat to view the development's progress.

"Do you see that, Bayo and Remi?" Chief asked as he pointed to the massive machines that pumped sand into partially formed islands.

"Yes, Dad," we said.

Chief continued, "One day that will all be land. And it will belong to you and me and your mother forever. No one can take it because we built it where it never existed."

I stared out, not able to grasp the enormity of what my father was doing. "That's small, Dad! It needs to be bigger so me and my friends can play on it."

Chief and my mom laughed. Then he said, "Oh, it's going to be big, Remi . . . so big that you're going to have to get a lot more friends."

"Hmmm . . . okay," I said. I started pointing to parts of the water that hadn't been filled in and began to count.

"What are you counting, Remi?" Mom asked.

"I'm counting all the buildings that will be built so I know how many friends to bring for hide-and-seek."

Chief smiled and said, "You are truly my son . . . you are my son."

CHAPTER THREE

THRONE OVERTHROWN

Every day is for the thief.
—NIGERIAN SAYING

One day Mom was tending to her bird-of-paradise flowers that surrounded our estate while Bayo and I played next to her. We were disrupted from our activity when we heard the rattling of our compound's gate.

"What is that?" Mom asked. We focused our eyes on our twelve-foot-wide gate.

"It looks like a man, Mum," I said.

A tall, slender local was trying to squeeze through a sliver of an opening to gain access to our compound. There was a metal box on our side of the wall that he must have thrown over before he started his slide. It was so funny that Bayo and I couldn't help but watch and laugh as Mom sternly stared on.

When he got through the gate, we noticed he wore a government service uniform, which for us meant he probably wasn't a threat. He picked up the box and approached Mom.

"Good morning, madam. I just checked the meter box, and it looks like you've gone over your allotted electricity for the month."

Mom didn't have the slightest clue what the man meant.

"Madam, if you want your electricity to stay on, you have to pay me two thousand naira. If not, I have to shut down the electricity right now, and you will have to go to the downtown office and make an appointment for someone to come to your home to turn it back on."

Knowing that the process of going downtown and back could take hours, she blurted, "You can't be serious!" Bayo and I stood on each side of her like two little bodyguards.

The local noticed my mother's accent. "Ah, American are you? I am sorry . . . I was mistaken. The fee is . . . four thousand naira. I see that this meter has not been serviced for quite some time now. So the added price includes the service as well."

"Wait right there! I'm going to call my husband!" She grabbed our hands. "Come on, boys."

Before she could turn to go inside the house, Felix, our family chauffeur, opened the gate and pulled into the driveway with my father. Mom beelined directly to Chief as Bayo and I followed. Knowing the man had upset Mom, I kept my head turned in his direction.

Mom told Chief what had happened. And, man, oh man, was my father mad! When Chief stepped out of the car, he gave the meter man a stern stare as Mom babbled on. Dad's look was so intense that the man's posture changed from one of confidence to absolute timidity. When my mother finished, Chief started screaming something in Yoruba as he walked toward the intruder. By the time Chief was nose to nose with the man, he was done with his speech. With his head down, the man muttered something in Yoruba, then shuffled off our property.

Though the situation seemed to be resolved, Mom was not happy. She looked at Chief and said, "John . . . I'm tired of this! Every week it's something different. I can't even go to the store without someone trying to bribe me for a . . . freakin' shopping cart!"

"Nike [the endearment was short for Morenike, the Yoruba name my father had given her], it's over now. It's okay; I'm here."

She calmed down a bit. "What . . . what would I have done if you hadn't arrived when you did?"

"Nike, the next time that happens, just give me a call at the office." He placed his hands on her shoulders. "But I can assure you that you will never see that young man again."

Mom believed him, but deep down she knew that even if that meter man never came back, someone else would. Situations like this led her to continually ask Chief to send money to the States. She didn't trust the system of her husband's country, which was so unfamiliar to her.

. . .

Nigeria is one of the most fascinating countries in Africa. It has an abundance of natural resources and is renowned for the sweetness of its oil. The beauty of Nigeria is in its people. While the three noted tribes are the Yoruba, Hausa, and Igbo, the richness of the Nigerian culture can also be noted in its more than five hundred ethnic groups. This diversity produces foods, music, and art that I am almost certain surpasses all others on the continent of Africa.

The talents of Nigerians are so vast that their contributions to medicine, engineering, science, and the arts can be noted around the world. Many times I heard my mother say that she had stimulating conversations with every Nigerian she met. "They make you want to be more intellectually versed on a range of topics because they certainly are." The bookshelves on our V.I. estate hosted the literary works of Nobel laureate Wole Soyinka (the first African to win such an honor), Chinua Achebe, and Helon Habila.

Sadly, corruption overshadows the attributes of the majority of Nigerians. Transparency International (the global coalition against corruption) has consistently ranked Nigeria in the bottom tier of their corruption scale.[1] Politicians pocket millions of dollars intended for infrastructure development, schools, and hospitals. As my father experienced with Maroko, one minute you can own property, and the next minute the government can seize it for no valid reason. Some police stay in uniform after working hours in order to cite and bribe innocent people. Customs agents threaten to deny entry for minor infractions unless they receive a "Christmas gift." And it's not uncommon for a fish, snake, or monkey to break into a government safe and steal millions of dollars.[2] Sounds crazy, but those excuses have been used, and yes, the government officials who committed the crimes were set free.

The sad thing is, the people suffer. And because the billions of dollars of oil revenues never trickle down to the people, the suffering comes in the form of severe poverty. Kids as young as six and seven have to drop out of school to panhandle just so they can eat. When it comes to medical treatment, God forbid you're poor and have to go to the hospital. In some cases patients leave in a condition far worse than when they arrived. The rich, on the other hand, fly to London or the United States for routine issues and procedures.

As it relates to my mom's meter man experience, the lack of social assistance programs, coupled with widespread poverty, leads some who are in a position to bribe, well, to bribe. Bribery in Nigeria is such a way of life that locals coined the famous phrase "Every day is for the thief."

My dad hated the political landscape and the role that blatant corruption played in politics. Anytime the idea of running for office was presented to Chief, he would say, "Most aspiring politicians don't run for office to serve people; they run to get rich! I have everything I need and more. The Lagoon development is my way of serving Nigeria. And unlike politicians, who *take* money while serving their people, I'm going to *spend* my money to serve my people."

. . .

Chief was a strategic master, but even though he had this gift, the dark clouds of governmental corruption slowly began to encroach on his dream of uniting the country into a dominant economic force. Years after the dredging started, officials and people in general began to look across the Lagos Lagoon and see hundreds of acres of newly developed land! As plots of land formed, Chief received inquisitive and threatening remarks from Lagos State Government officials.

"You won't be able to hold on to it."

"This does not belong to you."

"You think you're smarter than us."

The continual murmuring began to grow louder and would eventually form into a thunder that erupted into a treacherous storm.

One evening Chief came home from work in a rather uncharacteristic disposition. The first thing he would usually do when he arrived was grab Bayo and me, and we'd jubilantly wrestle around on the ground. On this particular evening he just walked straight by us without saying a word. Chief was upset, and his posture made it obvious that something wasn't right.

As Felix followed Chief with some bags, Chief abruptly turned to face him and shouted in pidgin, "I told you to have the other car washed by the time I got home. If it is not done within the next ten minutes, then it's coming out of your pay! Do it *now*!" It was obvious to us that his irritation did not pertain solely to a dirty car; something else was taking place.

"John, what's going on?" my mom asked as a strange nervousness crept over her. She'd seen her husband agitated before, but not like this.

Chief threw the newspaper on the coffee table and said, "Morenike, they're doing it again."

"Doing what?"

"They're trying to confiscate the land . . . the lagoon!"

"But how is that possible? Your proposal and application for approval were granted by the Lagos State Government. And you paid the fifty-thousand-dollar fee on top of the land you were compensated with for Maroko. Didn't you say that the fee was paid and approved?"

"Yes!"

Mom continued, "There's no way Westminster would have started the dredging if there wasn't approval by the government, right?"

"It was all approved! *Everything* was approved!" my father said.

Mom sensed that the questions she put forth made his mood worse. Felix had taken the packages to the kitchen, and as he headed back to the front door, my father reiterated his threat.

"Felix, the car better be washed in ten minutes. If not, your pay will be reduced! Do you understand me?"

The driver nodded and scurried out in shame. Without looking at Mom, he muttered, "'Night, madam."

My mom replied softly, "Good night, Felix."

Chief sat down and just stared at Bayo and me for about five minutes. Naturally, I didn't understand what was going on, so I continued playing. Then he started laughing. A sense of calm seemed to come over him. It was as if he was calculating in his mind the reasons why the government would not be successful in seizing the land, which was once water.

"They can't do it this time, Morenike! They're not going to get away with it."

"You're right," my mother said. "It's simply impossible. But, Bayo, I really think we should put some funds in the States. You know it's not safe to have all our money wrapped up here, especially in one project. And with what you just told me—"

"Nike, just trust me," Chief said.

Mom had every right to be concerned. She knew Chief had poured his entire life into the Lagoon Project. He thought about, smelled, surveyed, and discussed every single aspect of the project from the minute he woke up until he fell asleep from exhaustion. Not only was he consumed with it physically and mentally, but the project was solely financed by him. He had invested all of his money as well as leveraged his companies for the project. If the lagoon was taken, there was a high likelihood we wouldn't have anything left.

A month later Chief ran into another roadblock, or in my opinion, another excuse from the Lagos State Government to stop my father. The Nigerian Ports Authority stated that the approval he had received to start the dredging was only preliminary. In short, it wasn't official. To move forward, he would have to conduct a hydrological test, and others, to ensure that environmental safety standards were met. Chief would have to hire an outside company and spend another several hundred thousand dollars.

One would think that all of this would make Chief quit, pull his money out, and take his business ideas to the West. But he was a resilient risk taker, and quitting wasn't in his DNA. He hired a Canadian survey company and continued on with the project.

All of the setbacks and corruption weighed heavily on Mom. She supported Chief, but watching him go through all that he was enduring caused her stress to the point of illness. She felt she needed to be in a place where she could be strong for her boys. Both of my parents decided that it would be best for my mom, brother, and me to fly to the States for a couple of months. So in 1987, we returned to my mother's home state of New York.

• • •

One evening, while Mom made dinner for Bayo and me, the phone rang—it was Chief.

"Hello, Morenike. How are you and my boys doing?"

"Great," my mom responded. "We miss you. How are things going in Lagos?"

"It's challenging, but I'll manage. Look, Nike, I don't want to alarm you, but I had an incident last week that I need to tell you about. I'm okay, but I was bitten by a dog."

Mom was in the kitchen, and we could hear her frantic cry from our bedroom. "A dog! What happened?"

"I'm taking a walk to clear my head, and out of nowhere the neighbor's dog runs up to me and bites me—"

"Oh my God, John! Did you go to the doctor? No . . . you need to fly to the States now for proper medical treatment! Please!"

"I went to the doctor last week—"

"And?" Mom replied.

"I tested positive for rabies today. But I received medication, and I should be fine."

My mom couldn't speak for a few seconds. Knowing how bad health care is in Nigeria, she was devastated. When she finally spoke, she deescalated her tone and said again, "John . . . please . . . you have to get a ticket and come to the States today! Please."

"I can't . . . I'm dealing with a bigger issue that I must stay here for."

"What can be bigger than your health?"

"They're taking the lagoon. The state says I can't have it. Since the water was compensation for Maroko, I'll have to go to court to get back the money I used to pay for Maroko."

The second seizure was the result of a disagreement between the federal government and the Lagos State Government. Chief's Maroko deal was done with the Nigerian Ports Authority, which was the federal government. The NPA had what's known as literal rights over the lagoon foreshore, which meant everything that was coastal foreshore belonged to them. So when Chief won the case years earlier, it was the federal government that compensated him with what he wanted, the water.

Around the time of my departure from Nigeria, the Lagos State Government conveniently conducted an investigation and concluded that the lagoon foreshore belonged to the State of Lagos. They claimed the federal government had no right to dispose of it without the state signing off. Keep in mind this is a *big* government, not street hustlers on a corner, making up rules on a whim.

Chief essentially became a victim of conflict between the state and federal governments. And with Lagos exercising its authority, the federal government had no leverage or motive to come in and fight for Chief. Even worse, by the time the Lagos State Government realized the federal government's legal error, they decided it wasn't in their best interest to sign off on what Chief had already possessed and worked on for years.

In retrospect, due to the nature of the country's corruption, I'm not surprised that it worked out that way. With all the money my dad invested in the project—without a single building built on it—it was already worth multiple millions of dollars. And in the years to come—depending on how it was managed and what was built on it—it could be worth multiple *billions*. Someone had to be watching and waiting for Chief to get it to where it was, and that someone was about to get very rich off of all of Chief's hard work.

Mom was in a daze after Chief delivered the double dose of bad news. "I don't care about it all anymore," she told him. "I just want you to come to the States so you can get the proper treatment. We'll figure out the lagoon business after you're healthy."

"I have a meeting in Detroit next week. I'll take the rest of this week to work through the lagoon case; then I'll fly to Detroit and then New York. I promise, I'll get treatment when I get there."

The following week my father flew to New York. He was very upbeat, but my mom sensed his weariness.

In his typical joking form, he pulled up his pants leg to show Bayo and me the bite. "Look at what that dog did to me! Do believe that he tried to eat me!"

The way he said it was so funny that we couldn't help but laugh. "How big was it, Dad?" I asked.

"Oh, it was enormous. I thought it was a werewolf for a second." He started growling, which prompted us to mimic him.

We had a great week together in the city. We dined at our favorite Indian restaurant in Manhattan, went shopping, and even snuck a peek at Halloween costumes. I didn't have the slightest clue that my father was in a battle. He never complained or walked around saying, "Oh, they cheated me! I am a defeated man." No, even in the midst of betrayal by people he desired to edify, he maintained his jubilance in the presence of his sons. Nor did he seek medical treatment for the bite while he was there. He was adamant that he was fine.

The week sped by, and as fast as he flew in, he was back out in the direction of his beloved country.

Three days later, on a chilly October evening, Mom was startled out of her reading when the phone rang.

"Hello, Pauline. This is Shirley," my father's secretary said.

"Hi, Shirley, how are you?" Mom replied.

"I have some very difficult news to tell you." After pausing to compose herself, she finally said, "I'm so sorry, Pauline . . . but . . . but . . . Chief has died."

We later found out that my father had died from a combination of rabies and an adverse reaction to medication he received in Nigeria. Our nanny, Jane, was the last one to see him alive. She ran his bath, and when he didn't come out for hours, she discovered his lifeless body and called for help.

. . .

"Where are you going, Mum?" I asked as I watched my mom carry her suitcase to the door.

"I'm flying home to see your dad. I'll be back in a couple of days, okay? Grandmommy is going to watch you and Bayo."

"Okay, I love you. And tell Daddy I love him too."

Mom stood there with tears rolling down her face and said, "I will."

I didn't know why she was crying, because she had decided to wait until Chief was buried before delivering the news to Bayo and me.

She flew to Nigeria, buried Chief, then had a long meeting with my eldest half brother, John. John was intrinsically connected to Chief's company. He was a British-trained lawyer to whom Chief had entrusted the intricate details of all his businesses.

John and my mother stood in the living room of our house on Victoria Island. She was a stranger in her own home.

"Please tell me that your father set something aside for the children," she pleaded. "They're only five and six years old! I talked to him about this many times, and he assured me in the event of his death there would be nothing to worry about . . . the boys would be financially set for life. Please tell me that there is something, somewhere, set aside!" Tears streamed down her face.

"Pauline, I'm so sorry, but when Dad told you that, he was thinking along the lines of the Lagoon Project. He didn't account for the fact that he would die so unexpectedly. You see, he poured every dime he had into the project. *All* of his finances. There's nothing left. The government has stripped him of the land, but I promise you, Pauline, I'm taking them to court. Once this is settled, I can assure you that Bayo and Remi will be taken care of."

"What about the millions he paid for Maroko! Since they took the lagoon back . . . and since it was compensation for Maroko, aren't they required to pay us back?"

"They are. But this is a different system here, Pauline. It's not like the States." Mom could tell that he wanted to explain it, but even if he did, she was too upset to understand.

Mom continued, "But he had an insurance company! Surely he knew the importance of having a policy. The boys are just children, John. I can't believe there was nothing set aside for them."

"I know it sounds ludicrous, but everything was tied up in the Lagoon Project. There are no funds. . . . There is nothing!"

"But what about our home in Lomé; what about this house?"

"*Everything* was funded through the business account, and right now there's less than a thousand naira in it!"

My mother sank into the living room chair, not wanting to believe the words that were coming out of John's mouth. The reality hit her. She wasn't rich anymore. She was penniless. Seeming to read her mind, John put his arm around her shoulder and said, "I promise you that I will fight the government with every ounce of energy that I have, and we will win the land back. We will do exactly what my father wanted to do with it. You, Bayo, and Remi will be taken care of."

"But how am I supposed to feed my children? When I get back to New York . . . what do I tell my boys? John . . . I mean, seriously, how am I supposed to make it with two little boys?"

"We're all hurting, Pauline, and I promise you, I will pursue this case until we win."

Mom only had twenty-four hours left in Nigeria. She was hurt, deflated, sad, angry, disappointed, weary, and confused. That night she slept in her master suite for the last time, the same room that I would often sneak by when my parents hosted lavish parties. She later told me that as she lay in bed that night, all she could see were my brother's and my faces. A part of her wanted to die, but a part of her knew that she needed to live, for us.

She fiercely wiped away her tears and said, "I will make a way. . . . I have to for my boys. I have to."

CHAPTER FOUR

COMING TO AMERICA

Some days I wish I could be a kid again.

Africa is my birthplace, but the Bronx is my home. There's no place on the planet like the Bronx. The food, the people, the culture, the music—it's a melting pot of everything chaotic yet beautiful. On one block Italians serve up thin-crust pizzas, while right outside a group of Dominicans play dominoes and talk Yankees. Salsa and merengue music blast from souped-up Civics; Black Israelites stand on the corner, taking questions from critics. Haitians, Jamaicans, Vietnamese, and Puerto Ricans; hustlers and ballers, both literal and figurative, all locked together with a few eastern Europeans. It's "the Bronx," not "Bronx," "*the* Bronx"! You know a person, place, or thing is special when you have to put *the* before it. We fight hard; we love hard. As a matter of fact, doesn't *the Bronx* sound hard? That's because it *is* hard!

The Bronx contains the poorest congressional district in the United States,[1] but the borough is rich in passion: Roscoe Brown passion, J. Lo passion, Al Pacino passion, Mary J. Blige passion, Sonia Sotomayor passion, KRS-One passion, and Stan Lee passion. The Bronx molded me, formed me, and trained me in ways that no other place has. This was my environment. Africa is my birthplace, but the Bronx is my home.

I can't tell you much about the land of my birth, but I can tell you all about the Bronx. I love the Bronx, both the good and the bad.

"Remi! Yo, Remi!" my best friend, Ricardo, screamed up to my third-floor apartment from the sidewalk while six other friends stood with him.

As I sat by the window screen, I overheard another kid say, "He's probably still on lockdown, hahaha!"

Ricardo Regalado, who had been my friend since the first grade, added to the insult.

"Remi, you still on lock? Hahaha, I bet your moms tore you up. Hehehe!" Laughing through his joke, he continued, "See if your mom will grant you parole. It's been two weeks!"

I nodded in shame, then muttered, "Imma see what she says."

It was August 1991, I was nine years old, and it was the last week of summer break. While all my friends were running around outside, having fun, I had been locked up in my apartment for two weeks, writing reports and reading newspaper articles. Why was I "on lock"?

Two weeks earlier Bayo and I had been fighting in the living room, and we ended up breaking our mother's coffee table. We played many risky games around that table, and she had warned us multiple times, "Don't play around my coffee table, because if you break it, I'm going to break you!" To make matters worse, the rumor in the neighborhood was that she "gave it to us."

"Five dollars says his mom won't let him come out." That's the last thing I heard as I backed away from the window.

I glanced at the wooden frame of the coffee table, the only part still intact. The wood was African, and that table meant a lot to her. Along with the table, Mom kept a collection of African statues, paintings, and furniture. We had a bookcase full of African literature and art books, and even our dining room table was designed with traditional African wood and carvings. She always said she didn't like Nigeria much, but she always kept our little two-bedroom, one-bathroom apartment full of Nigeria.

She probably wasn't going to let me out to play with my friends, but at least I had to try. As I made my way through the living room toward the "Warden's Chamber," I grabbed the reports I had been writing off the dining room table, then made a stop in the room I shared with Bayo.

"Yo, Bayo," I whispered.

"What?" he asked.

"I'm going to ask Ma if she can let us go outside for the last week of summer. Come with me. It's better that both of us go than me alone."

Bayo, deep in writing, said, "No, go by yourself! I'm still writing my report. You know she's not going to let us."

My mom, being a teacher in the South Bronx, was well aware of the elevated high school dropout rate among African American males who lived in the borough. She also knew that the college graduation rate among Bronx natives at the time was extremely low. Because of this, when she punished us, she would make us read articles in the *New York Times*, then write long reports about the articles. And if she read the reports and saw that we had sandbagged the writing, she would make us start all over again with a different article. I guess this was her way of ensuring we wouldn't negatively affect the Bronx's educational statistics.

"All right, but if I ask her and she says yes, *you owe me!*"

"Leave me alone, Remi," Bayo said with his head down. Bayo was always the one to play it safe. I, on the other hand, never had a problem taking risks.

I stepped out of our bedroom and turned left down the apartment's only hallway, which ran adjacent to our only bathroom. I paused outside Mom's door to get a sense of the atmosphere. Her album of the decade, Anita Baker's *Rapture*, was on repeat, which meant she was probably in a good mood. Or it might have meant nothing. Whether it was Sade, Stevie, Anita, or Gladys, I would sometimes stand by Mom's closed door and sing along as if I were onstage in my own miniconcert, but this time I was all business. I needed to get outside to my boys.

I opened the door and saw my mom sitting on her bed with her notepad and pen, writing.

"Ma?"

"Yes, Remi?"

I walked closer to the bed and asked cautiously, "What are you doing?"

With her eyes staring at her pad and her pen moving swiftly, she replied, "Writing lesson plans for my new group of students. What are you doing?"

"I finished all my reports, and I did them right. Here; you can check them." I handed her my reports.

She took the papers and placed them to her side. "What is it that you want,

Remi?" Mom knew my games inside and out. I figured I could keep playing the game and act like I didn't want anything, or I could just get straight to the point.

"Can we go outside now?"

She put down her pen and pad. "Will you and your brother listen to me when I tell you not to do something?"

"Yes, Ma. We won't do it again. I promise."

"When I tell you not to do certain things, it's not because I'm trying to keep you from having fun. I'm trying to protect you. It's not just about the table. You and your brother could have been seriously hurt."

"Yes, ma'am. We're sorry." I had learned years earlier that when it looks like you're winning, say as little as possible or keep your mouth shut. Saying too much could turn a half yes into a no!

"Okay, you and Bayo can go outside, but tell your brother to come here with his report."

"Yes, ma'am!"

Looking back, I know it wasn't my mom's pleasure to punish or discipline us. But she knew the odds were stacked against us, and she didn't want to take any chances. She always did what she had to do, even if we hated it.

I left the room in quiet jubilee and ran straight back into my bedroom. Bayo was still writing. With my hands on my hips and my head tilted up, I said in my preacher voice, "FREE AT LAST, FREE AT LAST, GOOD GOD ALMIGHTY, WE ARE FREE. AT. LAST! AH! TAKE, AH, YOUR BLACK ASS, AH, INTO YOUR MAMA'S ROOM, AH!"

Bayo looked up. "Really?"

"Yup, I got us out of another one. Peace. I'm going outside."

Before Bayo had gathered his papers, I had my sneakers on and was out the door. I ran through the third-floor hallway—passing the hallway light that was *always* buzzing, then another apartment—straight to the staircase. As always, I sprinted down the first flight, jumping the last three steps, turned the corner to the second flight, and sprinted down even faster. When I arrived in the lobby, I stopped to take a quick look in the lobby mirror, then ran out of the building.

Ahhhh, freedom! Two weeks of punishment felt like a twenty-year prison sentence to this nine-year-old. It was good to finally breathe that good old-fashioned Fordham Hill air again.

We lived in a co-op called Fordham Hill Oval, which I referred to as the Hill. My father didn't leave us much of anything, but he did leave us the apartment in the Hill, which was probably the greatest thing he could have left us. The Hill, which was oval shaped, was located on Fordham Road and Sedgwick Avenue and consisted of nine tan buildings, each with sixteen to seventeen floors, a playground with a community center, and a constant security presence. The Hill was an amazing place to grow up. Why do I say this? It was a middle-income, working-class co-op located smack-dab in one of the poorest districts in New York, University Heights. I grew up with one foot in a bit of stability and the other foot in the instability that characterizes the Bronx. It was the best of both worlds.

It wasn't easy to keep our apartment. Mom struggled to keep up with the required monthly maintenance fees. I remember going to the maintenance office with her on multiple occasions and standing there as she pleaded with the property manager to give her more time to pay. "I just need five more days to come up with the money, please." It was always embarrassing for me, but I'm sure it was more embarrassing for her. She knew the Hill was above her means, but to her, slaving to make the payments and putting her pride aside to plead for extra time was worth it for her boys.

Our Hill crew consisted of Dante, Elijah (a.k.a. E), Charles (a.k.a. Showtime), Desean, Erica, Dennis, Kenny (a.k.a. Monkey), Douglas, Chris (a.k.a. Joker), Ricardo, Roberto, Victor, and sometimes my brother, when he wasn't punishing himself at the library. Dante, the leader of the group, was always good at leading us into trouble. E, who was second in command, was very athletic. Showtime's dad was also Nigerian *and* strict; because of this, Showtime was the obedient one, always questioning whether we should or shouldn't do something. Desean was the oldest and could get us things we were too young to get on our own. Erica the tomboy was meaner than most of us and could do everything we could do, from play football to partake in summer league slap-boxing championships that *always* turned into a fight. Dennis was the one most likely to succeed in life, and Monkey was the one who could climb anything. Douglas was funny and tough; Chris always had a smile like the Joker; Ricardo and Roberto were the Dominican duo; and Victor was the smooth, calm, and collected one.

During the summer months, we were inseparable. And though this was the era when Sega Genesis, Nintendo, and PlayStation reigned, we all wanted to be outside and active—and that, we definitely were. Whoever was the first one outside in the mornings would go building to building using the intercoms or their loud mouth to call down the rest of the crew. Once we were all gathered, havoc would ensue until we dispersed, spent from a good day's work, back to our apartments.

With my prison release from Building 4, Apartment 3G, it was like Voltron had finally been re-formed!

I found Ricardo first. "So what were you saying, Bed-day-key?" His mom would always yell through the intercom, "Ricky! Bedakey!" when it was time to come home.

"I can't believe it!" Ricardo replied as he giggled. "Yo, when you broke your mom's table, I called up seeing if you could come down, and she yelled like she wanted to whup *me*!"

"Your mom let you out?" another kid said. "You must have gotten lucky!"

"Yeah, I got lucky with *your* moms," I replied.

"Oooooooh," the group echoed.

"You fell right into that one! I'm *baaacckk*!" I said proudly, as if I hadn't been in trouble the past two weeks. "So what's it going to be? I'm free, and I'm ready."

Dante suggested, "Anybody down for kicking some doors?"

Damn, son. I just got out of the pen, and you already trying to get me back in!

Ricardo piped up, "The last time we did that, a dude came out of his apartment with a machete."

We played many crazy games on the Hill: Manhunt, where one team maneuvered through the complex, trying to avoid capture and abuse from the other team. Suicide, where one person would throw a tennis ball at the wall and whoever caught it had to blast the person who threw it as hard as possible in the back. Slap boxing, where the older kids would pick two younger kids about my age to fight it out with slaps instead of fists. Two-hand touch football, which never sounded bad until someone was accidentally pushed onto the concrete. That happened a lot, and when it happened, it usually wasn't an accident. Then there was snapping, where two people would enter into a joke competition, cracking on each other's mothers, clothes, features, and social status until someone cried or gave up. But by far, kick the door and run had to be the most exhilarating.

Here's how kick the door and run would play out. We would decide on a building in the co-op. After a decision was made—as a group—we would go to that building, take the elevator to a top floor (between eleven and seventeen), find a door, kick it repeatedly while a group held the stairwell door open, and then, when we were discovered, sprint all the way down to the lobby.

Before anyone could add to Ricardo's machete comment, Dante yelled out, "Duggy!" As Douglas made his way up to us, everyone turned and in unison repeated, "Duggy!"

Douglas was playful and outspoken. The combination of the two made him one of the most picked on in the Hill, but also one of the strongest. When you get picked on the way he was, it will either break you or make you unbreakable.

"Yo, Duggy, you down for kicking doors?" I asked, trying to deflect my stress and hoping he would be the one to say no.

"Come on! Do you have to ask? Of course I'm down."

It looked like I wasn't getting out of this one. We moved from the front of my building to the community playground entrance. This was where we devised our plan. I can't remember who came up with the plan, but this time Douglas and I were going to be the only door kickers. Dante was going to be the door holder. The rest of the team would wait for us a flight down.

As planned, we arrived on the fifteenth floor and found a door to kick. Dante held the door to the stairwell wide open, and Douglas and I put our backs to the apartment in the mule-kick position. On cue we both started mule kicking the door repeatedly. Douglas's head was shaking all over the place as he kicked the door. One kick, two kicks, three kicks. On the third kick, the door flew open.

"Uh-oh!" we both said.

A gentleman in his forties lunged to grab us, but we took off. All I heard as we made our way down the steps were the echoes of laughter from the kids below.

Yeah, we were wild, but that was a memorable time in our lives, a time that made me forget about all my problems.

In the nineties rapper Ahmad wrote a famous song called "Back in the Day." In the song he reminisces about being a kid again—wishing those fun days could go on for eternity. Well, *back in the day* was exactly how the Hill made us feel. Like Peter Pan, we wanted to stay kids forever: no responsibilities, no commitments, no jobs, just each other and the Hill.

When I think back to that time, lyrics to another song play diametrically in my head: "Keep Your Head Up" by Tupac Shakur. See, the Hill wasn't an oasis by any means. It was located in the West Bronx, and we were exposed to the same problems as everyone else living in that area. Even at the early age of nine, I had a keen awareness of my environment's imperfections.

CHAPTER FIVE

BAD TIMES

*Trust what you're going through now; it's
preparing you for your biggest opportunities.*

So what did they take?" a police officer asked my mom as she stood in our living room in a daze. A second police officer stood by, taking notes.

"I don't know. All I had in the house was twenty dollars," Mom responded.

It was a Sunday. Bayo, my mom, my half brother John (who was visiting from Nigeria), and I had just returned home from church. When we got off the elevator and made our way to our apartment, Mom noticed the door was ajar. Not a good sign. As soon as she pushed the door open, all she could say in a low tone was, "Oh my God. We've been robbed."

Not only had our apartment been robbed, but the entire apartment had been ransacked. It was a mess.

This was 1991, the same year as the Rodney King beatings in Los Angeles, so I was not too enthusiastic about the police. I had no filter; to me, they all were bad, even if they were trying to help my mom.

Acting like a mute with my hands in my church-suit pockets, I suspiciously stared at the officers while they questioned Mom.

"How long were you and your family gone?"

"We left . . . around eight," Mom said as she began to search for the arrival time in her mind. "And we must have gotten back thirty minutes before you got here. So three hours." She shook her head and asked, "How could some-body do this?"

"Do you have any idea who may have been behind this?" one cop asked.

"Yes, I think I do," Mom said cautiously.

A month earlier my mother had hired one of the maintenance men in the building to install an air-conditioning unit in her bedroom. When he arrived and got to work, my brother and I, as usual, were outside, running wild with our friends. Mom, realizing she had forgotten to tell us something important, told the maintenance guy she would be right back.

Mom later found out he was a crackhead. He must have thought her departure was a great opportunity to search the apartment for the cash he needed for his next fix.

Mom kept her money under her mattress. So when the crackhead pulled up the mattress, he found the money and pocketed all of it. Meanwhile, Mom delivered the message to my brother and me, then went back upstairs to the apartment.

About fifteen minutes later the maintenance guy finished the installation and asked mom for payment. When she went into her bedroom and lifted up the mattress, all the cash she had was gone. When Mom went back into the living room and told him she couldn't find her money, he threatened to uninstall the unit. Mom didn't have any more money—all she had was under that mattress. So he went into her room, uninstalled the AC, placed it on the floor, and left.

"I think it's the maintenance guy who works in the building," Mom told the officers. "I'm 100 percent sure he robbed us last month. I really think it's him."

The police later set up a sting, which eventually led to the crackhead's arrest, but Mom never got her money back.

Even though Mom was never repaid, we were more fortunate than another Fordham Hill neighbor. About a year later Leo Collins, a restaurant and club owner, would be robbed and shot to death right in the hallway. His killers were never caught, and like most murder cases in the Bronx at the time, his was never solved. Yeah, we lost some money and learned a valuable lesson—never leave a crackhead unattended in your home—but at least we didn't lose our lives.

• • •

The history of the Bronx is a fascinating one, and like most inner cities in America, the Bronx has always had a reputation for crime and turmoil. I guess that's what makes it as hard as its name. During the days of Prohibition, which took place between 1920 and 1933, gangs and bootleggers wreaked havoc on the borough. Organized crime factions such as the Irish Mob, Polish gangs, the Italian Mafia—specifically the Genovese and Lucchese crime families—and many others saw Prohibition as a lucrative black market and set up shop in the Bronx to take advantage of it. Prohibition was created to reduce crime but instead became a recipe for the borough's destruction.

Multiple crime factions bidding for the control and sale of liquor in their various territories would eventually lead to all-out war between the parties. Blood spilled in the streets of the Bronx, people went missing, and brazen heists would take place all in the name of liquor. The crime rate increased by 24 percent across more than thirty major US cities between 1920 and 1921.[1] In 1926 the Bronx recorded one of its highest crime rates since recording began.

By the 1930s, old sections of the Bronx began to fall into poverty. Over the course of thirty years, the Irish, German, Italian, and Jewish populations gradually made their way out, relocating to the New York suburbs, Florida, or other thriving states. The migration later known as "white flight" left the Bronx with a large population of Puerto Ricans, Dominicans, Haitians, Jamaicans, and African Americans, all minorities concentrated in one area during the peak of racism in America. As jobs left with the previous inhabitants, unemployment rates rose exponentially, neighborhood development halted, and the city government began a pattern of neglect. Just like that, the Bronx declined from a predominantly moderate, working-class neighborhood to a lower-income borough. The shift would reinstate the same high rates of crime that the Bronx saw during Prohibition, as well as establish a state of poverty that had never been seen in modern Bronx history.

By 1970, property values had plummeted, racial tensions due to the civil rights movement had flushed out large numbers of the middle class, and scores of buildings were vacated and left empty. High levels of poverty reached as far north as Fordham Road (the street I grew up on), and living conditions were so bad that some landlords resorted to burning their own buildings to receive insurance money. The wave of arsons, which took place in the poorest communities, specifically the South Bronx, would be commemorated in a nonfiction book and TV miniseries titled *The Bronx Is Burning.*

Along with poverty, another element also peaked in the Bronx in the 1970s: heroin. During that decade New York City was known as the heroin capital of America, with more than forty thousand recorded addicts.[2] With scores of vacant buildings (in some cases entire city blocks), a plethora of economically struggling customers (who had the highest rates of use), and police precincts already spread thin, the Bronx proved to be a perfect location for street gangs to carry out their narcotic enterprises. Addicts would literally line up in broad daylight outside of vacant buildings to buy heroin, then move to other vacant buildings, where they would shoot up.

By 1980, the decade of my birth, crack had overtaken heroin as the drug of choice. Addicts could buy a dose of this simple-to-produce and ready-to-use drug for as little as $2.50.[3] But though the monetary cost of the drug was low, the physical cost to the Bronx would be high. Homicides, prostitution, robberies, and assaults skyrocketed, all in the name of crack. Crackheads stole to support their habit, prostitutes sold their bodies, and gangs went to war with each other to control sales territories. It was the era of Prohibition all over again. Violence was king. But this time, instead of the Italian Mafia, Irish Mob, and Polish gangs spearheading the carnage, it was the Bloods, Crips, Latin Kings, Mexican Mafia, and other high-level drug dealers. By 1990, one year before the crackhead maintenance man robbed us, the Bronx was the site of 197 murders.[4]

My mother and the Hill tried to protect me from the violence the best they could, but sometimes I led myself right into it.

• • •

Growing up, I didn't have any connection to Chief's side of the family, except for my half brother John. On my mother's side, the Darlingtons were to me the definition of *family.* Of the Darlington boys, my cousins Corey and Romell were closest to Bayo and me. The girls outnumbered us, so during family reunions we always took off on our own little adventures. Romell was the eldest of us four; he lived in Teaneck, New Jersey, but would sometimes make the trek across the Hudson to spend time with us. Corey, the youngest, reminded me so much of myself because his mouth and antics would *always* land him in a lot of trouble. Sometimes I would shake my head with a smile and think, *This kid knows how to get into more trouble than me!* Corey lived down the street from the Hill on the corner of Claflin Avenue and 195th Street.

One evening Corey and Romell came over to our apartment to visit. We were doing our usual, watching the NBA game while debating which dream car would be the best to buy if we ever struck it rich.

"Mercedes 600! That's my car!" I yelled as I snapped my fingers.

"What? Why?" Bayo, being the analytical one, asked.

"Because it would be big enough to fit all my girls in. If I'm gonna be rich enough to buy that car, you know I'm gonna have to have a lot of girls. And the 600 could fit all 600 of them," I said in my high-pitched preacher voice.

Romell shook his head and said, "Cuz, come on, I know you ain't thinking . . ."

I laughed before I spoke. "I'm just kidding, but I know I could fit at least . . . six in."

It was around 8:00 p.m. and getting past Corey's bedtime. My mom came into the room, unannounced as always. "Corey, your dad called and said it's time for you to come home. Should he come pick you up?"

"Mom, we can walk him home," I suggested.

Romell confirmed, "Yes, Aunt Pauline, it's no big deal; we can do it. Uncle Kirk doesn't have to drive over."

"All right. Well, you need to leave now. It's late," Mom responded.

We got our stuff together, shut off the TV, made our way out of the apartment, and exited the building. To the left was one of the Hill's three entrances, which led out to Sedgwick Avenue. Taking Sedgwick to Corey's place was the fastest route, but at that time in the evening, it wasn't the safest.

As we exited the Hill and walked north on Sedgwick Avenue, we continued our car debate. Romell and I were in front on the narrow, northbound sidewalk of the two-way street, and Bayo and Corey were right behind us.

We walked, we talked, we laughed, and we joked. Cousins. Four boys with hopes and dreams. Yes, our dreams may have been superficial, but to us, those moments of dreaming brought us joy that no reality could.

In the midst of our dreaming, chaos intruded. *Pop! Pop! Pop!* The shots started off few, then erupted into a barrage. A car pulled up on the southbound side of the street directly to the left of us and started shooting up the building at 2559 Sedgwick. The targets of the drive-by started shooting back in our direction, and before we knew it, we were in the midst of a shootout. I froze, not knowing what to do. It was like everything was happening in slow motion. I can't remember what Bayo was doing, but Romell took charge.

He looked at me and yelled, "Come on, Remi!"

Instead of moving, I slowly turned my head to look back in the direction of the Hill. Romell grabbed Corey and threw him over his left shoulder to shield Corey from the bullets. Then he pushed Bayo, which prompted my brother to start sprinting back to the Hill. After receiving one last verbal lashing from Romell, I snapped out of my frozen state and started sprinting to catch up. We all ran as fast as we could. I don't know how Romell was able to do it, but he was way ahead of Bayo and me the whole time, even while carrying Corey over his shoulder.

Just when we thought we had made it out of the furnace, the car started speeding south in our direction. I will never forget the thought that popped into my mind: *They have to kill us. We're the only witnesses. They're coming to kill us.* Despite that thought, I kept running as hard as I could. As the car got closer, I thought, *This is it.* Then, just like that, the car sped by, running the red light where Sedgwick and Bailey Avenues met.

We sprinted back to the entrance of the Hill, stopped to check each other for bullet holes, then made our way in. Let's just say that when we got back up to the apartment and told Mom what had happened, she didn't let us walk the other way to Corey's apartment. Instead, Uncle Kirk made the drive over to pick up Corey, and my Army vet uncle made sure to bring his gun.

I'll never forget 2559 Sedgwick Avenue for two reasons: One, it was the first place I recall almost losing my life. Two, a few years later it would be the same building where Deena Taylor—Bayo's close friend and classmate—would be murdered. Just like us, Deena wasn't bothering anybody. We were all just kids who happened to be in the wrong place at the wrong time. But at the end of the day, it was my mouth that got us there. *We can walk him home.*

. . .

That wasn't the only violence my mouth had led me into at a young age. Right outside the Hill—along Fordham Road—is Devoe Park. Over the years, murders, robberies, drugs, and assaults have given the park a bad reputation. But to get to the stores that line Fordham Road, or to the buses and the 4 train, I would have to cut through the park. As a kid, I grew accustomed to seeing bags of drugs passed between people, smelling the weed smoke from older dudes congregating by the b-ball court, and passing the occasional strung-out crackhead who called the park home. If I learned anything from playing basketball there and constantly walking through that park—especially at night—it was to keep your head down, mind your business, and don't say anything. As long as I abided by those rules, I was fine. But one day I decided to break the most important one: keep your mouth shut!

It was a fall day in 1993, the leaves were beginning to turn colors, and I was shaking and baking on the Devoe Park basketball court.

"Who wants it? Who got next?" I said after shooting a jump shot that ended a one-on-one game. I was a master at running my mouth, or as we would say, "talking junk."

As the kid I had just defeated walked away, another kid walked up and said, "I'll play you." He was a little bit shorter than me and about a year younger. I was eleven at the time. I had seen this particular kid at the court many times but didn't have much of a relationship with him. Despite the fact that we were minimally acquainted, I was aware that his older brother was named James and sold drugs in and around the park. I also knew they both lived off of Andrews Avenue, which was across the street from Devoe. We started our game.

"Check up!" I said as he tossed me the ball. One bucket, two buckets, three. I kept scoring on him; the competition was nonexistent. I ran my mouth the entire time. I wasn't saying anything about him directly. I was just talking about myself and the game.

"Another one!"

"I *can't* be guarded!"

"Yeah, boy!"

"This game is *over*!"

The kid got fed up and yelled at me. "Shut up!"

I didn't pay much attention to him. I just continued dribbling the ball. Then he said it again, this time with a tougher tone.

"Shut up, yo!"

I felt disrespected, so I stopped dribbling the ball and said, "Or what? Don't be mad 'cause you're losing."

I could tell my response made him angrier because his next comment was a threat. "Okay, keep talking, and I'm gonna go get my brother!"

Then my mouth proceeded to write a check that my skinny eleven-year-old body couldn't cash. "I don't care; go get your brother!"

Remi, what are you thinking? You know who his brother is!

The reality was, I wasn't thinking. I was trying to play the tough street kid. And to make matters worse, as soon as the kid left the court to go get his brother, I stayed right there and waited for them to show up. I could have swallowed my pride and run as fast as I could to the Hill, but I didn't.

Thinking back to that time, I probably didn't leave because I was always open to a fight, no matter the size of my opponent. In the Hill we fought each other all the time, and our fights weren't little wrestling bouts. I'm talking full-on fistfights.

About fifteen minutes later I saw the kid with two much bigger guys standing at the Fordham Road crosswalk, waiting to cross the street. I recognized James immediately. He must have been about seventeen at the time.

Once the light changed, the three figures sprinted across Fordham Road and entered the park. Now that all three of them were in the park, I was able to get a better look at the third individual. I didn't recognize him at all, but he was older, late thirties, and had a 'fro that shot straight up and a nappy black beard. The guy looked exactly like the character Jerome from the hit TV show *Martin.* I would later find out that the Jerome look-alike was the kid's uncle and had been recently released from prison.

They stopped at the court and looked around as though they were looking for someone. The courts were full of players that day, maybe fifteen in all, and a steady flow of people passed through the park as usual. I kept dribbling and shooting the ball as if nothing had happened while watching James and his companions from the corner of my eye. Finally the kid pointed at me.

"That's him right there."

My heart started racing, and my body got really hot, probably from the nerves.

The three approached me, led by James.

"That's him. He was talking all kinds of junk," the kid said.

James asked me, "Do you know who I am?"

"Yeah, I know who you are," I replied humbly.

James continued, "Who's your brother?"

"My brother?"

"Answer his question, little nigga!" Jerome said. They were all obviously upset.

"Bayo is my brother," I replied. I didn't understand then, but the reason they asked was to make sure I didn't have a family member they were friends with—or shouldn't mess with.

Once they realized that Bayo wasn't a name they knew, the beatdown commenced. James punched me in the face; then Jerome slammed me to the pavement. All three of them started kicking me all over. I covered myself in the fetal position, protecting my head the best I could. When I thought it was over, James pulled back one arm and Jerome pulled back the other so I couldn't cover my face. They held me down and gave the kid the cue to repeatedly punch me in the face.

I'll never forget this: I looked to my right toward the west entrance of the court and saw an older gentleman who lived in the Hill. He just stood there and watched me get beat up. There was no point in screaming for help or trying to fight back. No one was going to help me, and fighting back could have made my situation worse. My mouth got me into this, so I had no choice but to take the beating.

Finally, after being pummeled by a ten-year-old, a seventeen-year-old, and a thirty-year-old, the beating stopped, and there I was, an eleven-year-old kid with a knot on my head and blood coming from my face, wishing and hoping for someone bigger than them, perhaps my father, to come to my rescue. But no one came, and my father was long gone.

Jerome pointed his finger straight in my face and said, "Don't ever mess with my nephew again."

I nodded. The episode ended with the kid spitting in my face while Jerome and James stood by to make sure I didn't retaliate in any way. Then, just like that, they left. Everyone at the basketball court stared at me for a moment, and then, as if they had seen that scene play out many times before, went back to playing basketball. I walked off the court, bruised and embarrassed but alive.

The older gentleman who had seen me get beaten to a pulp approached me as I limped back to the Hill and said, "Why didn't you fight back?"

I looked at him, thinking, *Why didn't you help me fight back?* Then I shook my head. "You don't know who those people are."

Bayo must have heard what was happening, because he came running up to me as I made my way to the Hill. He asked me what happened, I told him, and he put his arm around me and walked me home as the older man followed, continuing his talk about why I should have fought back.

But still, though Africa is my birthplace, the Bronx is my home.

• • •

Violence wasn't the only obstacle we faced. Due to the district we lived in, another major obstacle was the subpar public school system. History states that desegregation of schools in America took place in 1968, but since then, economically poor minority students, especially African Americans and Latinos, have been increasingly segregated in schools.[5] And the decades-plus reigning champ of "most segregated schools" in the US has been New York State.[6]

Why is segregation an issue? Because it plays a major role in school funding, which is dependent on local tax revenues. Schools in predominantly white neighborhoods typically receive more funding because tax revenues there are higher.[7] These schools have more money to spend on tools and resources such as tutoring programs. Lower-income communities, predominantly communities of color, draw lower tax revenues, which means fewer school resources and greater responsibility placed on the parents, who are often less educated or stretched thin trying to provide for a family.[8]

Studies show that when a school is able to invest more money into their student body, the graduation rates increase, which leads to higher rates of college acceptance, which subsequently leads to earning more disposable income, improving the cycle of school funding for the next generation.[9] The cycle is reversed in schools whose funds are reduced.[10] Our enrollment in the Bronx public school system put Bayo and me into the latter category. The quality of the school buildings and classrooms was abysmal, and the resources were either outdated, worn, or nonexistent.

A second educational obstacle we faced was the heavy use of standardized testing. During my elementary and middle school years, more emphasis was put on this new form of measuring students' performance, and thereby the teachers'. Being a teacher in the South Bronx, my mother recalls, "The teachers taught students how to take a test instead of teaching them how to think critically." Schools that had high test scores received incentives, while schools that received low test scores received interventions, which meant the school was put on a sort of probation while the teachers and principal were monitored—and sometimes replaced. Most Bronx schools that didn't have the proper tools, resources, and high levels of parent involvement usually received low scores, thus interventions, while the schools with the resources received higher scores, thus more funding and incentives. The rich got richer education and the poor got poorer education.

I think that's probably why I always sensed that some teachers never really cared about me; all I ever felt like to some teachers was a potential test result. Mom would confirm this notion every time Bayo and I objected to writing reports for her.

"Boys, those teachers don't care about you. . . . All you are is just a number to them. So get to the table, pick up the *New York Times*, and write those reports so you can learn how to think critically and prove the school system wrong."

Mom always took education seriously. Sometimes too seriously, I thought. Despite working two jobs, she was always at every parent-teacher conference. She reviewed every homework assignment, and if she received a phone call from a teacher saying I had fooled around in class—which happened often— I automatically got a spanking. Her goal was to smash any educational roadblock that stood in our way.

Teachers had it almost as bad as we did. Mom had no problem marching to the school and confronting a teacher for not maintaining the proper teaching standards. If a teacher gave us a project that Mom thought was too easy, the teacher would hear about it. If a teacher taught something incorrectly, that teacher would never do it again as long as Bayo or I were in the class. And God forbid, if a teacher disrespected or said anything inappropriate to one of us, *Diary of a Mad Black Woman* would be in full effect!

One day Bayo came home from school in an unusual mood. Now, anytime Mom sensed any bit of abnormality in our demeanor, she would get straight to the point. "What happened, Bayo?"

With his eyes staring at the ground, Bayo shook his head in a way that meant "nothing." At this point Mom really knew something was wrong.

"Bayo, did somebody do something to you?"

Bayo finally said, "Yes, the teacher made fun of me in front of the entire class."

"*What?* What happened?" Mom asked as I stood by.

Bayo explained he had a new teacher that day. When the teacher took attendance, she couldn't pronounce our last name. It's hard for most people to pronounce, so we were used to it. But instead of asking Bayo how to pronounce *Adeleke*, she began to jokingly mispronounce it multiple different ways. "A-day-lake," "Ad-ee-leek," "Ad-Lincoln," and so on. The class started laughing, so she kept on going. Finally Bayo corrected her.

"It's pronounced Ad-day-*lay*-kay!"

The teacher paused, gave Bayo a stern look, and said, "A-day-leek whatever," then moved on to the next name on the attendance sheet.

Mom was furious, but Mom's furious state was not like that of other parents I knew. Just as Mom was able to easily identify when there was something wrong with Bayo or me, over the years I had learned to identify when Mom had reached her boiling point: she became quiet, using few words; her posture became straighter; she was calmer and stiller than usual; and sometimes she would just stare into space. When I saw Mom like that, I got scared! To this day, I'm convinced that if a person could see the images in Mom's mind when she was in that state, they would see the equivalent of a thousand hells spilling over, but on the outside all they would see is a person as cool as the other side of the pillow.

After Mom began to come back into her normal self, she softly said, "You did the right thing by trying to correct her, Bayo." Then with a smirk she continued, "Don't worry. I will teach her how to say your name tomorrow. Let's get ready for bed."

I couldn't help but think, *OOOOOOOOh, tomorrow is gonna be a good day!*

Bayo and I were both attending PS 122, which was about a mile north of the Hill on the corner of Bailey Avenue and Kingsbridge Road. The next day Mom walked us to school. When we arrived, the teachers were at the entrance, waiting to collect their students for the day. Bayo pointed out the new teacher right away, and Mom made a beeline to her, with Bayo and me on each side.

"Hello, Mrs. . . . ?" my mom asked pleasantly, as she reached out to shake the teacher's hand.

The teacher accepted Mom's greeting and said, "Mrs. Rosenberg."

"Nice to meet you, Mrs. Rosenberg," Mom said with a smile. "You know my son, Bayo, I take it . . . and this is his brother, Remi. I'm also an elementary school teacher. I work in the South Bronx."

I could tell from Mrs. Rosenberg's look that she knew exactly why Mom had showed up. The woman was nervous. "Um, oh, that's nice. How are—"

"Bayo told me about a little incident that happened in class yesterday. Can *you* share with me what happened?"

Nerves overtook Mrs. Rosenberg. "Um . . . mm . . . yeah . . . I . . . did have a hard time pronouncing his . . . your . . . last name yesterday."

That was all Mom needed to hear. "How dare you humiliate my son in front of the class!" Mom got in Mrs. Rosenberg's face. "You are a teacher . . . let me start over again. You're an *adult*. Don't you ever make fun of my son's name or my name ever again! Do you understand me?"

Mrs. Rosenberg nodded.

Then Mom proceeded to give Mrs. Rosenberg a pronunciation lesson in front of everyone, "Ad-day-*lay*-kay! Say it!"

"Ad-day-*lay*-kay," the teacher nervously mimicked.

"Again! Ad-day-*lay*-kay." Mom made her repeat it as Bayo and I, along with a few other students, teachers, and parents, stood by and watched.

"Ad-day-*lay*-kay. I'm sorry," Mrs. Rosenberg said.

"Apology accepted."

The teacher walked into the school as embarrassed as Bayo had been the day before. Mom looked at us both, gave us a hug, then went on her way. Bayo walked into the school as proud as could be, with his head up and his chest out. And let's just say that teacher never mispronounced *Adeleke* ever again.

When we got home that night, Mom told us, "Never let anyone make fun of or defame your name. Your name is who you are, and you are royalty."

"Yes, Mom," Bayo and I said in unison.

"Do you know what *Adeleke* means?" Mom asked.

We both shook our heads, so Mom explained, "*Ade* means 'crown,' and the full translation for *Adeleke* is 'the crown is above.' Its meaning can be summarized in three words: *royalty*, *power*, and *completeness*. In European culture, royalty is described using names such as duke, monarch, king, queen, prince, or princess. However, in Yoruba culture, like Native American culture, royalty is referred to as chief or, in some areas, *ade*. Bayo, your full name, Adebayo, means 'the crown meets with joy.' And Remi, your full name, Aderemi, means 'the crown has appeased me.'"

As usual, I had to throw in humor. "Wow, Mom. So we're like Prince Akeem from *Coming to America*?"

"You can say that," Mom responded. As she had many other times, Mom went on to share our Nigerian history with us. She talked to us about who our father was and what he had tried to accomplish, the lavish lifestyle our family used to live, and what life would have been like if my father hadn't died. As always, I was mesmerized.

"Do you think we'll ever get the money back from the Nigerian government?" I asked.

Mom gave a response that I would hear a million times. "I wouldn't hold your breath for it. All we have to work with is what God has given us. . . . Don't count on anything else."

. . .

Many nights later, as I sat on our trundle bed, I began to reflect on my life in the Bronx. Bayo was in the living room, watching TV, and I was in our room alone, thinking about Mom's financial struggles, the bad things I had experienced in my short life, and the life I felt we should have been living—the life that was stolen from us. We had one lamp in our bedroom that sat on our only dresser, and the lampshade had been thrown away, probably because we broke it. Right below the lamp was a framed picture of Chief. I got up from the bed, walked over to the picture, and picked it up with both hands. And for the first time, it finally hit me: *your father is dead, he's never coming back, and this is your life*. I was so young when my father died that I couldn't understand it, but it was in that moment of reflection that I finally grieved my father's absence for the first time. I broke down crying.

My life wasn't structured for me to succeed, and I was finally realizing it. Inner-city life, a single mother, financial hardship, violence, a subpar school system, and fatherlessness.

My mom must have heard my cries from the living room because she quickly rushed in and asked what was wrong. It took me a while to get it out, but finally I told her, "I miss my dad. I wish he was here so we could have a better life." Mom put her arms around me and comforted me. She assured me that everything would be all right; we would make it. In her demeanor, if not in her words, she summarized the title of that Tupac song: "I know it looks like things will never change . . . but, my son, you must *keep your head up*."

Mom did the best job she could, but as I grew older and taller, my fear of her maternal presence began to wane, and the absence of my father loomed large.

CHAPTER SIX

ALL I EVER WANTED

I needed a father, and I found one in the arts.

I once heard author Roland Warren say, "Kids have a hole in their soul in the shape of their dad. And if a father is unwilling or unable to fill that hole, it can leave a wound that is not easily healed." Statistics show that children who grow up in fatherless homes are more likely to drop out of high school and are at a greater risk of poverty, drug and alcohol abuse, juvenile imprisonment, and teenage pregnancy.[1]

Though I wasn't aware of it at the time, that night when I grieved over my father would be the first step of a journey to find the treatment for my wounds and something to fill my paternal void. And that journey would lead me to the art of hip-hop.

By the time I was twelve, instead of sending Bayo and me to the local barbershops, Mom would sometimes send us about ten floors up to our friend and neighbor Chad. Chad, who was four years older than me, was a modern renaissance man, a smooth brother full of knowledge and an assimilator of black culture and experiences. Cutting hair was his art form, and his barbershop—which was his bedroom—was a sanctuary for deep discussions.

I looked up to Chad for many other reasons. The lectures he gave me as he would cut my hair always seemed to be laced with wisdom. He also blasted music that my mom would never in a million years let me listen to! It was almost like a foreign-exchange event every time I visited Chad for cuts, because although he was born and raised in New York, he loved to hear about Africa. With an insatiable hunger for knowledge, Chad would pepper me with questions.

"What was it like?"

"How are the people?"

"What language did you speak?"

"What was the meaning of that?"

"Tell me about cultural trends."

"Will you ever go back?"

I would share stories with him that I had heard from my mom, and in exchange for my knowledge about Africa, Chad gave me an education in hip-hop. The dude was like a rap encyclopedia. He knew about everything that pertained to the art of hip-hop, as well as every popular rapper: Nas, Pete Rock, Jay-Z, WU-Tang Clan, Rakim, A Tribe Called Quest, KRS-One, and many others.

As he carefully cut my hair, his head nodded with the cadence of the beats, his words mimicked the lyrics precisely, and the confidence that flowed from the music seemed to pulse through his veins. It was like he lived and breathed the very essence of hip-hop culture. In retrospect I believe that just like me, he was looking for the same thing I would find in it—a father figure.

One fall evening in 1994, Chad's lessons cemented me as a firm believer in the art.

I knocked on Chad's apartment door.

"Who is it?" a female voice yelled.

"It's Remi, Mrs. Brown. I'm here to see Chad for a haircut." My voice echoed through the hallway.

As I stood at the door waiting, I heard Chad's mom say, "Chad, Remi's at the door for you."

Within seconds he opened the door. "What's up, brother? You ready?"

"Yeah," I said, and Chad led me into his bedroom.

I was used to hearing music pulsating from his room, but this time my ears were entranced by the sounds of a new rapper. This guy wasn't just rapping; he was telling stories. He was dynamic, lyrically astute, and the beats he rapped over sounded a little like the old-school music Mom listened to.

I raised my voice over the blasting rhymes and beats. "Yo! Who is that?"

Chad grinned. "Biggie, Notorious B.I.G.! It's his new album, *Ready to Die*."

I blurted out, "Biggie? Whew . . . this dude is legit!"

As the music kept playing, my head nodded like a bobblehead on the dash of a car. I couldn't stop moving. When Chad was cutting my hair, my feet were tapping, and when he took a step back to take a look at his work before moving to another section of my head, I was back to nodding. It was like a synchronized haircut exhibition in Chad's room.

"Who the hell is this? Paging me at 5:46 in the morning, crack of dawn, now I'm yawning. Wipe the cold out my eye, see who's this paging me and why?" Though the album was just released, Chad had all the lyrics to "Warning" memorized, so he rapped along in sync as he cut my hair. *"Remember all your people from the Hill, up in Brownsville, that you rolled dice with, smoked blunts and got nice with."*[2]

"Yo! Biggie just mentioned the Hill!" I pointed out. In my foolish excitement I didn't realize he was rapping about the Hill in Brooklyn, not the Bronx.

Chad laughed. "Nah, man, different place."

Chad and I usually had long discussions as music played in the background, but this time the music did all the talking while we became the backdrop. By the end of that song, I was hooked, and just when I thought the hook couldn't go deeper, a song by the name of "Juicy" came on, laced with lyrical inspiration.

"This album is dedicated to all the teachers that told me I'd never amount to nothing. To all the people that lived above the building that I was hustling in front of [that] called the police on me when I was just trying to make some money to feed my daughter. (It's all good.) To all my peoples in the struggle. . . . It was all a dream. I used to read Word Up! *magazine. Salt-n-Peppa and Heavy D up in the limousine."* Being a dreamer, I was hooked by the opening monologue and lyrics. Like a hopeful church member listening to his pastor, I felt like Biggie was talking directly to me; I was that person who felt like he was in the midst of a long struggle; I was that person stuck in a world that said *"I'd never amount to nothing;"* I was that kid who would spend hours a day dreaming with friends about a future that I thought could never be.

As the song continued, Biggie mentioned the struggles he faced growing up in the inner city, living in a single-parent home, and being broke, but all those experiences were only things of the past. Biggie had made it! He came from nothing, and whether the world liked his methods or not, he became something. As Chad kept rapping alongside the lyrics, I just sat there in a trance.

"Living life without fear; putting five carats in my baby girl's ear . . . Super Nintendo, Sega Genesis, when I was dead broke, man, I couldn't picture this. Fifty-inch screen, money green leather sofa, got two rides, a limousine with a chauffeur. . . . Thinking back on my one-room shack, now my mom pimps an Act with minks on her back. And she loves to show me off, of course, smiles every time my face is up in The Source. *. . . Damn right I like the life I live, 'cause I went from negative to positive, and it's all good."[3]*

There was no more head nodding or foot tapping, just stillness and contemplation. By the time the song ended, I had eaten up every word, and the nourishment had manifested itself in the form of hope. In retrospect, that evening was a major turning point in my life. For the first time I thought, *I can make it out. I can make my mom proud and provide for her. . . . I can rise above my circumstances. It doesn't have to be a dream that never comes to fruition—it can be a reality!*

After the album finished playing, I left Chad's apartment filled with the encouragement and the paternal direction I had been searching for. Like many fatherless kids growing up in inner cities across the country, I found a father in hip-hop.

• • •

One thing that family and friends have always loved about me is the fact that I have an "all in" personality. And one thing that family and friends have always despised about me is the fact that I have an "all in" personality. This trait of mine has always been a blessing and a curse. It's a blessing because if I want something positive, I will run through hell and back to get it. And it's a curse because if I want something negative, I will run to hell without careful consideration, put my foot on the Devil's throat, and snatch what I want out of his hands.

My newfound paternal presence was a mixture of both blessings and curses. I wanted all that my "father" had to offer me, so naturally I was all in.

I dubbed every rap tape and CD I could, I studied music videos when Mom was out of the apartment, and I even began to mimic my father by writing music myself.

While some dads use a ball to play catch with their sons, I used rhymes and beats to play catch with my dad. And the more time I spent with him, the more I fell in love with him. I fell in love with his display, his confidence, his allure, his portrayal of rags to riches, and his conspicuous representatives (the rappers). Why? Because I was now able to see men like Biggie, who had come from where I came from, who grew up in single-parent homes, and who seemed to be successful in life, then draw a blueprint for my life from their words. And not only did I study my father for the purpose of mimicking his art, but also for the purpose of mimicking the life he often imitated through his art—this is where the curse would soon manifest.

On the other side of the battle, my mother kept my brother and me immersed in her definition of the arts. From the time we were small, we frequented the Metropolitan Museum of Art, the Schomburg Center for Research in Black Culture, the Studio Museum in Harlem, and the Lehman College Art Gallery—all places where Mom worked at one time or another. She would take part-time jobs at these various places for two reasons: One, she loved the arts. And two, it became a way for us to learn about her passion at no expense. By the time I was twelve, I had been so exposed to my mom's artistic realm that I was well aware of the Met's masterpiece paintings; Michael C. Rockefeller's exhibit of famous African art; jazz pioneers, such as Coltrane, Gillespie, and Davis; and writings from Langston Hughes, Zora Neale Hurston, Richard Wright, Marcus Garvey, Lorraine Hansberry, and James Baldwin. The arts were so much a part of our family life that Mom recalls people staring in amazement as Bayo and I would enthusiastically but peacefully study exhibits while taking notes.

I must admit, I loved the arts that my mom exposed me to. They gave me depth, showed me the immense creativity of black people, made me aware of other world cultures, and kept me somewhat connected to my African heritage. But they didn't give me the hope I was now receiving from my self-appointed father; therefore, his art began to overtake what Mom had given me all those years. With that, a war between both parents for my future ensued.

• • •

"What . . . the hell . . . is *this*, Remi?" Mom screamed as she stood in the entrance of my bedroom.

As if I didn't know what she was talking about, I replied, "What?"

"You know what! Stop playing with me, Remi! This!" With one hand she held up the Snoop Dogg *Doggystyle* cassette tape, and with the other hand she pointed to it.

Aw, man, I'm in trouble now, I thought. The cover art was a cartoon of a female dog wearing a G-string with her head in a doghouse while Snoop was on top of the house, reaching for her backside. At the top of the cover three other dogs looked on while at the bottom right a dogcatcher and a rat peeked from behind a corner. A large "Parental Advisory Explicit Lyrics" sticker covered the bottom left corner. And to make matters worse for me, the J-card unfolded into a comic strip that detailed—let's just say—a very explicit day in Snoop's life.

I knew that my mom would never approve of me listening to rap, especially *Doggystyle*, so after listening to the cassette, and other cassettes that I had bought or dubbed, I would hide them in the apartment. My hiding skills must have diminished because Mom found the most visually explicit one of the bunch.

"It's music, Ma. And the cover, that's art," I said timidly.

She took a deep breath. "You know you're not allowed to listen to this kind of music in *my* house. No, you're not allowed to listen to this kind of music, period!"

I stuttered through my reply. "But . . . Ma . . . it's my kind of art . . . I mean . . . it's art. Like Coltrane, Maya Angelou . . . all those other people you introduced me to. It's just a different kind of art."

Mom fought back her anger and frustration and uttered words she knew she shouldn't say. "Bitches . . . and hoes, and killing '*nig-gaz*' . . . and . . . hustling . . . is not art, boy! You done lost your mind, haven't you?"

"Uh . . ."

"Don't answer the question. Just tell me this: Are there any more of these tapes or CDs in this house?"

I stared at her for a second, contemplating whether to tell the truth, then said no. But there were more, a lot more.

"This is a warning, Remi. Don't let me find any more of *this* in my house." Mom gestured at the cassette.

"Yes, ma'am." Then she walked me out of the apartment to the hallway garbage disposal and made me throw the cassette, cassette cover, and case down the incinerator chute. Like I said, my parents didn't get along too well.

• • •

Though there was debate between my mom and me as to which music was and wasn't art, there was one creative expression we both always agreed on wholly and cherished as a form of art, and that was acting. I'll never forget Mom taking my brother and me to see our first play, *Show Boat*. I didn't want the play to end. The acting and singing were so good that it teleported us into a world that allowed us to forget about our problems.

"Old man river, that old man river, he don't say nothing but he must know something, he just keeps rolling, he keeps on rolling along. / I get weary and sick of trying, I'm tired of living and scared of dying, but old man river, he just keeps rolling along."[4]

For weeks I annoyed my mom and brother by mimicking Michel Bell's flawless performance.

I mimicked other plays as well: *Kiss of the Spider Woman* and *Bring in 'da Noise, Bring in 'da Funk* with Savion Glover. If Mom could score free tickets or save up some cash, we attended, we observed, and we learned about the power of acting. And, oh, the conversations that the plays would spark among us as we took the train from Broadway back to the Bronx were priceless. We shared questions, debates, theories, and laughs, all in the name of acting. At times it was as though we were the only ones on the train, a mother and her two sons savoring art as if it were a reality of our own.

Little did Mom know that *this* art was silently playing tug-of-war with the father I had fallen in love with.

In the spring of 1995 and summer of 1996, the tide of the battle began to turn in Mom's favor.

At least once a month Mom made it a habit to take us to the cinema. We would take the 12 bus across the Hudson River to the 1 train, then head toward the heart of Manhattan. Our theater of choice was the AMC Theater on Eighty-Fourth Street and Broadway, which was conveniently located across the street from Barnes & Noble—another place we would often frequent and where we even wrote reports.

On the weekend of April 7, 1995, we saw a movie we'd been anticipating since the first preview was released. The name of the movie was *Bad Boys*, directed by Michael Bay, an up-and-coming filmmaker with a unique style. It was his directorial debut. While Michael Bay's name was foreign to us at the time, the stars of the film, Martin Lawrence and Will Smith, were definitely not. They both had shows on prime-time TV. Will Smith's show, *Fresh Prince of Bel-Air*, aired on NBC, and Martin's show, which was named after him, aired on Fox. I can't tell you the number of laughs Bayo, Mom, and I had around the TV as we watched their shows, but there were a lot.

We arrived in a packed theater, found our seats, sat down, and waited in giddy anticipation. After the previews ended, the opening scene started.

Vroom! A black Porsche sped down a highway in Miami on an early morning. In the passenger seat was Detective Marcus Burnett, played by Martin Lawrence, and in the driver's seat was Detective Mike Lowrey, played by Will Smith. As the Porsche rolled down the road, the jokes kept rolling and rolling and rolling, and the entire theater kept erupting in laughter. I smiled at everyone's enjoyment.

There was comedy, there was action, there was suspense, but most importantly for me, there was a source of inspiration. Having an analytical mind like Chief, I was able to recognize something in *Bad Boys* I had never seen in a film: two men (Burnett and Lowrey) who looked like me and had my demeanor, but instead of playing gangbangers or hustlers or athletes or deadbeat dads, or other typical roles that African American men were known for playing at the time, they were playing heroes with swagger, running and gunning and saving the day.

Like the night I left Chad's house after I first heard Biggie, I walked out of the theater heavily impacted by Michael Bay's film. *Bad Boys* allowed me to see life through a different lens. Yes, there was cussing, and yes, there was violence, and yes, I was thirteen and it might have been too much for me to absorb at the time, but the movie planted a lesson in me that no other speech or sermon or art had been capable of planting. For the first time I got this little thought that said, *I don't have to be a drug dealer or a hustler or a rapper or an athlete or work some menial job that people expect of me because of my background and environment. No, I can be like Mike . . . or Marcus. In some way I can be a hero too.*

I filed the inspiration deep down within me and continued on with life. Providentially, a year later Michael Bay's second film, *The Rock*, was released.

The Rock was advertised as another action-packed film, lighter on the comedy in comparison to *Bad Boys*, but much heavier on the suspense. I wasn't as familiar with the actors as I had been with Martin and Will, but knowing that Michael Bay was behind it, I knew it was going to be good.

I made my way to the theater, sat down, and watched. The premise of the movie entails a group of rogue special forces marines who seize control of Alcatraz with tour-group hostages, then threaten to launch nerve gas into San Francisco if their ransom isn't paid. The film held my attention. I was thoroughly entertained. And then something unexpected happened. A group of men by the name of Navy SEALs was introduced.

I had never heard of Navy SEALs. In the Bronx we didn't get many military recruiters who visited schools to educate inner-city kids about special forces, and I definitely never saw any advertisements about Navy SEALs around town. It was the Bronx; no one comes from there and becomes a Navy SEAL. So when this mysterious group dressed in black showed up in the movie, my attention quickly shifted to intrigue.

"Green-light the SEAL incursion," a character in the film said. The SEALs received the go-ahead to sneak onto Alcatraz, rescue the hostages, and defuse the missiles. As I sat on the edge of my seat, I got my first insight into who these bold men were and what they did. Their gear was state-of-the-art, they didn't seem uptight the way other military units were often portrayed in film, their movements were smooth and precise, and each member of the team—though unique—operated cohesively with everyone else. I would later find out that the guys playing SEALs were so convincing because Michael Bay hired real Navy SEALs for the roles.

Then came the iconic shower shootout scene. Spoiler alert: the SEALs are discovered, a shootout ensues, and the marines kill all the SEALs. One might think that would leave a bad impression with me, but it didn't. Even after the movie ended, I couldn't get Navy SEALs out of my mind. The scene of the SEALs rising out of the water to sacrifice themselves to save others kept replaying in my head. I recognized something honorable in that. Something special about that group of men somehow resonated with me.

Bad Boys planted the seed that I could one day be a hero. *The Rock* planted the seed of the type of hero I would want to be if I ever could. In the weeks that followed, I learned as much as I could about the Navy SEALs, and one day I made the commitment to myself: *Remi, if you can ever be something special, it's going to be a Navy SEAL.*

CHAPTER SEVEN

HUSTLER

There's a way around every obstacle—
but some ways are worse than others.

Imagine a group of five-year-olds dreaming about their future. "I want to be an astronaut when I grow up," one kid says. Another jumps in with, "Oh, oh, I want to be the president of the United States when I grow up!" And, finally, the shyest in the group speaks up: "No, I have a better idea. I want to be the person who finds the cure for cancer when I grow up!" Like these kids' ideas, my thought of becoming a Navy SEAL was just another far-fetched and unattainable dream. So as time passed, the inspiration died out, the dream was forgotten, and the seeds were locked in an impenetrable box and buried deep within.

My teenage years were diametrically opposite those of my younger years, when I slap boxed with my friends or played kick the door and run. We all grew up too fast and went our separate ways. Some friends, like Ricardo and Roberto, moved north to the suburbs. Some, like Chad, went off to college, and others spent time trying to figure out their own future. The Hill playground became a ghost town, and the streets outside of the Hill became my second home.

By the time I was fifteen, I was all about getting money. My self-appointed father preached through Jay-Z's *Reasonable Doubt*: "*We hustle out of a sense of hopelessness; sort of a desperation.*" I was desperate to have the things Mom couldn't give me: Jordans every time a new pair was released, top-of-the-line clothes (Coogi, Iceberg, Sean John), a car, financial security, and whatever I desired. And along with my desperate hustle, I would quickly learn to live with the regrets for the choices I made to get what I wanted.

"Where are you going, Remi?" Mom asked as I walked out of our apartment.

"I'm headed to the store on Fordham Road. I should be back in an hour," I replied. I was fifteen.

"Okay, be careful," she said as she walked into the kitchen.

I went straight into the stairwell, closed the door behind me, and stood there, pondering. *You shouldn't do this. . . . This is bad. Remi, you can't do that to your mom.* But then a thought counter to that came rushing in. *Your dad has been dead for years. She doesn't need it anymore. And besides, this will help her detach from him.*

My thoughts duked it out like well-matched boxers in the ring.

Remi, it's the only thing he left her. You won't be able to turn back from this.

But Remi, once you make it, you can buy as many of them for your mom as you want. Plus, she hasn't worn it in months, so she won't miss it.

I reached into my pocket, pulled out the engagement ring my father had given to Mom, stared at it, then said, "She won't miss it. He's been gone for years."

Walking to the local pawnshop that day was one of the hardest walks I had ever taken down Fordham Road. I cut through Devoe Park, and within minutes I had arrived at the Fordham Pawnbrokers, which was located next to McDonald's between Grand and Davidson Avenues.

"Yo, yo, yo," I said as I knocked on the thick ballistic glass.

"What do you want?" the overweight pawnbroker said.

"I have something worth a lot of money." I pulled out the engagement ring and dropped it into the transition box. He pulled the box back slowly and picked up the ring to examine it.

"That ring, man, that ring is worth at least . . . ten thousand dollars." At this point my shame and regret had dissipated. I was in total negotiation mode, a rookie against a pro.

The pawnbroker examined the ring as though he were looking at a pebble he had just pulled out of his shoe.

"Yo, what's wrong with you, man?" I said with a bit of frustration.

Finally he looked up at me and said, "A hundred fifty dollars."

"What?!" I yelled. He dropped the ring back into the transition box and began to push it back toward me. "Wait, wait, wait. How about five hundred?"

"One fifty is my only offer. Take it or leave it," he said, still expressionless. The thoughts I had in the staircase resurfaced. *Your mom doesn't need it anymore. Your dad is dead and has been dead for a long time. She won't know that it's gone . . . so you can either take the money or let it continue to sit in her jewelry box with the rest of the dust mites.*

"I'll take it," I said bitterly.

"Are you sure? Because all transactions are final." He pointed to the large All Transactions Are Final poster taped to the door behind me.

I was so frustrated. "Yeah, man, I'm sure. Just give me the money."

I left that pawnshop with a mixture of deep regret and greedy joy. In time I learned to live with both emotions.

· · ·

The more I stole, the less it bothered me. Theft would define the beginning of my hustle. I had started out small, stealing a little bit from my mom, stealing from the local bodegas when the employees weren't paying attention. I worked myself up to stealing the engagement ring, then stealing from employers. I got so good at theft that I was always able to figure out creative ways to steal.

When I was sixteen, I took a job at a sneaker store in Manhattan. In 1998, minimum wage was $4.25, and I would get a little commission for every pair of shoes I sold. But for me, that wasn't enough. I wanted more.

One day I was in a section of the store alone, which was typical during slow hours and around closing time. As I stood by the door, staring out the window, a guy who looked like an investment-banker type rushed in and said, "I'm late for a meeting, and I need sneakers right now!"

"I got you. Do you have anything in mind?"

"No." Looking at the display wall, he pointed at the first sneaker that crossed his eye. "I'll take those . . . right there, size 10."

I sprinted to the storage room, grabbed the sneakers, then sprinted back out. He snatched the box out of my hands, took the sneakers out of the box, then gave the box back.

"Can you ring me up while I put these on?"

"Yeah, man," I said with a slight attitude. I didn't like the way he had ripped the shoes away from me.

I went to the register and scanned the box as usual, but for some strange reason the computer froze. Glancing back and forth between him and my computer, I said, "Um . . . excuse me . . . my computer froze. So you're going to have to wait a bit while I reset it."

"I don't have time to wait!" the customer replied.

"I don't know what to tell you, man. You can't leave without paying. I'm sorry, but you're going to have to wait or come back when you have more time."

Then the customer made a suggestion that got the wheels in my head turning. "All right, you're a smart and trustworthy guy, right?"

"Yeah, why?" I replied.

"How much are the sneakers?"

"Eighty-nine ninety-nine." As I gave my response, the guy pulled out his wallet, counted out five twenty-dollar bills, then handed me the cash.

"Keep the box; I don't need it. When you get your computer up and running, ring me up, pay for it with this, and because you're smart and trust-worthy, keep the change."

The customer turned and ran straight out of the store. Standing behind the register with the cash in my hand, I began to contemplate. Once the computer was up and running, I decided, *Easy money; this cash is mine.*

I took the empty box, grabbed some old shoes that were returned damaged without a box, placed the returned shoes in the empty box, wrote "damaged shoes" on it, and pocketed the hundred dollars.

For the remainder of my time at the sneaker store, when I saw an opportunity, I took it. I got so bold that I would say to customers as I fitted them for shoes, "If you don't need a receipt and can pay me cash, I can sell you those sneakers for three-quarters of the cost." It's a miracle I never got caught.

The money allowed me to buy whatever I wanted. At DeWitt Clinton High School, it made me who I wanted to be, *the man*. I walked the halls of Clinton (where James Baldwin, Stan Lee, Tracy Morgan, Ralph Lauren, and Neil Simon also walked) with a Nokia cell phone, the latest Sean John gear, and a pair of the latest sneakers every month. I would eventually expand my sneaker-selling enterprise by inviting students to bring cash to the sneaker shop in exchange for the latest kicks. I guess that's one thing that can happen when a young man doesn't receive affirmation from a father; he'll seek it from another source. For me it was from anyone who would give it.

. . .

The gimmicks I ran outside of high school were no different from the gimmicks I ran inside. No longer fearing spankings from Mom, I was the typical attention-seeking and teacher-manipulating class clown. I didn't get along with most of my teachers, I cut school often, and I rarely turned in my assignments on time. Between traditional school and Mom's homeschooling, I felt I had been in school so much that I just wanted it to be over. Furthermore, money and girls were more important to me than calculus and Olympe de Gouges.

My grades fluctuated between Ds and Cs, with a rare A and B when I chose to apply myself. The grades weren't low because I was stupid; I just wasn't motivated. When I *was* motivated (typically at the end of a semester), I became the black Einstein, somehow squeezing in the right grades just in time to avoid the dreaded double S: summer school.

But in the spring of 2000, just as I was due to graduate, my educational antics caught up with me.

During the last month of the spring semester, I was on track to fail half of my classes. I was so enveloped in my sneaker scam, music, and girlfriends that I had cut classes frequently—especially the last two classes of the day—and failed to turn in key assignments. Being a senior, that meant if I couldn't pull this one off, I wouldn't graduate as scheduled.

Realizing my impending doom, I shut down all illegal sneaker operations, took a light shift at the store, picked up my books, and did what I should have been doing the entire year—work! I finished any incomplete projects teachers would let me turn in. I did extra credit to boost my GPA, and as related to my nemesis, math, I studied linear functions, differential equations, exponential functions, and derivatives, all to pass my final math exams. From an educational standpoint, that was the hardest I had ever worked at that point in my life. I have no doubt that if I had put that much effort into my entire four years of high school, I could have received a full-ride academic scholarship like Bayo did. He followed in Chief's footsteps, studying engineering at Syracuse University.

The day before graduation, I walked into my counselor's office with my head high and my chest out, expecting to have passed every class.

"Hello, Mrs. Rodriguez. You're looking beautiful as always," I said with a smile.

As she thumbed through her cabinet, she replied nonchalantly, "Hello, Remi. Here for your report card, I take it."

"Yup. Looking forward to being done with this place and able to focus on my music," I said as I stood there in anxious excitement.

"That's not good!" she said.

"What's not good?"

"I can't seem to find your report card."

Not thinking anything of it, I said, "Oh, that's cool, I don't need it. I'm sure I passed all my classes." I turned to walk out.

Mrs. Rodriguez stopped me. "Wait . . . give me a second to check the graduation list."

As she made her way toward the long list posted on the wall, another counselor said, "Did you check the box of report cards for students that didn't meet the credit requirements for graduation?"

"Oh, that's right!" Mrs. Rodriguez said.

With a chuckle, I jumped in. "There's no need to check that pile, I should be—"

"Just give me a second, Remi," Mrs. Rodriguez said as she walked to the pile.

Within seconds of checking the pile, she pulled up my report card and said, "Here it is. *Remi Adeleke.*" I immediately got hot and woozy. Shock ran through every cell in my body as she looked it over.

That's impossible, I thought. *Who could have failed me?*

As she handed me my report card, she said, "Sorry, Remi. You passed every class except English."

"*What?* I did everything I had to do. I made up assignments. . . . I turned in my final report. Why would Mr. K fail me? What does this mean?"

"It means you won't be graduating tomorrow, and you'll have to go to summer school to make up the class. After you meet the requirements, then you can graduate."

I thought of all the plans I had for the summer and how embarrassing it was going to be to miss graduation. Worst of all, I thought of the women who were at the apartment, preparing for my graduation the next day: my mom, my grandmother, and my grandmother's closest sister, Aunt Dokey.

I went into survival mode.

"No, I can't go to summer school. I have to graduate tomorrow."

"Remi, it's *impossible*. . . . It's too late. I'm sorry. There's no way."

"Damn, damn, damn!"

"Excuse me!"

"I'm not talking to you, Mrs. Rodriguez. Sorry. I'm thinking out loud. . . . There's got to be a way!" I paced in her office as if I were a lawyer trying to figure out a way to get a serial killer acquitted.

"Maybe if you talk to Mr. Kozlowski," she said hesitantly.

I stopped pacing and stared at her. "Excuse me?"

She continued, "If you talk to him . . . I don't know. . . . Maybe he can change your grade. He's the only one that can do it."

"Are you serious?" I replied.

"I've never seen a teacher do it before, especially right before graduation. But . . . it won't hurt to try. He should be in his office now."

That was all I needed to hear. Before she could say another word, I was out the door.

It was the end of the day, and the teachers were beginning to depart. I sprinted to Mr. Kozlowski's office. When I got to his door, I peeked through the window to see if he was there. He was,

Thank God, I thought.

Seeing him seated, I dusted myself off, took a deep breath, then made my way in.

"Mr. K, why did you fail me? That's not cool, man! It's the day before graduation. You shouldn't have failed me!" Let's just say I thought my aggression would intimidate him into changing my grade.

With his eyes focused on the paperwork he was attending to, he said, "*You* failed, Remi. You missed a high number of classes, you only showed up consistently in the last month, and though you turned in make-up assignments, they weren't enough to fix the damage you'd already done."

"Come on, man. You can't do this to me."

"I didn't do this to you. You did it to yourself. Look, Remi: you're a bright kid, and I know that. That's why in good conscience I couldn't pass you. You didn't deserve to pass."

He was right, and with every cell of my body I knew he was right, but a part of me couldn't give in. I couldn't just quit. "Listen. I did the extra work. You know that. And if you know I'm not stupid, why can't you just pass me?"

"I'm done listening to you, Remi. All I can do is recommend an English teacher I think you should take for summer school."

"No, I'm not going to summer school!"

The back-and-forth went on for several minutes, and somehow, the longer it went on, the more hope I started to get. I made up stories. I got more aggressive, then less aggressive. I apologized, but most important, I just talked and talked and talked about why I should graduate.

Finally I sensed something break in him. He stood up suddenly and said in a rather loud tone, "Okay, you want me to change your grade?"

"Yes, please," I replied.

"I'll change your grade . . . but only if you can complete an assignment for me!"

"Anything. What's the assignment?"

Mr. Kozlowski sat back down, looked me directly in the eyes, and said, "I want you to write a fifty-page report as to why English is important in modern society. Have it on my desk by eight a.m. If you can do that, I will change your grade in time for you to graduate."

With my chest out, I nodded enthusiastically and said, "Yeah, I can do that. Eight a.m."

What made the situation even more entertaining is that right after I agreed to the terms, a girl by the name of Shania, who was in the same English class as me, busted into the office with the same question.

"Why did I fail?"

Because Mr. K had given me an opportunity to pass, he had to give it to her, too, so he did.

When I got home, I discovered Mom had somehow already received the news from the school that I wasn't graduating, and she was not happy.

"Remi, I can't believe you're not graduating high school!"

"Ma, it's okay. I got it all worked out. I'm going to graduate."

"According to whom? *The school told me you failed English and can't graduate tomorrow!* Of all the classes, Remi, how could you fail *English*?"

"Mom, I worked it out with Mr. K. I just have to do a little project for him; then he's going to change my grade. Tell Grandma and Aunt Dokey to put on their best tomorrow," I said in a smooth, New Yorker–type tone. "And, Ma, you too. I'm going to graduate."

Mom's response was one I've received a million times. "Oh my goodness, Remi, you are *crazy!*"

"Trust me, I'm going to graduate, Ma."

Full of frustration and not believing a word I said, she turned and walked away.

Instead of going directly to Mom's Compaq computer to start my report, I went into my bedroom and procrastinated for two hours. Finally I got myself out of the room, went into the living room, and started writing.

I don't know how I was able to pull it off, but I finally finished the report of exactly fifty pages at around five the next morning. I showered, took a quick nap, woke up, threw on my slacks and collared shirt, then jumped in a cab to Clinton.

When I got to Mr. Kozlowski's office and peeked in, I saw he was already there, all decked out in his faculty graduation attire. I waited a second to see if Shania would make it in time as well, but she didn't. I later found out that she decided not to do the report because she failed a second class as well and would have to go to summer school even if she turned in Mr. K's assignment.

I crept into his office cautiously. "Mr. K . . . um . . . I'm here . . . and I . . . completed your assignment."

Without saying anything, Mr. K gestured for me to hand him the thick stack of papers. After handing him my assignment, I stood there wondering what would happen next. Two days earlier I had expected to pass every class and was wrong, so I tried not to anticipate any outcome this time. I just stood there in suspense.

Mr. K flipped through the papers as if they were a deck of cards, stopping to scan a few pages intermittently. He asked me a few questions about the report. When he was done with the questioning, he gave me a speech I will never forget.

"Remi, do you see what you just did? I wish you had done this through-out the entire semester. You have so much *potential*, and I hope as you move forward in life, you will tap into it and not try to take the easy way out. I'm going to change your grade to a C, which means you will pass my class and can therefore walk with your graduating class. Good luck with your future!"

"Thank you, Mr. K," I said.

He nodded, and then, as if I were a ghost, he refocused his attention on the work he had been doing before I walked in. I departed in a bit of shock, not because he changed my grade but because I had pulled it off. I had talked with him, debated him, stayed up all night, written a fifty-page report, and turned it in on time.

As I left Mr. K's office, I thought, *Man, I can talk my way in and out of anything. If I can do that, there's nothing in life I can't do if I put my mind to it. Nothing.* I never expected that the greatest lesson of my high school years would come on the last day and through a lesson I created on my own.

• • •

With high school out of the way, I was off to the races. I quit the sneaker store, teamed up with a hustler I met along the way named Roderick, and we started selling drugs. My grandmother lived in Washington Heights, and in our younger years Bayo and I spent many days and nights at her apart-ment. Having spent a lot of time in her area, I knew it was where Dominicans had control of the vast drug market. So that's where I built relationships and brought my "work."

But soon Rod and I realized that with Dominicans controlling the Washington Heights area down to the southernmost border of the Bronx, gangs running the Bronx drug trade, and the Queens and Brooklyn territories too risky and unfamiliar to impose upon, we had to find a less-saturated and safer place to sell. We were just a two-man operation—there was no way we were going to go to war with anyone over a corner—so we did the next best thing. We jumped on the Metro-North and set up shop in Upstate New York for a few days at a time. One week we'd be upstate; the next week we were back down in the city, replenishing our inventory or tending to other hustles.

After a while we decided to expand our operation by bringing in an old friend from the Hill, Ricardo. Seven years earlier, Ricky and his family had moved to Poughkeepsie to escape the trappings of the inner city. By the time Rod and I had partnered with him, he knew the people and surrounding areas of Poughkeepsie like the back of his hand. Ricky's knowledge meant we spent less time trying to find unpoliced areas where we could sell, which in return meant less time on the streets.

We were the three amigos, the rebellious three out to conquer Poughkeepsie like Bundy and Sin from the movie *Belly*. We watched *Scarface* on repeat during the day and hit the college town of New Paltz or Poughkeepsie house parties at night. We did well, and the money was good, but it wasn't good enough for what I was trying to do.

I had big dreams of launching a record company that rivaled Roc-A-Fella, Bad Boy, and Murder Inc. Not only did I want to make music; I wanted to produce and control music. So, if I was going to be able to do that, I was going to need to generate a lot more money in a shorter amount of time. I needed a new hustle. And I would quickly find what I was looking for.

"Nice to meet you," I said to Ms. Green, a manager at one of the biggest cellular companies at the time. "My name is Remi Adeleke, and I'm here to interview for the cell phone sales position at WCT."

CHAPTER EIGHT

OUT OF CONTROL

A kingdom built on sand will eventually sink.

I'm still that kid with the multiple
flows, with multiple hoes.
When I spend I spend multiple
dough, reaching multiple goals!

There we were, Dios, Gift Man, and Desean, in my Lincoln LS. I was speeding at 120 miles per hour on the westbound side of the Norfolk–Virginia Beach Expressway while we all screamed in unison lyrics from our first compilation album. In the next lane, speeding and swerving alongside us, were Moreno, his cousin JR, the Twins, and Murdock in a Chrysler LHS, blasting the same music. It was about eleven in the evening, and we had just departed from the Atlantic Avenue Virginia Beach strip, where we were selling copies of our new album.

The year 2001 was one of the craziest, most financially rewarding years that a skinny kid like me from the Bronx could ever imagine. At nineteen years of age, I had accumulated thousands of dollars from my cell phone and two-pager scams, much of which fulfilled its purpose: to launch and fund my record company, 8th Wonder Records. The money I made, along with a few funds from investors, covered 100 percent of the studio time, travel expenses, and other materials needed to generate and promote our music. Within two months of our launch, my team—which consisted of three friends from the Hill (Elijah, Desean, and Charles), eight rappers (including myself), and an R&B singer—had already completed our first studio album. It was the highest point of my teenage years. I had a goal to make music, I put my mind to it, and though I went about it the wrong way, I created something out of nothing. Like Biggie, I had made it, and we were all ecstatic, especially me!

"Slow down, Remi! Damn, man. You gonna get us killed!" Desean yelled as I raced Moreno down the 264.

"Shut up, man! Stop being soft. I got this!" I said as I kept rapping in sync with my own lyrics. *"Niggas wish they could try us . . . mess around . . . and I'll catch a sudden case of Suge-Knightus."* Tapping Desean next to me as I swerved to dodge another car, I continued, "Get it? Suge-Knightus? I'll hang a nigga off of a building the way Suge Knight did!"

"Remi, stop playing, man! Pay attention to the road! You're gonna get pulled over!" At this point Desean was clearly aggravated.

Jerking the wheel back and forth, I laughed and said, "They love me! Ain't nobody pulling me over!" His fear was a joke to me. I loved Desean, but that was the way I used to be when I got excited about something. I pushed people, and I was too foolish to realize I was pushing them away from me.

"What's wrong with you, D?" I asked.

"I don't want to die, that's what's wrong with me!"

At this point I stared at him instead of the road. My pride wouldn't allow me to face forward. I wanted to prove to him that I had *everything* handled—the music business, the money, the crew, the cell phone hustle, everything—even driving 120 miles per hour down a highway with my head turned in his direction.

"Look at the road, Remi!" Desean commanded.

My eyes stayed locked on him.

"Look at the damn road, Remi!"

Still I didn't shift focus.

"Remi, c'mon, man!" Though the music was still blasting there was a cold silence from everyone in the back seat.

Finally the governor kicked in, which prompted me to refocus just in time to violently swerve and miss a car. I lost control for a second, cranked the wheel in the opposite direction to realign the car the best I could, got us down to a safe speed, and finally drove the way a sane person is supposed to drive.

Honestly, I was shaken, but I hid it from the crew. Desean stayed quiet for the rest of the ride back to the hotel. From what I remember, he was so upset that he didn't talk to me the next day either.

· · ·

Money from my cell phone hustle gave us new opportunities to promote our album. My ultimate goal was to build 8th Wonder to the point where we could shop the album and company to a major distributor (Interscope, Def Jam, or Universal) for a label deal. I was trying to follow the pattern set by other self-started record companies, like Roc-A-Fella, Murder Inc., and Ruff Ryders. But to acquire a label deal, we needed to sell a large number of records on our own to prove the concept and create a groundswell through promotion and marketing.

In the winter of 2001, with CDs in hand, most of the 8th Wonder artists and staff made our way to the epicenter of product marketing and promotions, the Virgin Megastore in Times Square. Until 2009, the Megastore was a hub for both famous artists and those just starting out. I say that because not only was the store notable for the music played and sold inside its walls, but also for the music created right outside its doors.

For years aspiring rappers from all across New York City would meet in front of the Megastore on Friday and Saturday nights to engage in rap battles. Some came with hopes of getting discovered by a big-time record producer or executive, some went for the thrill of embarrassing an opponent, and others attended to promote their music. We needed to expose 8th Wonder to the world, and I could think of no better place to do it than Times Square.

The lights were blaring, the crowd had gathered, and the proverbial fighting bell had rung. It was a beautiful scene. Tourists from all over the world dropped their cameras to focus on a group of inner-city kids as they debated in rhyme. People from Singapore, India, Japan, Italy, Australia, and London formed a circle of amazed onlookers. Their giddiness, claps, and laughs lifted us up.

"Oooooh!"

"Ahhhh!"

"Aweee!"

For a moment in time we were all kings, and the people of the world were our subjects, delivering the expressive applause our lyrics commanded. Everything outside of the rap radius was irrelevant; it didn't matter if you were a Democrat or Republican, white or black, American or Czechoslovakian. If you stopped your sightseeing to be entertained, we would not disappoint.

I felt like P. T. Barnum as I mingled with the crowd, pointing out my artists and soliciting our album while the 8th Wonder crew picked apart their opponents.

After about two hours of rapping and promoting, we decided to take a break and head to the Times Square McDonald's, which was one block up on Forty-Sixth Street and Seventh Avenue. As usual on a weekend winter night, it was packed. Each line had about ten to twelve people in it, and every seat on the first floor was taken. It was almost impossible to move without bumping into someone; we were all packed in like sardines.

It was quickly apparent that the awe the tourists felt when they watched us rap had disappeared. Upon seeing a group of black teenagers in baggy clothes and backward hats, women clutched their purses, fathers corralled their kids, and the only security guard in McDonald's—who happened to be white—stared at us with suspicion. As it usually did, reality set in. One minute we were all high from our subjects' applause, and the next minute we were low, looked upon with scorn and judgment. Though we were aware of the sudden change, we were all familiar with the treatment, so we did what we usually did in situations like that: we smirked with our chins high and shook our heads with our arms crossed.

After about ten minutes in line, we finally got to the counter.

"Welcome to McDonald's. How may I help you?" the cashier asked.

I ordered first. "I'll take the two Big Macs for three dollars special, no pickles or onions, please, large fries, and a Sprite with no ice." I looked out of the corner of my eye at the security guard, who was still staring in our direction. At that point I knew he was watching us, and only us. For the security guard to gradually follow us from the door to the counter left no doubt in my mind that he saw us as trouble.

The cashier interrupted my sideways gaze. "Will that complete your order?"

Trying to ignore my anger, I gestured to Dios. "Nah. Whatever he wants, put it on my ticket." I stepped out of the way so Dios could order.

We paid, collected our food, then made our way to the upstairs seating area to search for seats.

"Yiiiikes!" I exclaimed. The upstairs seating area was just as packed. There wasn't a single seat available.

"Let's see if the boys were able to grab a table downstairs," I said to Dios. The rest of 8th Wonder had also ordered and stayed downstairs in hopes of grabbing a table when someone left.

Back down on the lower level, I approached Charles and said, "No luck up there. Is it looking like anyone's about to get up down here?"

"Nah, man. Nothing," he replied.

Pointing to the corner, I said to everyone, "Let's just grab a corner over here and eat before our food gets cold. Hopefully someone will leave soon." Our only other option was to eat outside in the freezing temperatures.

We made our way to the southeast corner and proceeded to eat. Within seconds the security guard beelined in our direction.

"What's up with this guy?" I said under my breath as he walked up to us.

"You guys have to leave!" were his first words.

As the leader of 8th Wonder, I spoke up. "What? Why?"

"You can't stand here and eat! Go eat outside!"

"Hahaha. We're not going anywhere!" Dios said.

"Yo . . . we paid for our food here, and look around." I gestured to the crowd, including others who were standing as they ate. "There are no seats down here or upstairs. We have as much of a right to eat here as everyone else."

At this point everyone's eyes shifted to us. It was as though we had validated their preconceived notions. We were just a bunch of troublemakers who didn't belong in their midst. No one stood up for us, not even the girl at the register who had just filled our order, or the manager.

"If you don't leave now, I'm going to get the cops! Do you hear me? I will get them."

"I don't give a f***!" I was livid at this point. "We paid for our food. So if you feel like you need to go get the cops, go get them. We'll be right here waiting."

The security guard turned and walked outside to find the NYPD.

Just as I had at the Devoe Park basketball court, I stood there and waited for the unknown. I could have grabbed the crew and said "Let's leave," but I didn't. I was doing a lot of other things wrong at the time, things that actually warranted a cry for the police. But in this situation I knew we were right, and I wanted to fight for it.

"What you going to do, Remi?" Charles asked.

"I'm going to wait right here and have a conversation with the boys in blue. If things get out of hand . . . they get out of hand," I replied.

At that time in New York City, there was a lot of contention between the minority community and the NYPD. In 1997, Abner Louima was sodomized with a broomstick and beaten by a group of police officers in Brooklyn's Seventieth Precinct. Two years later, police officers in the Bronx fired forty-one shots at Amadou Diallo, striking him nineteen times as he stood in front of his apartment building. His wallet was mistaken for a gun. And over the years I had personally witnessed police officers unjustly throw people to the ground, talk to minorities like they were garbage, and threaten unnecessary force to impose their will.

Since the Rodney King beating in 1992, I'd had great disdain for the police. And what I had witnessed in New York City over the years since then made it exponentially worse, to the point where I even began to disdain the country that produced them, America. I had no filter.

Like many African American moms, my mother had given me "the talk" many times. "Remi, when dealing with cops, keep your hands visible at all times. *Do not* make any sudden movements, give simple yes and no answers, and for God's sake, Remi, please keep your mouth shut unless spoken to."

Let's just say I was about to break a few of those rules.

About two minutes later a group of five officers approached, led by their sergeant. The patrons looked on in intrigue.

"Is there a problem here?" the sergeant asked.

With bold confidence I replied, "No . . . there's no problem. Just eating the food that we bought here."

"It's time for you guys to go," the sergeant said.

I quickly said, "We're not going anywhere."

"What?" he asked with a surprised look as the other officers took a step forward.

I took a bite out of my Big Mac, looked at him, and said with a mouth full of burger, "We're not going anywhere. Listen: I could understand if we'd bought food at the hot dog stand across the street and brought it in here to eat. But we didn't. I paid for this food [I gestured at my McDonald's bag] right here, at that cash register, with my hard-earned money. And because of that, we're not going nowhere."

Dios jumped in with a few choice words, and by the time he was finished, both Dios and I had been pushed up against the wall, handcuffed, patted down, and arrested for disobeying a "lawful" order. The rest of the 8th Wonder crew was let go, and Dios and I were taken to two separate jails downtown.

That night in the jail cell was interesting for two reasons: One, I felt great pride for standing up to those whom I felt had oppressed my people for generations. And two, I felt that with all the illegal activity I'd been carrying out, that jail cell was right where I deserved to be! I had sold drugs, stolen from my mom, robbed employers, and taken personal information from people on their deathbeds to illegally activate phones and pagers. I had always assumed that I would one day end up in a jail cell, but it was a quite humorous scene as I sat there thinking to myself, *Of all the bad I did, the police arrested me for this—a Big Mac, french fries, and a Sprite.*

But little did I know that in just one month the walls would all come crashing down.

• • •

"Remi, who was that at the door last night?" Mom asked the morning after Devan confronted me about the twenty blow-up phones that were cut off prematurely.

My nerves lit up. The last thing I wanted my mom to find out was that I might have dragged her into my mess. I probed to find out what she knew.

"What are you talking about?"

"I heard you talking to someone in the hallway," she said.

"It was a friend who's a WCT customer. He was having a problem with his phone."

"Please don't do that at night. If you need to have a conversation, go downstairs to the lobby and do it there. I don't want to have to deal with complaints from the neighbors. You know Miss Armenta is old and has a hard time sleeping, so keep your business dealings out of the hall."

"Got it, Ma." I was so relieved.

I paid Devan back. I resigned from WCT. I'd given up drug dealing with Roderick months before this, having made so much money on the phone scam. It was probably a good thing that we went our separate ways because Roderick would eventually be sentenced to ten years in prison for strong-arm robbery.

With all my hustles suddenly shut down and a record company that needed a constant flow of funds, 8th Wonder was in a bad position. If we were going to survive as a company, we needed a label deal immediately.

I saw a glimmer of hope in the midst of my downslide. Most of the beats from the 8th Wonder compilation album were produced by a Virginia-based producer named DJ Willy. Along with that, most of our albums had been recorded in his Virginia studio. Over the months of recording, I made him a lot of money by paying for his beats and renting his studio. And through our business dealings we developed a great relationship. But even better than our relationship were the relationships he had with key players in the hip-hop industry.

Willy told me early on, "If you ever want to meet with executives at Def Jam, let me know and I'll make the introduction." I wanted to wait until we got our exposure to the level necessary for a meeting of that stature. Mom always said, "First impressions are the most important impressions," and I wanted to make the best impression possible. But in our situation, with the company bleeding cash, I needed to take a meeting with what we had. It was my last chance.

In January 2002, about a month after departing WCT, I contacted Willy and explained my situation. Without hesitation he drove up to New York and set up a meeting with then executive vice president of Island Def Jam Music Group, Kevin Liles. At the time Mr. Liles also oversaw Def Jam Recordings, which was home to Jay-Z (Roc-A-Fella label), Ja Rule (Murder Inc. label), Ludacris, DMX (Ruff Ryders label), LL Cool J, and many other popular hip-hop artists. He was a major player, a decision maker, so to be in front of him was an opportunity to change the trajectory of 8th Wonder.

On an early February evening two 8th Wonder artists and I pulled up to the headquarters of Def Jam, which was then located at 825 Eighth Avenue in

Manhattan. Understanding the importance of this meeting, I was extremely nervous. My future wasn't the only one on the line. So were the futures of all my artists and partners.

Willy met me in front of the building. He was a short guy, about five six, with a thick southern accent. That night he wore sweatpants and an oversize leather jacket. The guy looked like a ten-year-old who had stolen his grandfather's blazer. He was swimming in the jacket. I was already on edge, but his dress made my nerves worse. I thought that security would view us as a bunch of wannabe bums trying to sneak into Def Jam. *Why did Willy wear that? He should have come in with something more professional.* But I was dead wrong.

"You ready?" Willy said.

"Let's do this," I replied.

As we approached the security desk, Willy spoke to the guard as though he had been there many times, and the guard responded respectfully as if Willy were cofounder Russell Simmons himself.

I went over my mental checklist. *Stay calm, have confidence in your product, speak clearly and concisely, and don't come off desperate.* I held a copy of the album, which featured at least one song from each artist and a collaboration song with the entire roster.

Willy said to the security guard, "This is Remi. We're here for a meeting with Kevin Liles."

"Can I see your ID please, sir?" the security guard said to me.

As the guard called up to Kevin's office, I said to Willy, "Kevin's got to like at least one of our artists, right? What you think, Willy? You think we can close on something?"

"You never know," Willy said in his southern accent. "It all depends on what the execs are looking for at the time. Whatever's gonna happen is gonna happen."

"Yeah, you're right," I replied.

The security guard hung up the phone and redirected his attention to us. "Mr. Liles is expecting you. Take the elevator to the right. You know the floor, right?"

"Yup. Thank you," Willy responded.

With his hands in his oversize-jacket pockets, he made his way onto the elevator, and we followed. Our arrival on the Def Jam floor was a surreal experience. Mr. Liles's assistant met us at the elevator and walked us to his office. A large Island Def Jam Music Group sign was facing the reception area. Multiple plaques that represented multiplatinum or gold album sales lined the halls, and all over the place were pictures of artists I had listened to since Chad introduced me to hip-hop. This was a dream come true. It was as if my life had come full circle and was about to get even better. My nervousness transposed into excitement. I felt good. I felt like we were going to win. I mean, how could we not?

"Mr. Liles, your visitors are here," the assistant said.

Mr. Liles stood up and said, "Come on in, guys." He had a warm, comforting spirit about him. He wasn't intimidating, but I could tell that he was all business.

Willy embraced him with a handshake and said, "These are the guys I've been working with. I think they got some good stuff for you."

After Willy made the introductions, he stepped into the corner and stood there with his hands in his pockets. What would happen for the remainder of the meeting was now on me.

"Okay, okay . . . what's your name again?" Mr. Liles asked.

"I'm Remi, and I'm the CEO and founder of 8th Wonder Records. And these are my artists."

"Do you have music with you?" he asked.

I handed our CD to Mr. Liles. "Yes, here's our compilation album that we produced."

He read the print on the cover. "'Who will discover the 8th Wonder of the World?' Interesting. Let's see what you got."

Mr. Liles popped the CD into his player and started listening. Our album was set up with what we thought were the best songs first, because we intended the CD to be a demo also.

As the music played, I watched Mr. Liles intently. He only listened to snippets of each song. He nodded a little, seemed disinterested in some songs and interested in others. The good news was he listened to some of every song. I honestly didn't know what to think. My assessment was that he could lean either way.

Finally he spoke, and when he did, he was direct. "Um . . . yeah . . . it's good . . . but . . . it's not there." My heart sank, but I maintained my composure.

He continued, "Let me play you something that's popping. . . . I just signed this artist named Joe Budden. His album isn't out yet, but check this out. This is the kind of stuff we're looking for, artists that pop!"

As he took out our CD and put in Joe's, I thought, *Man, listen . . . you just told me the music I poured my heart and soul into isn't good enough. The last thing I want to do is hear music from a dude I never heard of.*

As the music played, I tuned it out and just nodded the best I could. I'm sure I was out of sync with the beat, but I couldn't concentrate. My dream that had been inspired by artists from Def Jam was now dissolving at the headquarters of Def Jam. As I stood in front of Kevin Liles, watching him talk up Joe Budden while the music played, my eyes stayed locked on him, but my mind was focused on what to do next. The money would be gone in weeks unless I jumped back into something illegal, which I didn't want to do. I had no other connections to major players in the industry. There was still a chance the feds would lock me up for my cell phone scam. How would I explain to my artists that it might all be over? My short-lived excitement now transposed into sorrow.

We said our goodbyes to Mr. Liles, thanked him for his time and honesty, and made our way out of the building. When we were finally out, we stood at the southeast corner and just talked. I tried to motivate the troops the best I could, telling them we'd find another way. But deep down I knew it was over. There was no way I could keep funding 8th Wonder at the same level.

Despite my revelation, as the months passed and the money was completely depleted, I tried to get the remainder of the albums into the hands of anyone who might lead us to a person, who knew a person, who had a cousin, who could somehow catch the vision and sign the label, or at least one of the artists . . . but it never happened. And I found myself spending hours in my bedroom, worried about jail time, questioning my past, and trying to figure out my future.

When I thought I couldn't get any lower, one day my grandmother came into my room and confronted me about something I had long forgotten.

"Remi, I don't know how I know this, but I know you stole your mother's ring!"

She totally caught me off guard. For years my mom had searched the house for the ring and would even ask me if I'd seen it, but in the last few months she hadn't brought it up once. So what my grandma said was so random but so true that I just stood there in shock. There was no way she could have known, and she even indirectly admitted that herself. How did she know?

"You took it, Remi, didn't you?"

I just stared at her. The woman who from my young age had taught me and my brother to always walk with our shoulders back and our chests out, the woman who helped my mother raise us, the woman who always made sure our clothes were starched and pressed, the woman whose mind was failing from dementia, now stared at me for an answer. It was as though she was offering me a chance at redemption, not just for the engagement ring I stole, but for all that had transpired since. All I had to do was confess.

What are you going to do, Remi? This is the lowest point you've been at in a while. Maybe telling the truth can bring you some kind of good luck. Or maybe nothing will change. What are you going to do?

I made my decision.

"No, Grandma. I didn't take it. And I don't know why you would say that."

CHAPTER NINE

UNSUNG HERO

Though people make mistakes, that doesn't
mean they don't have potential.

B*eep, beep, beep, beep!*
Lying in my bed with my face still smashed into the pillow, I patted around my nightstand to find the alarm. It was June 2002, four long months after my failed meeting with Kevin Liles. It was 9:00 a.m., and I knew if I didn't get up and out of the bed soon, Mom was going to barge in and give me another lecture about finding a job.

"I'm not taking care of a grown man! It's been four months, Remi. . . . You need to get out of this house and get a *job*!" I'd been hearing that for weeks, and, frankly, it was annoying. I was already dejected from not getting a label deal, and I was dead broke!

I turned over on my left side and stared into the room. The blinds were down but the window was open, so the light breeze intermittently blew against the blinds like a sheet in the wind, illuminating the room in increments. But when the wind didn't blow, it was dark, like my expectations for my future.

Then unexpectedly, as I lay there in bed, I heard a voice say, *"You need to get out of here. You need to join the military."* It was the type of voice you hear off in a distance within a dream, the way someone speaks to you while you're asleep. But I wasn't dreaming; I was awake.

In a state of bemusement, I propped my head up to look around, but there was no one in my room but me. The voice said it two more times, but softer than the first, and even softer on the last: "*You need to join the military. You need to join the military.*"

Now, I'll be honest: I smoked a lot of weed in my teenage years, and in the process of getting high, I did experience some freaky events, but I hadn't been high for at least three weeks before this. I was clean, I promise.

Not only was the voice audible, but it penetrated my mind and reverberated through my very being. It got my attention! I sat up and just stared into the room. And as I stared, I actually began to entertain the idea of joining the military. *What do I have left? I have nothing else to do.* Then I shook my head and began a silent argument. *No, I can't do that. I hate the police! And anyone in a uniform is the police. No! Plus, I like my hats backward and my clothes baggy, so there's no way I'm slipping into one of those tight-ass sailor-boy costumes. No!*

Full of frustration and anger, I lay back down and stared at the ceiling. *Damn, damn, damn! I ain't got nothing left!* I took a deep sigh and began to whisper, "If you don't leave, man . . . you're gonna probably end up dead or in prison." I lay there for about thirty minutes, trying to figure out what else I could do in life, but nothing came to me.

Finally I capitulated. "All right, imma do it! What else do I have left?"

The decision was made. I was all in! I rolled out of the bed, still in a state of disbelief over what I was thinking about doing. I flipped the blinds up to let the full spring light into the room, threw on some jeans and a T-shirt, and made my way out.

Years earlier my mom had stopped teaching and started a creative-writing company, so she was at her desk in the living room, typing away.

"Ma."

"Good morning, Remi," she said as she kept typing. "What are you doing today?"

Knowing her next question was going to be about whether I'd look for a job, I wiped the crust out of my eyes and said, "Imma go to the store, and then imma go check out a job opportunity. . . . I promise, Ma."

I wouldn't dare tell her what I was really about to do. My mom's brother had a grenade go off next to him in the Korean War. He survived but was confined to a hospital bed until he died. Along with Uncle Brother (which was what we called him), many of her childhood friends who had been drafted during Vietnam came back in body bags. To Mom, the military was a death sentence for a black kid.

"I love you, Ma," I said.

"I love you, too, Remi."

I walked out the door, past the buzzing ceiling light, and made my way down the staircase. I couldn't believe I was about to do this. But when the fresh spring air hit my face, that dream I'd had—years earlier—of becoming a Navy SEAL reemerged. And when it did, I didn't walk to the recruiter's office—I literally began to run.

I ran past all the buildings where I'd grown up, then through the Fordham Hill gates. I ran past the Devoe basketball court where Jerome and company had beat me up, and past the crackheads slumbering on the park benches. The more I ran, the freer I felt. I ran past the pizzerias, the bodega where I once stole a twenty-five-cent bag of chips, and the pawnshop where I'd pawned my mother's engagement ring. I ran past the 4 train, which I'd taken to DeWitt Clinton High School; Sammy's Clothing store, where I'd spent thousands of dollars on clothes; and the video game store, where I bought all my PlayStation games. The more I ran, the more my dejection shifted to excitement.

"I have a future! And I think it's going to be bright," I said aloud.

The Army, Navy, Air Force, and Marine Corps recruiting offices were all located on the second floor of 2488 Grand Concourse on Fordham Road, about nine blocks east of Devoe Park. When I got to the entrance, I caught my breath, then made my way into the building. Over the stairs was a sign that said Military Recruiters Offices, with an arrow pointed upward. I slowly made my way up, not knowing what to expect.

When I got to the top of the staircase, I looked right and then left. Office doors lined the hall on each side. *Which way to the Navy?* I thought. I chose the right. As I made my way down the hall, my heart rate began to elevate.

Remi, you are crazy.

The first office I passed had the door wide open; it was an Army office. There were two recruiters inside talking to a kid. I walked by, then came to the second office on the right. Inside I saw a life-size special forces marine cutout. The guy carried an M4 rifle and had on night vision goggles and a wet suit similar to those the SEALs wore in *The Rock*.

This is it! Look at that dude! Ooooweee, that's what I'm going to be right there! I thought with my hand under my chin and my head nodding. I was sold. *Forget the SEAL thing. I'm going to be a marine, baby!*

I peered behind the cutout. "Hello? Anybody here?" Someone's hot coffee was steaming on the desk, but there wasn't a person in sight.

I figured the Marines recruiter, or whoever the coffee belonged to, must have gone to the bathroom. So I sat down in a chair and waited, still staring at the life-size cutout while periodically looking out into the hallway.

I talked myself up the entire time I stared at the cutout: *That's my gun. That's my night vision. That's your boy! Imma be a straight killer! What? Wait till the Marines get a load of me!*

Fifteen minutes passed, and no recruiter showed up. I stood up and looked at the cutout and said, "Yo, I'll be right back. Hold my spot, aight?"

I stepped back into the hallway and walked to the Army office. "Excuse me. I'm looking to join the Marines, but there's no one in the office. Would you happen to know when the recruiter's coming back?"

One of the Army recruiters raised his head, looked at me, paused for a second, like he was annoyed (which prompted me to glance behind me to see if he was looking at someone else), and just shook his head.

Frustrated at this point, I walked back to the Marines office, stood there for about thirty seconds, then decided to walk down toward the Navy office. I walked past the Army office again, past the stairwell, and poked my head into the Navy office.

I'll never forget it: standing in the center of the Navy recruiting office was this drop-dead gorgeous Puerto Rican woman in a Navy uniform. She was about five four, shaped like an hourglass, with golden brown skin. It was like the light of heaven itself shined upon her. I was in a trance. Immediately I forgot about the Marines *and* the Navy. I just wanted to be alone with this lady.

I strolled in as she continued a discussion with another recruiter. She had a thick Bronx accent.

"Um, hello," I said with my chin slightly up.

"Hello. How can I help you?" she asked.

I stared at her for about four seconds before I responded in a suave tone, "Yeah, my name is Remi Adeleke. I got a record company . . . and I'm thinking of giving that up to become a Navy SEAL."

She saw right through my foolishness and said, "Oh, really? That's impressive."

"Yeah, I know." Looking around, I continued, "Not too many dudes come from here and go SEALs."

At this point she couldn't hold back anymore. She began to laugh at me, and the other recruiter joined in. I'm sure she was thinking, *This fool thinks he can get with me. Well, I am going to get him in the Navy.*

"I'm Petty Officer Tiana Reyes, and I'm one of the Navy recruiters here. Do you know what it takes to be a SEAL?" she asked.

"Yeah, yeah, I know. Swim, run, push-ups. That's nothing. I can do that *all* day," I said as I stared at her. "See these muscles?" I put up my skinny arms and tried to flex through my baggy white T-shirt. "I got what it takes, I promise."

"Can you even swim?" she asked.

"No, but I'm a quick learner."

She wouldn't stop chuckling. "Okay, I see that you're strong, but I need to know if you're smart. See that computer over there?"

"Yeah, I see it. And yes, I am a genius. Graduated top of my high school cl—"

"Okay, I get it; you're the man. Now, go over there and sit at that computer. It's an ASVAB prep test. When you finish the test, come get me, okay?"

"Okay, okay." I stared at her while I walked to the computer. *Man, I love this girl! She is so damn fine, and that uniform? Mm mm mm.*

The test consisted of SAT-type questions, and the content was similar to the material students are taught in their senior year of high school. I had been out of high school for about two years, so I definitely couldn't remember how to calculate certain equations, and I was rusty in science and paragraph comprehension. All in all, I did well enough to pass, but not well enough to be a Navy SEAL. The ASVAB requirements were high for the SEAL program.

"Um, it looks like you're nowhere near the scores needed to go to BUD/S (Basic Underwater Demotion/SEAL training), but hey, at least we know you're eligible to enter the military," Petty Officer Reyes said with a smile.

"That's great, that's great," I said with a bit of shame. My score may not have gotten me into BUD/S, but it definitely did what it needed to do in that moment: it humbled me.

Sensing my shame, she said, "You'd be surprised how many kids from this area don't even pass the ASVAB. It's terrible. You're one of the lucky ones."

Despite my objectifying her, she was sincerely encouraging, and I sensed she was as beautiful on the inside as she was on the outside.

"Are you from around here?" I asked her.

"Yeah, I was born and raised right here in the Bronx. I joined the Navy to get out of here, get my education, and see the world. Joining the Navy was the best decision I ever made. That's why I'm back here, trying to help you . . . *my peoples* . . . get in."

"Hey, Tiana!" someone yelled from the entrance of the office, then addressed her in Spanish.

"Hey, Junior!" she also replied in Spanish.

I looked at him and asked, "Who's that . . . your man or something?"

She laughed. "No . . . that's Staff Sergeant Diaz. He's the Marines recruiter."

I laughed inwardly.

Tiana walked me to her desk. "Next we have to do a background check. Are you okay with that?"

I gave the same hesitant response that I'd given my high school guidance counselor when she tried to find my report card. "Yeah, no problem . . . I should be good."

But the truth was, I had no idea what would show up. Since I left WCT, I had been living in fear every day, wondering if the feds were going to kick down my door and arrest me for the cell phone scams. *Guess this is my moment of truth.*

I sat in her office chair, tapping my foot nervously while intermittently glancing at the exit right behind me. *Man, I should probably go. If she finds something, who's to say she won't call the cops on me?*

She took her time, and I couldn't read her expression at all. But when the other recruiter stepped out of the office, she looked up at me and said, "You popped up in the system pretty fast. I was just waiting for the other recruiter to leave. You have a warrant for your arrest in New York. *And* you have a warrant for your arrest in New Jersey. You've been busy, haven't you?"

Damn. I was frozen.

"Yeah," I finally said. "I made a lot of mistakes. Did some bad things."

She continued, "Technically . . . you can't join the military. I'm not even allowed to recruit anyone with a closed record, let alone someone who has an outstanding warrant!"

My heart sank, and my body got hot, as it usually did when I was extremely nervous. I wanted to die right there in the office. My introspection kicked in. *Are the warrants for the cell phone scam? They have to be! My life is over! I'm about to get my black ass thrown in jail! Why is this happening to me? What the hell was this voice telling me to join the military? I didn't want to join the damn military anyway.*

I was so scared I didn't want to know what the charges were for. With my head down and my mind spinning in every direction, I said, "Okay. Thanks for your time, Petty Officer."

As I got up to walk away, Tiana spoke up. "Do you have a suit?"

"Huh?" I replied.

"A suit, tie? You know, nice clothes."

"Nah, I don't have a suit, but I do have slacks, a tie, and a white collared shirt. Why?"

"It doesn't look like your warrants are for felonies, so . . . come back in three days, looking as sharp as you can be. I'm going to help you out. I may have a way in for you."

. . .

To this day I believe that Petty Officer Reyes was an angel. What are the chances of me hearing a voice telling me to join the military, then walking into an empty Marines office, and finally walking directly to the one military recruiter who was willing to *break* the rules in order to get me into the military?

Three days after I met her, Tiana did all the talking while I stood by her side in the New Jersey Court of Common Pleas. As instructed, I wore pressed slacks and a collared shirt with a black tie. I even got a fresh haircut.

"Your Honor, I am Petty Officer 2nd Class Reyes. I've served in the US Navy for eight years, and I've been stationed at the Fordham Road US Navy Recruiting Office in the Bronx for a year. Earlier this week Mr. Adeleke approached me. He shared with me that he has made some mistakes in the past but expressed that he is ready to turn his life around. And he wants to start his turn by joining the Navy. As you know, Your Honor, 9/11 took place less than a year ago. The military can use a young man like Mr. Adeleke. He is full of potential, and I believe that he can make a difference despite his mistakes. But according to recruiting guidelines, we cannot accept him if he has warrants or an open record. Therefore, Your Honor, I respectfully request on Mr. Adeleke's behalf that his record be expunged. If you do this, I will be able to process him into the Navy."

Standing there in nervous silence, I looked upon the judge with as much respect as possible and waited for his response. The tough guy who'd tried to intimidate a life-size marine cutout was long gone.

The judge looked at Tiana and spoke. "Petty Officer Reyes, I want to thank you for your service to this country, and I want to thank you for advocating on this young man's behalf. What you have done and are doing is very honorable."

"Thank you, Your Honor," she replied.

He focused his eyes on me and began his speech. "Mr. Adeleke, you are a lucky young man. And regardless of what my decision is, you should be grateful that this servant of our country is taking a chance on you. She clearly sees something in you. And being that an act of war, 9/11, has recently taken place, just miles from here, I see your choice to join the Navy as very patriotic. Therefore, as requested by you, Petty Officer Reyes, I will clear his warrant here in the state of New Jersey, and I hereby expunge his record."

I took a quick look at Tiana and grinned to say thank you; then I looked back at the judge.

The judge continued, "However, the court requires that you pay the necessary fines in the amount of three hundred dollars."

When we got out of the courtroom, Petty Officer Reyes said, "One down, one to go. Then you can go become a Navy SEAL." I didn't know if she was joking or serious about the last part, but I was grateful for the overall outcome. I wasn't so grateful about the fines, though. By then I barely had a nickel to my name.

. . .

The next day Officer Reyes drove me to a courthouse that was on the southern tip of Manhattan, mere blocks away from Ground Zero.

As we sat in her government vehicle, Tiana shuffled through some court papers that she had dug up the day before.

"McDonald's?" she said.

"Huh?" I replied.

"What . . . you were arrested for disobeying a lawful order at a McDonald's? Your record company couldn't afford to pay for your Big Mac?" she asked jokingly.

"It's a long story. We were black in the wrong place at the wrong time. I paid for a meal, security wanted us out, we didn't leave, cops were called, and I went to jail."

"Yes, but you never showed up to court," she said.

"Nah, I didn't think I needed to. I don't remember getting a court notice."

"Um . . . typically when you get arrested for something, you eventually go to court."

My mood changed to relief. "This is *good*!" The warrant wasn't for the cell phones! All I needed was to get this McDonald's thing clear so I could disappear into my new life.

"What do you mean, 'This is good'?" she asked.

Trying to avoid explaining my cell phone scam, I said, "Nah, I'm just saying it's good because it should be an easy case to clear. You go in there, do your thing, and I should be good to go. I seriously wasn't in the wrong in this case. Maybe with some other stuff, but not this."

Because of how well things had gone in New Jersey, I wasn't as nervous as I was then. Petty Officer Reyes gave the New York judge the same speech she'd given the New Jersey judge. Her words were formal but her heart was saying, "Though people make mistakes, that doesn't mean that they don't have potential."

As if we were in an episode of *The Twilight Zone*, the judge also gave the same speeches. "Thank you for your service. . . . She sees something in you. . . . This is a patriotic decision that you're making. . . . We will support you turning your life around by clearing your warrant and expunging the charge. . . . But you have to pay five hundred dollars in fines and court fees."

Two down! I breathed easier; my old dream was within reach. I didn't know whether to laugh or scream. I was thrilled. I finally had the opportunity to turn my life around, and I wasn't going to let the judges or Petty Officer Reyes down.

But, wait—how much exactly are these court fees and fines?

•   •   •

It was about time I told my mom what was going on.

"Mom! You here?" I said after walking into the apartment from the New York courthouse.

"Yes, I'm in my bedroom."

I made my way back to her, more nervous than when I'd met with the New Jersey judge. I loosened my tie and walked toward Mom's room. For a second I stood at her door, the door where I often stood and sang along to my mom's favorite R&B hits. This time there was no music playing; she was just sitting on her bed reading. We had lived together my whole life, and now I was going to tell her goodbye. And I knew she wasn't going to like where I was going. I stepped in.

"How are you doing, Remi?"

"I'm doing good, Ma. How you doing?"

"I'm fine. Why are you all dressed up? Did you have a job interview?"

I chuckled inside. *Oh yeah. Did I.* "Ma, I got to tell you something."

She put her book down and stared at me. "What happened, Remi?"

I sighed deeply and said, "I'm joining the military."

As soon as *military* left my mouth, Mom went from zero to *sixty*!

"No, no, no, no, you are not, Remi!"

"Mom, I need to get out of here. There's nothing here for me anymore."

Tears started pouring out of Mom's eyes. "Remi, please don't do this! *I don't want you to die!*"

"Mom, I'm not going to die."

"Remi, you will end up on the front lines! Remi, please don't do this to me! You are not going into the military!"

The tears kept flowing, and I hugged her to console her the best I could. But Mom knew me well, and she fought hard because she knew that when I made a decision, it was made. There was no turning back.

"I don't want you to die like your father! I can't afford to lose you, Remi!"

"I know, Ma, I know, but I got to go. I have to do this."

Hours later, after she calmed down, I told her what happened at the courts and how I just needed to pay the court fines of $800 so I could leave. She didn't have the money, and though she didn't want me to leave, she made it possible for me to go.

The next morning, as I lay in my bed trying to figure out how to come up with $800, my mother came into the room and handed me the phone. My eighty-three-year-old Aunt Dokey was on the line.

"Remi," Aunt Dokey said through the phone.

"Yes, Aunt Dokey."

"Your mother told me what's going on with you. I'd like to help. Can you meet me at the Apple Bank on 207th and Broadway? I don't want to carry that much money with me out of the bank."

I sat upright on the bed. "*Yes*, Aunt Dokey! Thank you."

She said, "I'll see you at the bank shortly, okay?"

"Yes, ma'am. I'll be there."

I looked at my mom and said, "Thank you, Mom. Thank you."

"You're welcome. I'm proud of you, Remi. I ever tell you how much I love you?"

"All the time," I replied.

"Hurry up and get to the bank before Aunt Dokey gets there."

I ran to the 12 bus stop, jumped on the bus, and took it right to the corner of 207th and Broadway, then made my way into the bank. Shortly after I arrived, Aunt Dokey, who lived a few blocks away, pulled up. We exchanged greetings; then she went to the teller to pull out the $800.

She gave me the money with one hand, then placed her other hand over mine. "Remi, I don't want you to ever give me this money back. This is for you. I just want you to be somebody special."

I'll never forget those words.

"Thank you, Aunt Dokey. I love you, and I won't let you down. I promise." I gave her another hug, walked her to her car, then met up with Petty Officer Reyes to get the money to the courts. I was free and clear, and now somewhat eligible to join the military.

CHAPTER TEN

MOMENT OF TRUTH

I will never regret trying, but I will regret not trying.

Petty Officer 2nd Class Tiana Reyes was somehow able to pull off a feat that most recruiters wouldn't even attempt. She got my record cleared so fast that by the time I started the MEPS (Military Entrance Processing Station) process, none of my warrants or expunged cases showed up in the system.

As I sat alone in the MEPS hall, Petty Officer Reyes emerged from an administrative office and approached me with a smile.

"Remi, you're clear. I just checked the system *again*, and nothing showed up." She whispered, "Did you fill out the form the way I told you?"

"Yes, I checked no on everything. Ever had a warrant? No. Ever been arrested? No. Have you ever been in any trouble with the law that your recruiter told you to conceal? No." I looked at her curiously in reference to the last question.

"Good. Now listen to me. You have to answer that way for the rest of your military career. Do you understand me?" I nodded. "If MEPS finds out what I did for you, that's the end of my career."

"I got it. I got you. I would never do that to you," I replied.

She continued, "As soon as you get to boot camp, there's going to be a segment called Moment of Truth." I turned my head to look down the hall for a second.

Snapping her fingers in my face, she continued, "Listen to me, Remi! The drill instructors are going to bring all the new recruits into a room. And they're going to challenge you all. They're going to ask if you've had warrants or misdemeanors or any infractions that were on your records that you didn't tell your recruiters about. . . . Pay attention!" She was stern. Since we met, I had never seen her that serious.

Tiana continued, "They're going to ask you if your recruiter told you to lie or hide the fact that you committed a crime. They're going to say, 'We don't care if it was a violation for littering!' And then they're going to try to intimidate you by saying that they have access to a more advanced way of checking your background than your recruiter did, FBI-level stuff. . . . Are you following me?"

"I'm listening," I replied.

She continued, "And they're going to tell you that if they find anything, you're going straight to jail, but if you confess, they'll let you go home. It's all lies, Remi. Whatever you do, when you get to Moment of Truth at boot camp, do not tell them what I did for you! And do not mention your warrants or your expunged record or the fact that you saw two judges last week. They won't be able to see it in their system. Do you understand me?"

"I understand," I said. But in reality I was stressed! *Damn. I haven't seen her like this. What kind of circus has this woman got me in?*

She started speaking in her normal tone. "So . . . your ASVAB score was subpar, but that's okay. Your scores qualified you for the corpsman rate. It's not a SEAL, but it's a medic."

"Medic?" I asked.

"Yeah, Marines don't have medics, so they use Navy corpsmen as their medics. You'll get to run around with a gun and a med bag."

"Oh, that's cool. So I'll get to be a killer after all?" I said, referring to the life-size cutout that I had eloquently conversed with at the Marines recruiting office.

"What?" she replied.

"Never mind; you won't understand." I chuckled.

"All right. You said bye to your mom, right?" Tiana asked.

"Yeah. She cried, but she's happy for me. I'm hoping the military will help me give her a better life one day. She's sacrificed a lot for me, so now it's my turn to sacrifice for her."

"Once you go through those doors to swear in, I may not see you again. They're going to bus you all straight to JFK to catch your flights to Great Lakes."

I stared at her and teared up a little bit, then said, "I can't think of anyone besides my mom and Aunt Dokey who's done what you did for me. I'm going to be great. I promise. I won't let you down."

Though she probably wasn't supposed to, due to fraternization policies, she leaned in and gave me a hug, then whispered, "You're going to be great. I believe in you." Then she turned and walked toward the exit. That was the last time I ever saw Petty Officer Reyes. Like I said, I believe she was an angel.

After Tiana exited the building, I turned in the opposite direction and made my way toward the Ceremony Room.

Tiana had done her part; now it was time for me to do mine. I was ready to start my new life and defy the odds I was up against. I walked by a row of desks that lined the hallway, then turned left and passed through a set of double doors.

The Ceremony Room was a circular room that had large emblems for each branch of service posted on the wall. American flags in stands lined the room. The space was filled with people getting ready to swear in: Caucasian, African American, Asian, Hispanic, Middle Eastern. Some were fresh out of high school, and a few were middle-aged. I had never seen such a diverse group of people in one room.

Within minutes the MEPS commanding officer walked in and requested we all line up in four columns facing the largest American flag in the room.

"I'm Major Armstrong, and I'll be swearing you all in today," he said.

I nodded, as focused as an eagle.

He continued, "Do you all understand the DOD separation policy and UCMJ Article 83?"

We all said in unison, "Yes, sir."

"Do you have any questions, concerns, or reservations?"

"No, sir."

"Are any of you reluctant to do this? Or has anyone forced any of you to do this?"

Again, we all said, "No, sir."

Then Major Armstrong yelled, "Room, attention!"

We snapped straight up with our hands to our sides.

Then he instructed, "Raise your right hands and repeat after me. I—state your name."

I raised my right hand. "I, Remi Adeleke."

The major continued, "do solemnly swear."

We repeated, "do solemnly swear."

Though there were about twenty of us in the room, I felt like I was the only one. Everyone was repeating Major Armstrong's words, but my voice was the only one that mattered to me. I was making the biggest change I had ever made at that point in my life.

Major continued, "that I will support and defend."

"That I will support and defend."

"The Constitution of the United States of America."

"The Constitution of the United States of America."

He scanned the room as he continued, "against all enemies, foreign and domestic."

"Against all enemies, foreign and domestic."

"That I will bear true faith and allegiance to the same."

As I continued, I felt more and more ready, like a caged lion ready to be loosed. "That I will bear true faith and allegiance to the same."

"And I will obey the orders of the President of the United States."

"And I will obey the orders of the President of the United States."

"And the orders of the officers appointed over me."

"And the orders of the officers appointed over me."

"According to regulations and the Uniform Code of Military Justice."

"According to regulations and the Uniform Code of Military Justice."

"So help me God."

"So help me God!" *I'm in, I made it*, I thought.

Then the major gave his closing remarks. "Today you made a very important decision by joining the military. Less than 1 percent of the US population wears this uniform, and you're joining us today in that 1 percent. Only 20 percent of applicants are accepted into the military. A lot of young men and women would love to stand where you are, but they couldn't meet the ASVAB, medical, or background-check requirements. This is a major accomplishment, and you should all be proud of yourselves."

Two weeks earlier I had strolled into Petty Officer Reyes's office as a hustling, sweet-talking fool. Now, on July 2, 2002, I was officially a serviceman.

• • • •

I, along with the other new Navy recruits, landed at Chicago O'Hare the evening of July 2 and was bussed to the Great Lakes Recruit Training Command in North Chicago.

The intake process at Great Lakes was a lot like I pictured an intake at a minimum-security prison. Our group from New York was quickly separated, and we were all placed in different divisions, which consisted of about sixty recruits each.

All the guys' faces and heads were shaved, and the girls' hair lengths were shortened. After our military-standard grooming, the guys went into a large changing room, where we were commanded to disrobe and issued a bag of military clothes. We received brown cardboard boxes for our civilian belongings, which were unceremoniously carried off as if they held no meaning at all. We were being stripped of our individualism and thrown into a new way of life.

In all honesty, it was fun for me. Drill instructors were screaming, kids were crying, and I was laughing—inside, that is.

After our boxes were carried off and we each had made our one phone call home to say we had arrived safely, the last part of orientation began: the Moment of Truth.

It was exactly as Tiana described, but more intense than I expected. The drill instructors shuffled us all into a large classroom.

A tall, muscular, African American drill instructor with a southern accent started, "Re-cruitsssss! This is what we call the Moment of Truth!"

Another instructor who was shorter and Filipino repeated in a swift and prominent Filipino accent, "Moment of Truth!"

As the black instructor continued, five more instructors paced around the room, scanning us for signs of fear or deceit.

"Your recruiters can't protect y'all no mo'! Sit your ass up!" He slapped the table where a white kid was slightly slouched. "Now, if any of you . . . were ever in trouble with the law—parking tickets, speeding tickets, breaking and entering, murd-duh—this is your time to fess up! What your con-artist recruiters won't tell you . . . is that we have a system . . . that's connected . . . to all the government computers in the country. And imma tell y'all somethin' . . . we all know the game! We all been recruits. And we all have friends who were recruits. So we know the lie that your recruiters probably told you about this here event . . . that it's just a game . . . but this ain't no game. *We the government!*"

Immediately a kid raised his hand and said, "I lied." Then another kid raised his hand and finally a third. One of the drill instructors directed the three confessors out of the classroom.

The Filipino instructor yelled again, "Moment of Truth!" and added, "Amen!"

The black instructor continued, "That's right! See them kids? They did the right thing! Now, because they just lied to get here, they'll be processed out and sent back home . . . but that ain't worse than what's gonna happen to you when we run our check . . . and find out that . . . three, four . . . maybe seven of y'all lied to the government!"

I started to get hot, but I knew I had to keep my composure and not show any signs of guilt. I repositioned myself in the chair, pushed my shoulders back like my grandmother taught me, and straightened my back so as to say, "I'm good! Y'all won't find nothing on me." But I'm not going to lie; I was scared to death!

The drill instructor continued, "We're going to give you five minutes to think real hard. If there's anything—we don't care if it's a ticket for taking a shit in public! I know how you country boys do. I'm a country boy myself—but whatever it is, you better fess up!"

After the black instructor finished talking, all the instructors, including him, stepped out of the room, leaving us to ponder. There was a dead silence. No one's head turned to the right or left. Everyone just faced forward silently.

I kept saying over and over in my head, *I'm good, I'm good. She told me I was clear. I'm good.* After three minutes, to everyone's shock, another kid got up and walked out. As the door was closing, I heard him say, "I have something. My recruiter . . .," and that was all I heard. I never saw that kid again.

Ten minutes later all seven instructors walked back in. The Filipino opened up with his normal tag: "Moment of Truth!"

Then the muscular African American instructor said, "Another one of your fellow brethren decided to come clean . . . get his sins washed away! I'm going to give y'all ten seconds to confess, and then after that imma start reading names off this list!" He held up a white paper with small black print. "Ten, nine, eight, seven, six, five, four, three, two, one! Time's up!"

Then he started reading, "Adeleke!"

Aw, shit!

"Get up and get out!" he said. Everyone in my view quickly looked at me like the little brother who was being carried away for his spanking.

I stood up and started to make my way toward the exit. My heart was racing a million miles per hour. Not only were the recruits in my view intermittently looking, but the drill instructors were all staring at me as well. One shook his head at me as if I were a murder suspect who just got caught. And when I stepped out of the room, a separate group of drill instructors were right there waiting for me. The three kids who had been first to leave when the Moment of Truth started were also there.

This is it. It's over. Tiana must have messed up or missed something! What did she miss?

Despite having my name called, I still held it together. I kept repeating, *I'm good, I'm good, I'm good.* When I got to the exit, I heard a second name called.

"Alvin! Get up and get out!"

I approached the first instructor that stood outside the classroom and said, "Recruit Adeleke reporting."

"Do you have anything to confess, Recruit?" the instructor asked.

I looked him straight in the eye—the same way I did when my grandmother confronted me about my mom's engagement ring—and with confidence said, "No, Instructor!" He pointed to the three kids. "Line up behind them anyway."

Everything was happening in slow motion. *This is definitely not good. Now I'm lining up with the group that's about to be kicked out the Navy.*

I heard a third name called as I made my way to the back of the line.

"Avery! Get up and get out." After hearing the third name, I began to consider that this may be part of the game. *They may just be calling everyone out of the room in alphabetical order. My last name, Adeleke, just happens to be first.* But I still wasn't sure. The innocent ones might be lining up somewhere else.

When I got behind the three kids who'd initially stepped out, I whispered, "Yo." None of them responded, so I tried again. "Yo." I leaned in closer. "Yo."

"What?" the kid in front of me finally whispered back while still facing forward.

"Why are we standing here?"

Alvin, the kid whose name had been called right after mine, came to stand in line behind me.

The kid in front of me responded, "They planted us."

"What?" I said.

He continued whispering with his head forward, "In order to encourage people to confess whose recruiters really told them to hide crimes, they planted us in the room and gave us a sign when they wanted us to stand up. The instructors figure that if a person on the fence sees someone stand and leave . . . they'll be more inclined to confess. We were just a trap."

"Damn, that's cold, man! So that fourth guy who stood up minutes after you guys left, he fell for it?" I said.

The kid in front of me continued whispering. "Yeah, we heard him say his recruiter told him not to mention a drug incident that got sealed years ago. He's done. Processing out."

I just shook my head and thought of Petty Officer Reyes.

Wherever you are, thank you.

After everyone's name was called, our newly formed boot camp division, 332, made its way to its new home for the next two months: the barracks. As I lay on my top bunk that night, staring at the ceiling and hearing multiple recruits literally crying themselves to sleep because they missed their mommies, I thought, *What a day! I went from the streets of the Bronx to Navy boot camp all in one day.*

It was as though I had been jettisoned out of my self-made chaos and into a second chance at life.

CHAPTER ELEVEN

THE PERFECT PLACE TO TRAIN

You can let people hurt you . . . or
choose to let them fuel you.

With tears streaming down her face, a Mexican lady in her midseventies fearfully recited the Hail Mary prayer. *"Dios te salve, Maria. Llena eres de gracia: El Señor es contigo. Bendita tú eres entre todas las mujeres . . ."*

She was rocking back and forth in the middle seat to my left, vigorously rubbing the rosary. Then came another violent shake, followed by screams from the majority of the passengers on the plane. For the past thirty minutes of our flight, the plane had been falling and rising like a roller-coaster ride. When the plane dipped, everyone screamed in unison, then stopped for a few seconds, then screamed again on the next drop. And when the plane snapped left, I could see everyone's head bend right, and vice versa.

The bell rang to inform us that the pilot was about to deliver a message. "Ah . . . ladies and gentlemen, we're experiencing abnormal . . ." The plane rattled violently and sent everyone into an even greater frenzy. About twenty seconds later he continued on the cabin speaker. "As you can see . . . ah . . . we're experiencing strong turbulence in our approach to San Diego

International Airport. We have suspended all cabin activities. Please keep your seat belts tightly fastened."

It was Saturday, January 4, 2003. Having graduated boot camp and corpsman medical school, I was officially a US Navy sailor about to serve at my first duty station, Naval Hospital Camp Pendleton.

As the plane continued to rattle and clatter as if it were about to fall apart, I held my right hand against the seat in front of me to gain more stability. *Damn. I survived boot camp and my rating school without getting caught for my spurious background! Now this? It seems like it's always something in my life!*

The Mexican lady, who was still reciting the Hail Mary prayer faster than I had ever heard anyone pray, slipped her right hand under my arm and held on tightly. I looked at her and gave her a warm smile as if to say, "It's okay. . . . You can hold on." The protective spirit that boot camp engrained in me was already beginning to manifest, and the tough street persona that would have made me feel awkward at the old lady's actions was beginning to slip away. I wanted her to know that I was there for her, and if anything bad was going to happen, she wouldn't be alone. I tried to maintain my composure for her.

After ten more minutes of chaos, the shaking stopped, the clouds cleared, and I was able to see the city lights of the San Diego night. It was beautiful, unlike New York City, with tall buildings and skyscrapers; here it looked like houses were everywhere. Since leaving Nigeria, I had never been this far away from home, so I was excited.

When the plane landed, all the passengers cheered as loudly as they had screamed. My Mexican friend unclutched my arm and said, *"Gracias, mi amigo."* Recognizing my dress blue sailor uniform, she then spoke these words to me in English: "Thank you for your service." It was the first time anyone other than my mother—at my boot camp graduation—had said that to me. I didn't know how to respond, so I just smiled and said, "Thank you, ma'am."

• • •

About eight of us men and women from our graduating corpsman class were headed to Camp Pendleton. We had plans to drop our bags at the base, then head straight to the Gaslamp Quarter to hit the clubs. Our shuttle driver found this amusing.

"You know it's about an hour's drive to base," he informed us.

It was already about 9:30 p.m., so I blurted out, "Hour drive? Damn. Where we driving to, back to Chicago? Our military orders say San Diego!"

The driver laughed as he focused his attention on the road. "Yes, Camp Pendleton is in San Diego, but not San Diego city . . . San Diego County. Camp Pendleton is in the most northern part of San Diego County."

Most of the group deflated, but I was determined. I told the group, "It's okay . . . it's okay. We'll get there about . . . say . . . 10:30 p.m., change as fast as possible, then rent this van for the ride back." Turning my attention to the driver, I asked, "If we paid you, can you give us a ride back?"

"I'm sorry, I can't. But you can try to get a cab."

"Okay . . . um . . . that's fine. . . . We'll just get a cab. Thank you." Turning my attention back to the group, I said, "See? It's all good. As soon as we get there, I'll call a cab so that by the time we're dressed and ready, it should be waiting for us. That way we can get to the Gaslamp . . . say by . . . eleven forty-five at the latest."

Everyone gestured as if they were on board; then I added, "We all still getting hotel rooms and staying the night there, right?"

Mostly everyone said yes, with some hesitation. I'm sure no one thought we could make it, but I did! I turned to a corpsman named Angie, who was sitting next to me, and whispered, "We still sharing a room, right?"

She giggled and whispered back, "Yes."

I grinned and whispered again, "What about a bed? We sharing that too?"

"If you still want to," she said with a cute giggle.

We arrived at Camp Pendleton's main gate around ten thirty. The gate was heavily guarded by eight marines with rifles. The guard matched each of us to our IDs one by one, and we were cleared to enter.

You wanted to be a marine; now you got it, Remi.

By this time everyone's excitement was reinvigorated, but after about five minutes of driving, I started to get frustrated. *Where is this hospital?* I thought as I stared out the window into the pitch blackness of the base. Then ten minutes passed.

"How far are we?" I asked the driver. "I thought it was just an hour drive."

He yelled back, "To the front gate. It's about twenty-five minutes from the gate to the hospital. This base is 125,000 acres."

"I'm a city boy; what's that mean?"

"That means it's *big* . . . about the size of Rhode Island. It's the largest expeditionary training facility on the West Coast. Notice. There's not many streetlights. Those mountains, valleys, and bushes you see out there, that's where your marines train. They even have areas where they can drop bombs. There are some wilderness areas where you can walk for miles and not see anybody. I doubt you're going to make it back down to the Gaslamp tonight. The hospital is one of those places that's off in the middle of nowhere. Just to get a cab out there is going to take forever. Might be better for y'all to make plans tomorrow."

Our crew fell dead silent. Trying to be positive, I said, "Listen: we can still make it!"

One of the other sailors, Carl, said, "You just heard him. We'll probably have to wait an hour for a cab. Then we'll have an hour-and-a-half drive down to the Gaslamp. We can't make it, Remi."

I looked at Angie, thinking of the time we were supposed to have alone in San Diego.

"Hey, driver! You got a number for a cab?" I asked.

"Yup." He rattled it off as I rustled through my sea bag to find my phone. I unlocked it only to see a large No Service alert on the home screen.

"My phone says no service," I said as I held it as high as I could.

"What?" the driver said.

"My phone . . . my damn phone has no signal," I replied.

The driver laughed again. "Yeah, there's little to no cell service on this base. When I have drop-offs at the hospital and have to call my company, I always use the landlines at the barracks or hospital quarterdeck."

I was more and more frustrated. "Can you at least speed up a bit? We're the only car on the road."

"Sorry, no can do. The speed limit is thirty miles per hour. The base police hide all along this road, especially at night. I can't afford to get pulled over on base for speeding. If I do, I can lose my base access, which means I'll lose work."

Wow, this night just keeps getting worse and worse. Despite all the obstacles, I was still determined to get down to the Gaslamp, even if it was just Angie and me. I didn't care if it was a hundred-dollar cab ride or if we didn't get to the Gaslamp until 2:00 a.m., I was going.

Finally we pulled up to the hospital, and just as the driver described, it was in the middle of nowhere. The large, eight-floor hospital sat in the center of a wide valley. To the east and west were massive hills. A storage facility was located behind the hospital to the north. Directly across the street to the south were dormlike barracks adjacent to a track and field. There was another building about a third of a mile south of the barracks, and next to that were a gym, a baseball field, campgrounds, a fire station, and Lake O'Neill. Other than that, there was nothing else but pitch-black wilderness and howling coyotes. I was not in the Bronx anymore!

We went straight to the barracks to check in with the petty officer on duty. Petty Officer 3rd Class Green, an African American woman in her midtwenties, was waiting to welcome us. "Welcome to Camp Pendleton. It's late, and I'm sure you all are ready to get some sleep."

I don't know what you're talking about. I'm about to find a phone and call a cab, I thought as I looked at Angie and nodded.

Petty Officer Green continued, "Males are on the first floor, two to a room, and females are on the second floor, two to a room." Looking at us sternly, she said, "Males, you are not allowed on the females' floor for any reason. If you're caught anywhere near the females' floor, you will be subject to captain's mast. Same goes for you, ladies. Do you all understand me?"

We all said in unison, "Yes, Petty Officer."

She began to call out our names for room keys. "HA [hospital apprentice] Adeleke, room 106." I politely took the key and quickly began to make my way toward my room to see if it had a phone. I was on a mission to call a cab for Angie and me. Right before my foot stepped out of the foyer, Petty Officer Green said, "Oh . . . please come back, HA Adeleke."

Hiding my frustrated expression, I made my way back to the group. Then she delivered the dagger to my heart: "Command has decided to secure liberty for the weekend for all of you. None of you are allowed to leave base. After you're all checked in Monday and have gone through orientation, you will be eligible for liberty next weekend. If any of you are caught leaving base, you will be subject to . . ."

I know, I know. Captain's mast. I walked away full of rage.

I was so angry I couldn't see at the time that this place was ideal for me! It was as though someone knew my dream and had strategically pulled me away from anything and everything that could stand in my way of fulfilling it. Having no car and no easy access to entertainment, people, or society itself, I had nothing to distract me from my efforts to qualify for SEAL training. This was the perfect place to train.

. . .

As directed by Petty Officer Green, I reported to the hospital for duty Monday at 0730. The hospital was a complete health-care facility with a clinic, an emergency room, surgical suites, patient rooms, a large lab, imaging facilities, and the ever-so-famous Docs Diner in the basement. It serviced everyone on the base, approximately thirty-seven thousand military personnel and their families. During the day it was as busy as Times Square. After getting fully checked in, I was assigned to the family practice clinic on the first floor.

Sporting the hospital's working uniform—black pressed pants, a black collared shirt, a National Defense Ribbon, and a tie—I made my way to the clinic with my check-in envelope in hand. As I strolled down the hall like George Jefferson, expecting to go directly to my supervisor and lay out my career plan, loud shouting abruptly stopped me in a T-intersection.

"Who do you think you are?!" a marine yelled. Straight ahead of me was the entrance to the family practice clinic. I could have made my way right in, but I decided to observe what was happening. I peeked around the corner to see a gunnery sergeant screaming at what looked like a junior marine.

"You better start sounding off with some freakin' volume!"

The junior marine, who must have been about nineteen, stood at attention. The gunnery sergeant had his right hand turned sideways near the kid's face, an angry gesture known as the knife hand. A girl about twenty years old stood shamefully behind the junior marine.

"No excuse, Gunny," the junior marine said.

The gunny continued in an extremely raspy voice: "You think you can march around this base, holding hands with your girlfriend . . . while your uniform looks like a freakin' soup sandwich, Lance Corporal?"

My eyes were wide open at this point. *Yo! This dude is disrespecting him in front of his woman!*

"No, Gunny. . . . She's my wife," the lance responded. "And—"

"Did I ask you who she is? At 0630 tomorrow morning, I want you and your platoon corporal on the 3/1 grinder!"

Before the lance corporal could respond, the gunny turned and made his way toward the corner where I was observing. I backed up against the wall and started prying through my check-in envelope as though I was looking for something. When he turned the corner, he looked at me, and I quickly looked at him, then back down into my envelope. Once he got a good distance away, I stared at his back, then whispered, "I would've knocked your ass out." I shook my head. "Thank God I didn't join the Marine Corps. I wouldn't have lasted."

That wouldn't be the last time I watched a marine-chewing session at the hospital. It happened on a regular basis.

I made my way into the family practice clinic. Two women were sitting at the front check-in desk—one African American and the other Filipino. They were civilian contractors in their sixties.

"Good morning, I'm the new check-in, HA Adeleke, and I'm here to see HM2 [Hospital Corpsman Petty Officer 2nd Class] Brown."

They were both jubilant and had a warm maternal presence.

"Welcome. I'm Mrs. Perez," the Filipino woman said.

The other gave me a big smile and said, "Yes, yes, so nice to meet you. I'm Ms. Francine. I'll go get HM2 right now." She got up and walked down the hall.

I sat down, placed my envelope in my lap, and looked around the clinic. The waiting room was full of patients, mostly women and kids. The national news played on a large TV in the waiting room, so after taking a look around, I focused my eyes on the news. As usual at that time a report about the Iraq War came on. I could tell by the concerned looks on the faces of some wives that their husbands were over there. They looked as though they were hoping to get a glimpse of the men they loved.

"You must be HA Adeleke," someone said. Taking my eyes off the screen, I looked up to see a short Mexican lady in a Navy uniform.

I immediately stood up. "Yes, ma'am."

"Nice to meet you. I'm the LPO [leading petty officer] for the family practice clinic, HM2 Brown."

"Nice to meet you as well, HM2."

"Follow me. I'm going to show you around the clinic and introduce you to some of the doctors you'll be working with."

"Roger that," I said.

"To the left of the check-in desk is where you're going to check patients in after they're cleared at the front desk. There's an electronic blood pressure cuff, but some doctors will request a manual blood pressure if the electronic reads are high."

The electronic BP machine was on a rolling stand along with a thermometer and finger pulse oximeter.

"Got it," I said.

"We require rectal temps for all babies that show signs of a fever."

I was taken aback. "I'm sorry?"

"Babies . . . if they have signs of a fever, they get rectal temps. Some will kick and scream, but some will be calm. Don't worry; you'll be fine," she said with a smile.

Oh my goodness, I thought. *This place just keeps getting worse.*

As we made our way out of the check-in room, HM2 spotted a female doctor leaving one of the patient rooms with a chart in her hand. "Dr. Ryan, this is HA Adeleke. He just checked in today. He'll be one of your medical assistants."

"Hey, great having you, Adeleke." Dr. Ryan extended her hand to shake mine. I was a bit taken aback. All the doctors were officers, and I was enlisted, so I wasn't used to interacting with officers so casually.

"How was corpsman school?" Dr. Ryan asked.

Because I hadn't gotten a chance yet to tell anyone my plans, I used Dr. Ryan's question as an opportunity to lay it out. "It was great. I finished top ten in my class." That was actually true. "I was hoping to get orders to a Marines battalion so I could get some operating experience. My goal is to be a SEAL, but . . . I'm here, so . . . I'm ready to do the best job I can where I'm at."

Dr. Ryan responded, "Well, I look forward to working with you. My husband is a doctor down at BUD/S, so maybe one day I can have him give you a tour. You can watch the guys train."

"Oh, yes ma'am! Thank you."

"You're very welcome. I'll see you around," Dr. Ryan said before walking away.

HM2 Brown continued the tour. When we got to the instrument cleaning room, she stopped me and said, "As your LPO, I'm not just here to manage you, but I'm here to help advance your career. You do a good job here, and I'll be your first advocate to help you get into BUD/S."

I looked at her, smiled, and said, "Thank you, HM2." She had a warm, servant spirit that reminded me of Petty Officer Reyes.

As she continued to walk me through the clinic and introduce me to the other staff and doctors, it didn't seem like I was really in the military. This seemed like a normal job without that *hooyah* mind-set I had gotten used to during boot camp. Unlike the gunny in the hall, everyone in the clinic seemed like civilians who just happened to work in a hospital on a military base. And then I met a woman who would totally reverse that premature notion.

As we stepped out of the instrument room, an attractive brunette approached us.

"Is this the new corpsman?" she asked.

HM2 replied with a sweet smile, "Yes, this is HA Adeleke. Adeleke, this is HM3 Trotter. I manage both sides of the clinic, but we're preparing her for my LPO position when I leave. So she's responsible for all the junior corpsmen on this side of the clinic . . . the side you'll be working on."

I had already become so used to everyone's relaxed demeanor that I said, "Hello. I'm Adeleke."

She smiled, then looked at HM2. "Do I have him now?"

"He's all yours, HM3. I'll see you around, Adeleke. If you need anything, just give me a holler."

"Roger that, HM2," I said as she began to walk away.

"It's H . . . A!" Trotter said intensely while keeping a low tone.

I smiled at Trotter, not understanding what she meant. "Excuse me, HM3?"

She stepped close to my face. "Stand at attention when I talk to you!" I slowly got into the attention position, totally unaware of what had just happened.

"You introduced yourself as [she enunciated every syllable in my last name] Ad-day-lay-kay! You're in the Navy. Therefore, you have a rank. So when you're in uniform and your superior approaches you, you state your rank, H . . . A, and then your name, Ad-day-lay-kay. Do you understand me?"

I'm not going to lie: a little Bronx attitude rose up in me. I thought of the junior marine who had just been punked in the hallway, and I wasn't ready to get punked like that! I rolled my eyeballs up toward the ceiling and said, "Yeah . . . I understand you."

"It's *yes, HM3*, not *yeah!*"

As I got ready to say it again anyway, I thought about Petty Officer Reyes. I had told her I wouldn't let her down. I had told her I would be great. By fighting with my superior, I wouldn't be keeping my word. So I refocused my eyes on Trotter and said respectfully, "Yes, HM3."

"Don't f*** with me, HA Ad-day-lay-kay!"

"Yes, HM3."

"Good . . . you're learning," she said sarcastically. "Now, Dr. Wilson has a pap smear scheduled in thirty minutes. I'm going to show you how to prep a room for a pap smear. During the exam, you will stand by and respectfully watch because you will be assisting on many while you're here."

"Yes, HM3," I replied.

. . .

I had expected to join the military, then pick up a gun and run around some forest with my face painted and a rucksack on my back, but my hospital assignment was nothing like that. My daily routine consisted of gathering vital signs for patients, giving babies shots, assisting with pap smears, administering birth-control shots, giving pregnancy tests, and moving boxes. I was miserable. I'd gone from running a record company to being Nurse Betty. It was all very humbling. But unbeknownst to me, I desperately needed this crash course in humility if I was going to be a SEAL.

As the first three weeks passed, HM3 Trotter got worse. I don't know why, but this woman *hated* me! She really did, and over time the sentiment became mutual. She tested my patience on a daily basis, and I didn't pass the test every time. But the more she antagonized me, the more she lit the fire within me to get out of that hospital and into SEAL training before I did something I would regret. Then one day she made a grave mistake and said something to me that turned out to be the greatest gift she could have given me.

"H-A Adeleke!" HM3 Trotter yelled as she marched down the clinic hallway in my direction. "H-A Ad-day-lay-kay! Come here right now!"

Oh God, what is it now? I said to myself.

"Meet me in the immunization room!"

I already knew what to expect: she was going to hoot and holler and try to do the knife-hand thing, and I was going to stare at her while I stood at attention and repeated, "Yes, HM3," until she got tired of looking at me.

As soon as I stepped in and closed the door behind me, I snapped to attention. I didn't want to have to hear her tell me to get there.

"What is it with you? Huh? You prepped the room wrong for Dr. Carter's two p.m. pap smear!"

"Yes, HM3."

"Well . . . explain yourself!"

I sighed.

"You tired, HA Adeleke?"

"No . . . well . . . yes, HM3." *Tired of you.*

"Well . . . what happened?" she asked again.

"I'm sorry. Dr. Carter has a specific way he likes the room set for paps, and Dr. Wilson has a different way. They both had paps at two p.m., and I mistakenly put Dr. Wilson's patient in room 6 and Dr. Carter's patient in room 8." I crossed my hands to gesture that I had mixed up the rooms. "So, you see, it was a mix-up. It's my fault. I'm sorry. Everything was in the rooms, just not exactly the way they wanted it. Again, I'm sorry."

With her hands on her hips and her face screwed up with disgust, she stared at me as she nodded her head for about five seconds, then said, "Huh. And you want to be a Navy SEAL! There is no chance in hell that you'll ever make it. You probably won't even get into BUD/S! You can't even set a room right for a *pap smear*!" She turned and stormed out of the room.

If Petty Officer Reyes was an angel assigned to me, Petty Officer Trotter had to be a devil assigned to me. But both gave me priceless gifts.

After Trotter left the room, I stood there for a second, then turned to the mirror. I started talking to myself aloud. "Did you hear what she just said to you? She said you won't make it! That biatch said you don't have a chance in hell. Whatcha gonna do?"

The next day I walked into HM2 Brown's office. "HM2, I respectfully request a moment with you."

"Yes . . . of course, come in." Before I could sit down, she asked, "Is it about HM3 Trotter?" HM2 Brown, along with the rest of the clinic leadership, knew about the way Trotter treated me. It got to the point that anytime HM3 Trotter brought a charge against me, even if it was legitimate, HM2 Brown would do a cursory investigation and then write it off. In the short time I was there, my leadership knew that, yes, I was new to the Navy and made some mistakes, but I also had a strong work ethic, and for the most part I was respectful, and Trotter was, well, *Trotter*.

I chuckled. "No. No, it doesn't have anything to do with her. I'd like to request a change to my schedule."

"What kind of change?"

"As you know, I want to go to BUD/S, but I can't swim, I don't have the ASVAB scores, and I'm not in the proper physical condition. The pool at Mainside closes at five. So by the time I get off at four, get changed, and run the three miles there, it's pretty much closing time."

"You would like to take off during working hours to swim?" HM2 asked.

"Yes and no. I'd like to have the time to train but also give the clinic its eight hours. So, in short, I respectfully request to work four hours during the morning clinic from eight to noon, have the afternoon clinic off, then come back and work the evening clinic from five to nine or whenever it ends."

She sat back in her chair, squinted, and said, "Are you sure you want to do that? With your training hours, that's more than a full day's work."

"I'm absolutely positive. And I promise you, I will work as hard in the morning and the evening as I do now in the morning and the afternoon."

"Okay, I'll let you do it."

"Thank you so much, HM2. I appreciate your help."

"You're welcome, Adeleke." After I walked out of the office, I noticed HM3 Trotter in the waiting area, greeting a patient. I looked at her, and she glanced at me, then turned back to the patient.

As I kept staring at her, I said softly, "Thank you, HM3. You have no clue what you just did."

. . .

That Saturday I took the base bus from the hospital to the Mainside Center. I was on a mission to get everything I needed to train myself. I spent a whole paycheck on a black rucksack, swim goggles, an ASVAB study book, an iPod, a log book to log my progress, and a bunch of snacks. I also purchased the DVD set of the Discovery Channel documentary *Navy SEALs Training: BUD/S Class 234*. I loaded everything in my new rucksack and waited an hour at the bus stop for a ride back to the hospital. When I got back, I dropped my bag at the barracks, then walked to the gym about a third of a mile away.

The gym was empty. I asked the gym attendant, "Is it always like this?"

He laughed and answered, "Always! You Navy don't like to stay fit. Sometimes we'll get a few marines from the other side of base, but for the most part . . . this gym is for the hospital staff. You see any hospital staff?"

"Yeah, me."

"Well, it's all yours; have fun."

The last time I had worked out in a gym was back in my high school weight training class. I was as skinny then as I was now, but I didn't care. I was determined to acquire the strength needed to get accepted into BUD/S and prove Trotter wrong.

I walked around the gym, inspecting all the machines, and periodically stopped to strategize how they could be used. I took notes for about fifteen minutes, and when I was done, I made my way toward the exit.

The attendant teased, "I knew you Navy don't like to stay fit. Where you going? You just got here."

"Don't worry. Believe me. I'll be back."

I walked back to the barracks and popped in the BUD/S 234 documentary. I watched and took notes. I didn't have anyone to teach me how to work out or anyone to work out with. I was in the middle of nowhere and on my own. But, like my father, I was an auditory and visual learner, so I figured that if I could observe workout patterns in the documentary, I would be able to develop routines of my own.

After going through the first half of the DVD set, by Sunday morning I figured it out! Whatever workouts I created, they needed to be constant, similar to the fitness routines in each 234 episode. Recruits would run to the ocean, get wet, then run to another point and do more push-ups. Or they'd do pull-ups, drop down, do push-ups, then jump on a dip bar and do dips. I couldn't train like the typical fitness enthusiasts of the time who did a few reps, rested for a while, then did another set. My heart rate had to stay elevated. More importantly, I couldn't be comfortable during any part of my training.

With the notes I took at the gym the day before, plus the notes I took while watching the BUD/S 234 documentary, I developed six workouts for six days of the week. Mondays would be my chest/triceps/back circuit days, with a push-up test at the beginning. Tuesdays, I would run three miles uphill to the pool, try to swim, then run three miles back, with a mile-and-a-half run test in the beginning. Wednesdays were my pull-ups/abs/legs circuit days, with a pull-up test at the beginning. Thursdays and Saturdays would repeat Tuesdays as run-swim days. And Fridays I would do a mash-up circuit that hit every muscle group, with a sit-up test at the beginning.

After I planned the workouts, I created several charts to track my progress. Along with the many other requirements needed to get into BUD/S, I would have to complete a five-hundred-yard swim in less than twelve minutes and thirty seconds, do a minimum of sixty push-ups, a minimum of sixty sit-ups, a minimum of ten pull-ups, and finish a one-and-a-half-mile run in under eleven minutes and thirty seconds. At the time the only category I was semi-safe in was the run. Other than that, I could do only about thirty push-ups, fifty sit-ups, no pull-ups, and walk in the shallow end of the pool. Each chart was specific to each part of the test. For example, my push-up page looked like this:

2/6/2003 30 push-ups
2/13/2003 32 push-ups
2/20/2003 32 push-ups
2/27/2003 33 push-ups

My goal was to progress, not regress, and for me, the best way to do that was to see my growth in writing and create realistic goals throughout the process.

After I drew out pages of charts, I grabbed my new iPod, connected it to my Dell laptop, and uploaded workout music. Years earlier I had grown to like film scores, so I uploaded the most motivating ones: Hans Zimmer's theme from *Gladiator*, James Horner's theme from *Glory*, and Bill Conti's "Gonna Fly Now" and "Going the Distance" from *Rocky*.

I was ready!

By Sunday afternoon I had my gear organized and my fitness schedule squared away. Now it was time to crack open the ASVAB book and develop a study plan.

The book was broken up into sections that matched sections of the test: arithmetic reasoning, general science, mathematics knowledge, mechanical comprehension, word knowledge, and so on. Each section had about seventy pages of reading material. I started reading the first section, but after about an hour I said to myself, *This is not going to work. It's just too much content to memorize.*

I got up and paced. Some doubt began to creep in. *You've been out of school for way too long, Remi. It's going to take you a year to retrain your mind to be proficient with all of this content.* Then I thought of the time I almost didn't graduate high school because I had failed English. In that case I found a way to produce what needed to be produced. If I could do it then—in the short amount of time that I had—I knew I could do this now.

I sat back down at my desk and began to flip through the pages. *There's got to be a way to streamline this process. There's just got to be a way,* I thought. I kept flipping and flipping, and then I got to the sample test sections. There were five full tests in the book. I flipped past these and came to an answer key for all the tests, followed by a breakdown as to why the right answers were right and the wrong answers were wrong. A light went off in my head.

I got it! I'll take the test, then check my answers. For the questions I get wrong, I'll study the breakdown as to why. After that I'll take another test using the knowledge I gained from the breakdowns.

With my final piece figured out, I went to sleep Sunday night with a well-oiled plan that was going to help me prove HM3 Trotter wrong. More importantly, it was going to help me achieve my dream.

CHAPTER TWELVE

PLAN, PREPARE, EXECUTE

*If you're not uncomfortable when you're
training, you're not training.*

When my alarm went off Monday morning, I jumped out of my bed, pressed my uniform, put a fresh shine on my shoes, and made my way across the street to the hospital. I got there five minutes early. And when the clock struck eight o'clock, I immediately started checking in patients.

Right after I led the last morning patient to Dr. Ryan's room, I knocked on her door. It was cracked open.

"Um, ma'am?" I said.

"Yes, Adeleke," she replied.

"Your last patient is all checked in. Vital signs are normal. I told her you'll be right in."

"Thank you."

"Will you need me to assist on anything?"

"One second. Let me check the chart." She walked to the door, and I handed her the patient's chart through the small opening.

She looked at the chart for about a minute, then said, "No, you can take off for lunch. This is pretty straightforward."

"Great, thank you," I said.

I ran to the check-in room, cleaned up, then made my way down to Docs

Diner. Though the cafeteria was free, the food was not good at all, so I often opted to eat at Docs Diner instead. I got to know the civilian ladies who worked at the diner pretty well. They were always sweet to me. Knowing that I was a broke E-2 living in the barracks, the cashiers would always give me a discount and sometimes comp my meals.

After lunch I went back to my barracks and took my first ASVAB test while my food settled. I didn't do too well, but the answer explanations were so clear that I felt confident about how to fix my deficiencies on the next test.

I ran to the gym with two hours to spare, completed my workout, which was extremely difficult because I was so out of shape, then ran back to the barracks, showered, threw on my uniform, and got back to the hospital ten minutes before evening clinic started.

When the last patient left that night, I cleaned the waiting area and check-in station, turned off the TV, then made my way across the street to the barracks. When I finally got in bed, I said to myself, *See? It's not that bad. This is a perfect routine.*

But the next day would not be easy, because that was going to be the official start of my swim training.

. . .

"Come on . . . keep going . . . keep going . . . don't quit!" I said between breaths as I ran past Lake O'Neill on Santa Margarita Road toward Vandergrift Boulevard. Vandergrift was the mile-and-a-half point of the run. I was only one mile in and I. Was. *Winded!* I wanted to stop so bad, but I knew that pushing through the pain was the only way I was going to meet my goal for the day; and my goal was to get a solid baseline time from which I could improve.

A car drove by and honked at me as if to say, "Good job!" That would later turn into a ritual of the hospital staff every time they saw me running. The honk gave me a little boost, which caused me to pick up my head and maintain my pace.

When I could see the last tree at the T-intersection of Santa Margarita and Vandergrift, I started sprinting toward it. *Almost there*, I thought. At this point I couldn't talk. I needed every breath to grab as much oxygen as possible.

"Aweeeeeee!" I screamed as I passed the tree. I quickly looked at my watch to clock my time. Ten minutes, forty-five seconds. "Not bad, not bad," I said.

Then came what would be my nemesis during every run: the Vandergrift hill. The hill was a fifteen-degree incline for about 1.3 miles. Not fun. I had already struggled on the first half of the run, so I knew I was going to feel the pain. I had to press through. *Like BUD/S 234 showed, if you're not uncomfortable when you're training, you're not training*, I told myself.

"Drive, drive, drive, drive," I kept saying as I climbed. As I moved up past the tree line at the base of the hill, I began to see the vastness of Lake O'Neill to my left.

I had a simple goal for the hill: not to walk any of it. I didn't care how slowly I ran, I just wanted to maintain a runner's gait. My other goal for the day was not to drown when I entered the pool.

After a two-minute break, I took off up Vandergrift. The sun was shining, I had my *Rocky* theme, "Gonna Fly Now," on repeat, and I was feeling motivated! Call it corny, but hey, it helped.

Periodically I would yell, "Aw, this sucks!"

When I got halfway up, I switched songs from Bill Conti's *Rocky* theme to James Horner's closing credits music for *Glory*. At this point I could see the hospital off in the distance, and as I got higher, the hospital got lower.

Finally, after about fifteen minutes, I made it to the top! I stopped to take in the beauty of the land and what I had achieved. I could see the light of the day glistening off the lake; I could see the campgrounds, the hospital, and everything that surrounded it; I could see hills upon hills as far as the horizon. I didn't enjoy the pain, but the reward was worth it.

"If only my boys back home could see this," I said as the *Glory* soundtrack played through my earphones. Then I turned and finished the last leg of the run to the pool.

When I arrived, I walked into the locker room, changed, and made my way to the pool deck. As I walked past the deep end toward the shallow end, I couldn't help but think back to boot camp. At boot camp everyone had to pass a simple swim test in order to graduate. All we had to do was jump off a high dive, stay above the surface for two minutes, then swim to the other side of the pool. The recruits who didn't pass were labeled NQS (Non-Qualified Swimmer) and forced to show up to mandatory swim remediation training. It was always easy to identify NQS recruits on their way to remediation, because it was always a group of twenty to thirty African Americans marching in ranks, with two to three other races mixed in. If a recruit still didn't pass the basic test after they were remediated for two months, they were eventually discharged from the Navy.

Standing over the edge of the Camp Pendleton pool, I thought back to the day I took my boot camp test. I was so sick that every part of my body ached. I had a sore throat and couldn't stop coughing. I didn't care. Though I didn't know what I was doing and was sick as a dog, I did not want to be labeled NQS. I jumped off the high dive, hit the pool, then fought my way to the top. When my face broke the surface, I lay on my back and kicked like a frog to stay afloat. And as soon as the drill instructors blew the whistle, which indicated that we could swim to the other end, I stayed on my back and *fought* my way to the other end. But that was surviving, not swimming.

I tried not to let that past experience discourage me as I stepped into the shallow end of the pool. At this point the lifeguard started staring at me. I pushed away from the pool wall and flailed around. This time I was on my stomach. I swung my arms like a windmill and kicked my legs violently.

Oh yeah . . . I got this . . . I'm moving. By the amount of effort I was putting in, you would have thought I swam the length of the pool. But when I picked my head up to check my distance, I was in the exact same spot! Both lifeguards were looking at me, trying to fight back laughter. I didn't let it get to me. I was well aware of my deficiency.

I kept up my fight for an hour; then I got my stuff and ran the three miles back to the barracks.

To the lifeguards' surprise, I'm sure, I showed up to that pool three days a week every week, as planned. There were times when I left very discouraged and even believed HM3's assessment of my future, but I kept coming back. I had no choice if I wanted to be a SEAL.

Then one day I decided to humble myself.

"Hey . . . hey!" I yelled at the lifeguard as I stood in the shallow end.

He lifted his sunglasses and looked in my direction without saying anything.

"Can you help me out here? Can you help me with my swimming?" I asked.

The young Caucasian guy with a California-boy accent said, "Sorry, dude . . . I can't leave the lifeguard stand to show you how to swim!"

I looked down at the pool for a second and then looked back up and said, "Okay. Can you do me a favor and just talk me through what I have to do?"

"Yeah, dude! As long as I stay up here, I can do that!"

And just like that he started coaching me from the lifeguard tower. I held on to every word he said, and in three weeks I started to see improvement. I got better, but not as good as I needed to be. And then I met Lieutenant Colonel Murray.

After arriving at the pool locker room one day, I put my swim trunks on and got ready to head out to the pool. Right before I stepped out, I heard, "What unit you with, Marine?"

I turned around to face the voice. Not knowing what rank he was, and having witnessed other marines get filleted for addressing a senior marine in a lax way, I stood at attention and said, "I'm stationed at the hospital, sir. I'm not a marine."

"You're a doc?" he asked with shock, using the nickname marines use for corpsmen.

"Yes, sir."

"Wow. I'm impressed. You know, I've driven by you many times as you run up Vandergrift. I thought for sure you were a marine." He extended his hand. "I'm Lieutenant Colonel Murray. Stationed at 1st Reconnaissance Force Recon Battalion."

"HA Adeleke, sir," I replied as I shook his hand.

"What are you training for?" he asked.

"I'm training to be a SEAL, sir."

"SEAL, huh?"

"Yes, sir."

"How's your swimming coming along?"

"Not as good as I want it to be, sir."

"I tell you what. Meet me here this same time on the days you swim, and I'll work with you. How's that sound?"

"Of course! Yes, yes. Thank you, sir," I replied.

"Your training starts today. I'll meet you on the pool deck in five minutes."

"Yes, sir!"

Between the lifeguard's coaching and Lieutenant Colonel Murray's training, by mid-March I was swimming laps. Back and forth, back and forth, without stopping. I picked up every technique the colonel taught me pretty fast. I was hungry to learn. Hungry to succeed!

Not only did my swimming get better, but everything else did too. I passed the last three tests in my first ASVAB book and moved on to my second book of tests. According to my workout charts, my push-ups, pull-ups, and sit-ups increased dramatically. And with that, my body began to transform. When I looked in the mirror, I didn't see a skinny kid anymore. Lateral muscles began to pop out, biceps grew, abdominal muscles protruded, my quads were chiseled, and stretch marks appeared on my chest and my shoulders. Eight weeks earlier I had struggled to run up the Vandergrift hill. Now I would borrow a seventy-pound barbell from the gym, throw it across my shoulders, and take it with me on my run up.

• • •

Despite my successes, one night I almost flushed all my hard work down the drain. Though my determination had a habit of working for me, sometimes it turned against me.

On March 7, 2003, the Navy SEAL–based movie *Tears of the Sun* was released. I had to see this movie! But I didn't have a car, and most people living at the barracks didn't have cars either, so I was pretty much stuck. Two weeks passed. Knowing that if I didn't get to a theater soon I'd have to wait for the DVD, I got desperate!

The weekend of Friday, March 21, I had command duty, so instead of going straight to the barracks when my night clinic shift ended, I had to go straight to the hospital quarterdeck to check in with the duty petty officer for the weekend. My particular duty was duty driver, which meant if anyone or anything needed to be picked up or dropped off in San Diego County or on base, it was my job for the weekend to do it.

As I made my way to the quarterdeck, I wondered who my duty petty officer would be. I hoped it would be someone tempered. My hopes were quickly dashed when I came around the corner and saw HM3 Trotter!

"H-A Ad-day-lay-kay. Looks like we have duty together tonight."

The way she said my name made me cringe. I don't know why, but this crazy thought popped into my head. As I walked up to her, I thought, *Why don't we just go ahead and have sex? Maybe . . . you know . . . maybe that will make things better between us.* Like I said, it was a crazy thought.

I stood at attention and said, "Good evening, HM3."

In typical form, she started talking without greeting me. "The duty vehicle keys will remain here on the quarterdeck. Here's the duty pager. If I page you, you will respond immediately."

As she handed me the pager, I replied, "Yes, HM3."

"Since you're hard at following instructions, I'm going to reiterate. You are not allowed to leave the barracks for any reason but to come here to retrieve the vehicle keys if needed."

"Yes, HM3."

Then she said, "Dismissed."

"Yes, HM3."

I did a right-face and departed out of the main entrance of the hospital.

At the barracks a few guys were hanging out on the benches by the parking lot, so I made my way over to them.

"Here comes the machine!" a guy named Jason yelled.

"What up, fellas?" I said.

"Nothing. We're just chilling. You got duty tonight?" Jason asked.

"Yup. Trotter the Barbarian," I replied.

The hospital had what we called *temps*, who lived in the barracks. They were people stationed on the base who needed to be close to the hospital for a period of time due to medical reasons. One of the temps was a six-foot-four, bald, African American guy named James. He said, "Well, I'm about to jump in my whip and head down to San Diego."

"What you got planned?" Jason asked.

James replied, "I don't know . . . walk the Gaslamp strip . . . maybe check out a movie, get some food."

My ears perked up. "Movie, what movie?"

"Probably that new Navy SEAL joint. Tears of something," James said.

The wheels started turning in my head. *In the three and a half months I've been here, I've never been paged while on duty. It's probably not going to happen tonight. Imma go!*

I spoke up. "I tell you what. If you go to see that movie, I'll come with you."

Jason piped up, "You on duty, dog! You may not want to do that. You know, you get caught UA [unauthorized absence], you can kiss BUD/S good-bye for at least three years."

As I ran toward my room to change, I yelled, "I'm good. I've never been paged. It's not going to happen tonight."

After I got changed, I stuffed the pager in my jeans pocket just in case, ran outside, and jumped into James's car.

As soon as we got off base and my cell reception kicked in, I called up my buddy Luis, who was stationed in San Diego at Balboa Hospital. Luis and I met in boot camp and remained good friends. He had as much passion about being a SEAL as I did.

"Yo, Louie!" I said when he answered.

"What's going on, Remi?"

"Check this out: we're about to hit up the Gaslamp 15 theater on Fifth and G. We're going to see *Tears of the Sun*. You want to meet us there?"

"Sure. What time is the showing?" he asked.

"Ten p.m.," I replied.

"All right. I'll see you there."

James and I arrived at the theater about ten minutes early. Luis had seats reserved for us. I was anxious to be as inspired as I had been when I saw *The Rock* years earlier.

The trailers started on time at ten. About fifteen minutes later the theater went darker, the screen opened up a little wider, and the movie started.

As the opening credits were still rolling. I heard, *beep, beep, beep, beep!* The pager in my pocket started going off!

I got *hot* and whispered to Luis, "Aw, shit! I got paged!" I reached into my pocket and pulled out the pager. It was the naval hospital quarterdeck's phone number. As I ran out of the theater, I thought I had just ruined my life, once again. I tried to calm myself down. *Maybe it's just a test to check the pager.*

When I got out of the theater, I tried my best to find the quietest place possible. I found what I thought was a good spot and called the quarterdeck on my cell.

HM3 Trotter answered, "Naval hospital quarterdeck, how can I help you, sir or ma'am?"

I tried to act like I was half-asleep, "Uhhh . . . hello . . . I think I just got a page." I yawned.

As usual, the woman just vomited everything out, which worked in my favor. "HA Adeleke, I need you to get here right now, get the duty vehicle, and get to Balboa Hospital. A patient here needs IV medication, stat. The order is ready for pickup. Get out of bed right now and get to the quarterdeck!" Then she hung up on me.

I said out loud, "Okay, this is not that bad. Balboa Hospital is right down the street from here. We'll get the medication and race back up to Camp Pendleton." I sprinted back into the theater.

"James, Luis, we have to go now," I whispered.

When we got out of the theater, I explained what was going on.

Luis said, "Oh, that's easy. I know exactly where you need to go." That was a tremendous blessing because Balboa Hospital is a massive facility.

When we got there, Luis led me straight to the pickup site for the medication. By this time I had received three pages from HM3 Trotter. I didn't answer any of them.

"Hello, I'm HA Adeleke from Naval Hospital Camp Pendleton. I was sent here to pick up medication for a patient," I said to the duty nurse.

"Wow. That was fast. Wait . . . you're not in uniform," the nurse said.

"Yes, sir. I'm sorry. . . . I was told it was an emergency, so we just raced down as fast as possible."

He looked at me with a bit of suspicion, then handed me the bag of IV medication.

When we got out of the hospital, I said goodbye to Luis and jumped back in James's car. We raced as fast as we could back up to Camp Pendleton. It was about an hour-and-a-half drive, but it felt like three hours. At some points I wished I could have jumped out of the car while it was moving and flown through the sky to the hospital. My entire career was flashing through my mind.

I'm never going to BUD/S; I'm never going to be a SEAL. I'm going to go to captain's mast. . . . I might even get kicked out of the Navy! Dammit! You messed up again, Remi!

While my mind was spinning, my pager and phone were going off. HM3 Trotter kept calling and paging me back to back to back.

After we got on base, I told James, "Listen, man. I know we're not supposed to speed on base, but, please, do me this favor: speed! If we get pulled over, I'll just show them the medical bag and tell them it's an emergency."

He looked at me and said, "I got you. And listen: I'm just a temp here, so there's nothing anyone can do to me. However you need to use my name, use it. My Navy career is over. I'm getting out. I don't want to see you lose yours."

"Thank you, James, but regardless of how you help me, Trotter hates me, so she's gonna fry me."

James pulled right up to the hospital. I jumped out and ran up the steps to the quarterdeck as he pulled away. As soon as I walked through the doors, HM3 was right there waiting for me.

"Where. The f***. Have you been? Oh . . . you are so done!" Her voice echoed through the halls. "You are never going to BUD/S! I'm going to personally see to it that you go to captain's mast . . . that you are busted down in rank!" The woman's hands were shaking by her sides. I thought for a second that she was going to slap me. "You will be charged with unauthorized absence, dereliction of duty, and disobeying a lawful order!"

She was so blinded by rage that she didn't see the bag of medication I was carrying.

"Where were you?" she yelled.

I didn't say anything.

"I said, where the hell were you, Adeleke?" Her head shook.

I slowly lifted the bag of medication.

"What's that?!" Trotter yelled.

"It's the medication you requested, HM3."

"Wait . . . what? How did you get this?" she asked as a nurse from the ward approached her to retrieve the bag.

I watched as Trotter handed the nurse the bag. And as soon as the nurse grabbed the bag, she ran to the elevator to get it up to the patient. That's when it hit me that whatever that medication was, it was important.

"I asked you a question!"

I told a story that I had concocted on the way up. "After I got off the phone with you, I accidently fell back asleep. Then thirty minutes later I woke up, realized what happened and how I needed to get to Balboa. When I ran outside, one of the temps was getting ready to pull off, so I ran up to him and asked him where he was going. He said San Diego. I explained everything to him, and he sped me down and back to get the medication."

"Bullshit! *You're done!* Your liberty is secured for the rest of the weekend. You are not to go anywhere but to the hospital or the barracks. On Monday morning I'm going to have our chain of command charge you with *everything* that I listed. Get out of my face!"

"Yes, HM3."

I did a right-face and made my way back to the barracks.

Monday morning, HM2 Brown, HM3 Trotter, the clinic chief (senior enlisted), and the lead nurse for the clinic, Lieutenant Commander Richard, sat me down in a conference room to get my side of the story. I knew the gig was up and I was going to be charged, but I was determined to stick to my story. I was hoping that somehow it would work.

To my surprise, Trotter was on her best behavior. It was quite funny seeing her "normal." Since meeting her I had never seen her so calm. Then I was dismissed while the leadership convened over my fate. I went back to checking in patients and assisting on exams. After an hour HM2 Brown called for me.

"HA Adeleke, please come into my office."

I walked in and said, "Yes, HM2."

"Look: we know how she can be." With those words I knew I was, as the umpires say, *safe!*

HM2 continued, "Be careful with the choices you make, Adeleke. You probably should have taken the duty vehicle, right?"

"Yes, HM2. I'm sorry."

"It's okay. You got the medication to the patient in time. And that's the most important thing. You don't have anything to worry about. Just be careful and keep doing what you're doing."

"Yes, HM2."

CHAPTER THIRTEEN

"HE WON'T MAKE IT"

Sometimes you got to go uphill
in order to go downhill.

In January 2004, exactly a year after I checked in to Naval Hospital Camp Pendleton, I strolled through the main hallway of the hospital with my head high, my chest out, and my checkout envelope in hand. I was en route to the quarterdeck to get my last signature before I jumped into the duty vehicle waiting to drive me to SEAL training in Coronado, California.

A year earlier, HM3 Trotter had told me I'd never get accepted into BUD/S. I smiled from ear to ear as I made my way to the quarterdeck, knowing that in a short period of time I'd proven her wrong. I met the SEAL ASVAB requirements on the first try, passed my BUD/S screening test on my second attempt, and cleared the interview and medical evaluation with flying colors. It typically took a candidate stationed at a command two to three years to be accepted into BUD/S and released from a command. With help from HM2 Brown and my career counselor, Michelle Brick, great evals, and a lot of consistent hard work, I did it in half the time.

"I hear you're going to BUD/S," the quarterdeck petty officer said as I handed him my checkout sheet.

"Aye, Petty Officer!" I said jubilantly.

"You know if I don't sign this sheet, you can't leave?" he joked as he scrolled down the sheet to find the signature line.

I just stood there smiling, still in disbelief that I had pulled it off. I seriously thought I was dreaming, but it was a reality.

The petty officer went around to the back office, made a copy of all my checkout sheets, and came back to give me the duplicates. "What ya got in the bag?" he asked.

"Let's see . . . I got me some lumpia . . . mm . . . pancit . . . mm mm mm . . . *and* . . . fried chicken." I rubbed my stomach playfully. My clinic had just thrown a going-away potluck for me. The front desk receptionists, Mrs. Perez and Ms. Francine, tearfully made me a to-go bag and encouraged me to "eat it all up now, ya hear?" Along with many of the other women in the clinic, they had become like mothers to me. Everyone showed up to my going-away party except HM3 Trotter.

After I said my goodbyes to the quarterdeck staff, I ran out the main entrance and down the same steps I had run up when I frantically delivered the IV medication. I'd already stowed my sea bag in the duty vehicle, so as soon as I hopped in, the driver took off.

My departure from the hospital was somewhat of a sentimental drive. As we made our way down Santa Margarita Road, I couldn't help but reminisce about the hundreds of runs I'd done on that very road. When we pulled up to the stoplight at the Vandergrift intersection, I stared up the hill. I had conquered that arduous hill week after week. Hot, cold, raining, I ran it. Tired, frustrated, hungry, I ran it. It was painful at times, even monotonous, but I learned in that moment, as I stared at the hill, that sometimes you have to go uphill in order to go downhill. Sometimes you have to go through the grind to get to the goal. When the light turned green, the driver turned right, and I continued to stare at that hill as we drove off in the opposite direction.

. . .

Pulling into the Naval Special Warfare Center in Coronado was the most surreal experience I'd ever had at that point in my life.

After we cleared the heavily guarded gate, we passed the base exchange known as the surf mart. I saw a group of superfit guys with long hair, sunglasses, board shorts, and flip-flops walk through the parking lot. "Those have to be SEALs," I said to the driver. As we turned left on Trident Way, we passed a large building on our left, which I later found out was for SEAL Teams 5 and 7. On my right was another parking lot, where I saw a second group of guys who fit the same profile.

I continued chatting away as the driver stayed silent. "This definitely ain't a Marines base. No high and tights. Board shorts . . . flip-flops . . . *man* . . . I've only seen a few people in uniform!" It was then I realized I was in a totally different world, a world that went by a different set of rules.

The BUD/S compound sat toward the south end of the base, right before the SEAL Teams 1 and 3 building. When we pulled up to the BUD/S quarterdeck, I quickly stepped out of the vehicle and tried my best to smooth the newly formed wrinkles in my uniform. I didn't know what to expect upon checking in, but I did know I didn't want to run into an instructor with a half-baked uniform.

After getting all the wrinkles out, I grabbed my sea bag and said goodbye to my reticent driver.

He said, "Good luck," then did a U-turn to head back to the base exit.

I walked up to the quarterdeck doors and stopped to take one last look at my uniform, using the reflection in the glass. I took a deep breath and walked in. Behind the quarterdeck desk sat two Caucasian guys in the same dress-blue uniform I was wearing. I didn't know who they were or who was watching, so I immediately stood at attention after I handed them my orders.

"HN Adeleke, checking in for training."

The guys looked at me and laughed, then the younger-looking guy said, "Dude, we're students. Relax."

"Roger that. What class you guys in?" I asked.

Looking at my orders, the other guy said, "Your class . . . 250."

"That's dope," I replied.

"Where you from?" the younger guy asked.

"New York . . . the Bronx."

"Huh, I could tell from your accent you're a *New Yorker*," he said, trying to mimic a New York accent.

"Where you from?" I asked.

"California."

"Cool, cool. So what I gotta do to start the check-in process?"

"Walk through that entrance." The California boy pointed to a door opposite the one I had just entered. "That's the BUD/S grinder. Walk past the grinder and turn right. The second door on your right is the master-at-arms office. Check in with him first so he can stamp your orders; then head to admin."

"Got it. Thanks," I said as I made my way there.

"And hey, 249 is getting hammered on the beach, so if I were you, I'd get across the grinder as fast as possible before the instructors see you," he admonished.

"Roger that," I replied as I stepped through the doors.

I stepped onto the same outdoor grinder I had seen countless times in the BUD/S 234 documentary. It was where all pre–Hell Week classes did their early morning workouts. Though the guy at the quarterdeck told me to move as fast as I could through the grinder, I had to stop to take it all in; I didn't care. It had been a long road from the Bronx to here, and whether anyone knew my story or not, I had earned the right to process it all.

The grinder was a perfect large square. Pull-up bars lined the east and north ends. To my right was the infamous bell that dropouts rang when they decided they'd had enough. Below the bell was a line of about sixty helmets stamped with number 249, all belonging to students who'd quit. Though the rest of the class was hidden by a large sand berm, I could hear them yell "HOOYAH!" as they ran through painful remedial exercises.

"Damn, son! This is sick! I'm here!" I said as I turned around to view The Only Easy Day Was Yesterday sign.

I began to make my way across the grinder toward the MA office. When I was about halfway across, a sign in the center of the north end caught my attention. I walked a bit closer to make sure my eyes weren't fooling me. The sign read, Be Someone Special. That phrase was eerily similar to the phrase Aunt Dokey had used when she'd handed me the money to pay my court fines: *I just want you to be somebody special.* My heart rate elevated a little bit, and in that moment I just *knew* I was in the right place.

As I backed away from the sign, I nodded and said, "I will, Aunt Dokey, I will."

. . .

My father sent all my older half siblings to an elite boarding school in London. He was in the process of preparing to send Bayo and me to the same school, but his death derailed those educational plans. Though we missed the experience our older siblings had, Mom told us stories of kids from elite families who attended school with them: royalty, the children of world leaders, the children of billionaires and millionaires, and so on. Mom would tell us, "Your siblings didn't just get a stellar education, but much of their cognitive growth also came from the interactions they had with other elite students from around the world."

I mention this because most BUD/S students also came from such high-caliber backgrounds. There were Division I football players, wrestlers, and water polo athletes. There were Rhodes Scholars and guys who had graduated from Ivy League colleges. There were guys who had started careers as accountants and real estate brokers, even a lawyer who decided one day that he was tired of his day job and wanted to be a SEAL instead. There were even a good number of guys who came from wealthy families; I remember one guy in particular whose family was so rich that he didn't have to work a day in his life unless he wanted to, and he wanted to. And then there were just guys, like me, who'd worked hard to get there. Most of them were all-around great guys, guys who were simply a pleasure to be with. Honestly, at times, in my insecurity I thought, *These people are too good for me to be around. I don't measure up. I'm not worthy to be here.*

But the way my fellow classmates treated me was totally contrary to my insecure feelings. The indoctrination phase lasted about three weeks, and because I was one of only three African Americans in a class of 230 guys, by the end of INDOC everyone knew my name. It was quite funny because I was like the cool kid. Classmates were fascinated by my story because no one comes from Africa and the Bronx and attends SEAL training, but I did, and everyone wanted to know how.

The fact that I was indeed an anomaly made for a lot of great discussion, which was good and, for me, definitely needed. It's one thing to have a belief about a particular class of people, but it's another to actually sit and hear the unmitigated heart of a person who's from an entirely different culture, region, or class. We had deep discussions about racism, classism, what it was like being an African American in America, and what it was like being a Caucasian kid in Alabama. In the three weeks of BUD/S INDOC, I learned things from classmates that I never would have learned anywhere else. In retrospect the biggest effect those interactions with my classmates had on me was transforming the notion in my mind that if one civil servant was bad, *all* were bad. There was never any conflict during our talks because, to us, we were all brothers hungry to understand each other; our hearts were of the same fire, with the same dream—to make it out alive.

• • •

Ding, ding, ding! The entire class stood behind the BUD/S barracks, which were opposite the grinder, as we heard the bell ring. It was 4:30 a.m. in the second week in February. We were moments away from our first official evolution of BUD/S. The ringing came from a student who was so scared that he decided to quit before it even started.

Come on bro. You could have at least given it a shot, I thought.

Our class OIC (officer in charge) said, "All right, boys, it's time to line it up and head out to the grinder." We all got out of our seven-man boat crew ranks and formed three long lines. There were diverse levels of temperaments in Class 250. Some guys were extremely fearful, some guys were quiet, and others seemed stunned. As we stood in the early morning darkness, awaiting the inevitable, I felt like I was in the opening D-Day scene from *Saving Private Ryan*.

As planned, one of the students stood parallel with the ranks and began to lead cadence. "Two!"

"TWO!" the whole class yelled.

"Fifty zero!"

"FIFTY ZERO!" we repeated.

"Two!"

"TWO!"

"Fifty zero!"

As we made our way toward the grinder, our chant got more and more intense. "FIFTY ZERO!"

"Fire it up!"

"FIRE IT UP!"

"Motivated!"

"MOTIVATED!" When we arrived on the grinder, there were a dozen or so BUD/S instructors waiting for us. These men were all Navy SEALs who had done their time with SEAL Teams and returned to BUD/S as instructors.

"Fire it up!"

"FIRE IT UP!"

"Ded-i-cated!"

"DED-I-CATED!"

"Hooyah!"

"HOOYAAAAAH!" We all belted out as we dispersed and sprinted to premarked spots on the grinder. You could hear the echo reverberate off the surrounding buildings and into the darkness.

"Shut up and drop down, you turds!" an instructor yelled. We all immediately got in the push-up position.

Another instructor yelled, "Well? What are you waiting for? Push them out!"

Our OIC began to lead us. "Down!"

We all did a push-up, then yelled in unison, "ONE!"

"Down!" our OIC yelled.

"TWO!" we repeated.

"Down!"

"THREE!"

During First Phase, the typical push-up count was twenty. When we got to ten, an instructor said through a megaphone, "This is the first exercise, and you all already suck! You got guys who aren't going all the way down. You got guys who aren't counting. How about you start from one?"

So as suggested, we started all over. The game continued, and every time we got anywhere past ten, at least one of the 220 students did something wrong, which prompted the instructors to start us back at the beginning.

We were only seven minutes in, and my arms were already burning like they had never burned before. I wanted to drop to my knees so bad, but I knew I couldn't. Being one of three black students in the class, not to mention the tallest of the three, I stood out among the sea of white students.

While still in the push-up position, I turned my head to the right to see the helmet of the kid who'd quit before we started. His last name was on the front and back. I said to myself, *Nope, my name is not going to be in the same line as that guy's.* Seeing that helmet on the grinder was enough motivation for me.

A new voice yelled, "All right! You shit birds can't do push-ups right! Backs!" We all rolled onto our backs, and as we did, you could hear the collective *aaahhhs* of relief.

This instructor got on his back in preparation for the next exercise. "Flutter kicks!" We started kicking, and the instructor led the cadence. "One-two-three!"

We yelled, "ONE!"

"One-two-three!"

"TWO!" we yelled.

"One-two-three!"

"THREE!"

When we got to fifty, I heard, *ding, ding, ding!* Another student quit!

I just closed my eyes and kept repeating to myself, *I'm not quitting, I'm not quitting, I'm not quitting.* I felt water splashing on my face, which prompted me to open my eyes. Two instructors were hosing us down. It was a typical San Diego winter morning, around fifty-five degrees, so the water made us feel colder.

"Stop, stop, stop!" the guy on the megaphone said. "I have a better exercise. How about . . . say . . . hit the surf!"

Hit the surf meant we had to sprint about 110 meters to the beach, run up a twelve-foot-high sand berm, then back down the other side, keep sprinting to the ocean, jump in, and sprint back to the point where the command was given.

As instructed, we sprinted to the beach, jumped into the freezing ocean, and sprinted back to the grinder. When we got back, the instructor on the megaphone said, "Oh, I forgot to tell you—sandy too." So we all sprinted back to the beach and rolled around in the sand, then sprinted back to the grinder again. As soon as we got back to the grinder, we heard, "Oh . . . did I say sandy? How about wet and sandy?"

I could see weariness and doubt creep into some of the guys. After I made my third trip back to the beach, got wet and sandy, and began to make my way back to the grinder, I passed one student who was walking.

"Yo! What you doing? You got to go get wet and sandy. Run!" I said while passing him. He didn't say anything. Like a zombie, he just stared in the direction he was walking. It was a look I would later see in many other drop-outs. I called it the thousand-yard stare.

A minute after I got back to the grinder, I heard *ding, ding, ding!* I looked toward the bell to see the walking zombie place his helmet next to the others from the first few dropouts.

The instructors were in a frenzy over the quitters. When the entire class returned, we all stood at attention as we dripped a combination of water and sand onto the grinder. You could hear the sound of heavy breathing and see steam rise off the bowed heads of the students. We were only twenty minutes in, and it already sucked! I picked my head up and locked eyes on the Be Someone Special sign. I just nodded in agreement.

After another hour of shenanigans, Master Chief picked up the mega-phone and said, "This is just the first hour of training, and you clowns are falling apart. You want to waste my instructor-staff time? Well, I'm going to waste your time. Go line up on the beach!"

We all scurried out to the beach and lined up side by side with our backs to the ocean. The medical truck drove through a break in the berm and flashed its high beams on us. Then the instructors slowly walked over the berm and down to where we stood in silent anticipation.

The temperature was still around 55 degrees, and there was a slight breeze. Because of my lack of body fat and my wet clothes, I was already shaking. To make matters worse, I knew exactly what was coming next: an evolution called surf torture.

Through the megaphone, Master Chief gave the command: "About face." We all turned around to face the ocean. "Lock arms." We interlocked our arms. "Forward march." As a class, we all began to make our way into the ocean.

The water temperature in San Diego in February hovers around 57 degrees. In layman's terms, that's freezing cold. I had already been in the water, but it was a quick in and out. Now I was slowly walking in, and the only way I could stop was if I unlocked arms and turned to quit.

When the water got up to my ankles, I said, "Damn, that's cold," but I kept moving.

Then the water was at my thighs, then hips, and, finally, when the water reached my abdomen, Master Chief said, "Aaaand halt."

We all stopped and stood there as the waves splashed on us. I remember trying to stand on my toes to keep as much of my upper body out of the water as possible. Then I heard the command, "Take seats." We all slowly got in the sitting position. I could hear all kinds of cursing from the guys up and down the line. Our upper bodies were now submerged, and when the waves crashed over us, our faces would be submerged as well.

I quickly learned that I could take the name-calling (growing up in the Hill prepared me for that), the sprints and push-ups (my training at the hospital prepared me for that), and everything else they threw at me, but the cold was my kryptonite. My body wasn't built for it.

After fifteen minutes of lying there, shaking like a coconut on a tree, I heard the infamous *ding, ding, ding!* again. The instructors had brought the bell to the beach, and another student had quit.

"Feet!" Master Chief yelled through the megaphone. My body was so stiff and felt so heavy that when I tried to get up, I fell back down. As soon as I trembled to my feet, we got the command, "About face." The class turned and faced the beach. "Forward march."

As we stumbled our way back to the beach, I stuttered to myself, "Th . . . Th . . . Th . . . Thank G . . . G . . . G-God . . . it's over!"

Master Chief continued, "I told you I was going to waste your time! Take off your shirts . . . and pants!"

As instructed, we all stripped off our pants and shirts as fast as possible, then stood on the beach in our underwear.

"Now, raise your hands." You would have thought I was at a rock concert the way my entire body shook with my hands in the air. We stood there for about five minutes as the wind chilled us. I remember thinking, *This can't be legal!*

After five minutes Master Chief returned to the megaphone, "Hands down. About face. Lock arms. Forward march. Take seats." Back into the freezing cold water we went. Before I sat down—*ding, ding, ding!*—another student decided it was too cold for him to go back in, so he quit.

I'm here. I'm not going nowhere. It's freezing. I'm probably gonna die. But I'm not quitting. I have nothing else. . . . This is it.

Finally, after another fifteen to twenty minutes of surf torture, the morning evolution ended. I had survived! It was nothing to celebrate, though; we still had log PT (physical training), in which seven men, soaked and sandy, had to heft a 200-pound log up and over that high sand berm, then press it over our heads and carry it into the ocean and back. We had surf passage—rigorous small-boat training—and boats on heads, a spine-crushing drill that involved running through the soft sand with a crew balancing a 105-pound boat on our heads. We could also expect a uniform and room inspection, the infamous seven-stages-of-hell run, and a bay swim—all evolutions that were as painful as the two hours I had just endured.

But for me, there was nothing worse than the bay swim.

• • •

"You and your swim buddy will swim from the dock to the buoy, which is half a mile out," Instructor H briefed the entire class on our last evolution of the first day of training. The evolution was a wet-suit-appreciation bay swim, which meant no wet suit. All we had was our trademark UDT (Underwater Demolition Team) shorts, white stenciled T-shirt, goggles, a web belt with a knife, and our duck-feet fins. The instructor continued, "Instructor W will be in a kayak. When you get to him, give him your swim pair number and names. Once he checks your swim pair number, you will swim counterclockwise around him and the buoy, then make your way back to the dock. Do you understand?"

We all yelled, "HOOYAH!"

"All right . . . bust 'em!" On his command, we all sprinted to the dock and squeezed into our fins as fast as possible. Honestly, though I had made it through every evolution of the day—evolutions that were probably worse than this—I was tremendously worried.

Before showing up to BUD/S, I had done all my swim training without fins. I didn't know that swimming with fins was the primary method of swimming at BUD/S. During my first fin swim in INDOC, I jumped in the pool and kicked as hard as I could but barely moved. When that happened, I had a flashback to my first pool session at Camp Pendleton. The same discouragement that began to overtake me at the Camp Pendleton pool began to overtake me at the INDOC pool. I figured that three weeks of INDOC would help me get it down, but it hadn't.

"You ready, Adeleke?" Tyrone asked me. Tyrone was another African

American in the class. We already stuck out, but choosing each other as swim buddies made it worse!

I despondently said, "Yeah, let's get this over with."

"All you have to do is stay as close behind me as you can. I'll set the pace and guide, okay?"

"Roger that."

We both jumped in, surrounded by other students who splashed and kicked. Tyrone took off, and for a second, I lost him in the chaos.

"Adeleke! Adeleke! I'm right here!" Tyrone yelled. I looked around and couldn't see him. Then finally I spotted him and started kicking in his direction.

I finally caught up to Tyrone. Then he took off again at a normal pace. No matter what I did, I couldn't keep up. The water was freezing, but I was so focused on trying to figure out how to swim with the fins that I couldn't even pay attention to the cold. Tyrone stopped again.

"Come on, Adeleke!" he pleaded. "You gotta keep up, or we're going to get a safety violation."

During swims at BUD/S, there is a six-foot rule. The rule is simple: swim buddies can't be more than six feet apart. If they are, they could both get safety violations. Three safety violations means expulsion from the program.

"I'm trying, brother! I'm trying!" I replied as I kicked as violently as I could. I swung my arms and even tried to rotate my body to streamline the process, but nothing worked; I was barely moving. I got so frustrated I almost took off my fins.

After five minutes of stroking I lifted my head to see where I was in relation to where we started. The first thing I noticed was that the rest of the class was yards ahead of us. And when I finally got my head turned to look back, I also noticed we were only thirty yards from the starting point.

"Come. Here. Come. Here," Instructor W said through the megaphone in a robotic tone. Tyrone and I swam back to the starting point to meet the instructor. It took us longer to get back than it had to get out.

By the time we got to the dock, there were five more instructors waiting for us.

"Holy shit!" Instructor W yelled. "How the . . . ? Wait. This is too funny! How the hell do you show up to BUD/S and can't swim?"

"Hooyah," I replied. I didn't know what else to say. I thought I would be kicked out of training.

W said, "No, no, no . . . I really need to know. Drop all the *hooyah* crap and explain how you got here."

"No excuse, Instructor!" I replied, trying to avoid his question.

W shook his head in frustration, then turned to Tyrone. "Tyrone, you been here before . . . what? . . . two, three times?"

"Hooyah, Instructor W, two times I quit and came back," Tyrone replied.

"Okay, so you already failed the program twice. Can you . . . can you . . . explain to me, why would you pair up with this moron who can't swim?"

Tyrone replied, "Hooyah, I thought I could help him."

"What?" W asked.

"I thought I could help him!"

Instructor H chimed in. "Adeleke, the bell is right over there. Do yourself and everyone else a favor and go over there and quit. Look: you're not going to make it. Just go quit now and find another job."

"Negative, Instructor H," I said.

"What?"

"Negative. I'm not gonna quit. . . . I'm going to figure it out."

"Okay, well, get to the buoy and freakin' figure it out!" he yelled.

"Come on, Adeleke. Let's go," Tyrone said.

As I turned around to follow Tyrone, I heard an instructor say, "There's no chance in hell he'll ever make it. He'll be gone by the end of the week."

I swam away muttering to myself, "Well, it ain't the first time I heard that."

CHAPTER FOURTEEN

NEVER QUIT

You're either hard . . . or you're dumb.

It was March 3, 2004, the fourth week of First Phase. *Ding, ding, ding, ding, ding, ding, ding.* A bell rang in a sweet cadence as our class filed into the base chapel. But this wasn't the bell that dropouts rang when they quit. This was the chapel bell.

Two weeks earlier, on February 19, the remaining members of our class were on one of the toughest pre–Hell Week beach runs to date. Instructor G, who was known as the fastest distance runner in First Phase, led the run. Those who didn't keep up were periodically punished with a combination of push-ups, chase the rabbits, and hitting the surf. As you can imagine, after doing those exercises, it was even harder to keep up!

There's a saying in BUD/S: "It pays to be a winner!" From recent experiences the entire class knew that the punishment during the run would be nothing compared to the session that would take place at the end for students who weren't with the front pack when Instructor G stopped. The students in the front were winners, and the others were losers infamously known as the "goon squad."

I tried to muster the strength to reach the front of the pack. *Come on, Remi . . . you got to get up there. You don't want to be in the goon squad today! Hell Week is in two weeks, and your body needs a break.*

We had already run four miles and were quickly reaching the end point. I raised my head and started driving my legs as hard as I could. Then, when I thought I was getting close to the group, Instructor G started traversing the A-shaped sand berm.

Full of anger, I said, "Dammit! My legs are already burning . . . and I'm so close. Now this!" When I reached the berm, I put my hands on each thigh and pushed down with each step. "This can't be legal" had become my saying.

Behind me our class LPO, Robert Vetter, yelled, "Come on, boys! Let's get up there!"

About two minutes later, I heard, "Corpsman! We need a corpsman!" I turned to see another student kneeling over Rob's body. Being a corpsman, I sprinted back to him. Another class corpsman who got there before me started doing CPR, and when the instructor medic got to the scene, he took the lead and directed the student corpsman. Rob was unconscious—no pulse, no breathing.

Rob was rushed to Sharp Coronado Hospital and placed on life support. After ten days with no sign of brain function, his family decided it was time to let him go.

Ding, ding, ding, ding, ding, ding, ding. Rob's was the first funeral I had ever been to. I didn't even go to my father's funeral. I sat there in disbelief. Days ago Rob and I had sat together at a table, wet, miserable, and smiling, as we talked about Australia, of all places. And now his lifeless body lay in a casket, and his daughter, like me, was left without her father.

. . .

"Listen up! This is your last two-mile timed ocean swim before Hell Week," Instructor H said as he briefed us on the beach. "Most of you won't make it through Hell Week anyway, so if you fail today, I don't care! You know the rules. Swim out past the breakers. Instructor W and Instructor J will be waiting for you in the green safety boat." He turned and pointed to the safety boat that was sitting out past the surf zone. "You see it?"

"HOOYAH!" we all replied.

"Next to the boat is a buoy. After you check in, you will line up on the buoy in your swim pairs. When Instructor W gives the command, you will swim one mile, parallel to the beach, to a second buoy. Check in with the instructors at the one-mile buoy; then swim back to the starting point."

"HOOYAH!" we all said.

"Adeleke . . . Adeleke!" Instructor H yelled as he scanned the crowd to find me.

I made my way through the crowd and stood at attention in front of Instructor H. "Hooyah, Instructor H! I'm present!"

"I can see that, Adeleke!" he replied.

Holding up a thermometer at my eye level, he said, "The water temperature is about . . . 58 degrees today. The last two swims took you almost two hours to finish. The passing time is eighty-five minutes, Adeleke. I don't think you're going to want to be in that water [he pointed to the ocean] for two hours again. Go find the bell, ring it three times, and go home. It's okay! People quit all the time. Look around. Sixty percent of your class is already gone!"

"Negative, Instructor H!" I replied.

He was right on the first part. I did not want to be in that water again for two hours! Even though we wore wet suits for the ocean swims, by the end of each one I was either borderline hypothermic or downright hypothermic. My body would get so locked up from the cold that my classmates had to drag-carry me out of the ocean into the first-floor barracks shower and turn on all the showerheads to rewarm me.

Instructor H continued, "All right, Adeleke! I don't know which one it is: you're either hard . . . or you're dumb!"

"Hooyah! Hard. I'm . . . I'm hard, not dumb." I could hear some of my classmates quietly laughing.

"Well, what are you waiting for? Get out there!" he commanded.

We all jumped into the ocean, screaming, "HOOYAH!" It was our way of saying, "Damn, that's cold!"

The instructors' taunting didn't stop. When Tyrone and I got to the check-in boat, Instructor W sarcastically said, "Adeleke, you're still here?"

"Hooyah!" I replied.

"Dammit! I didn't bring my DVD player and two-hour movie to watch."

"Hooyah!" I replied again.

"Shut up, Adeleke."

Upon his polite request, Tyrone and I turned and swam into line with the rest of the class.

Instructor J gave the starting command: "Stand by! . . . Bust 'em!"

And we were off. Fins kicking everywhere, water splashing all around us, and salt water getting into my mouth as I tried to breathe.

Within minutes the chaos dissipated, and there we were, Tyrone and me, swimming as if we were the only people in the ocean. To this very day, I still don't know why Tyrone chose to keep me as his swim buddy.

"Adeleke, come on, man! We can't do this again!" Tyrone yelled.

I replied, "I'm coming, man!"

Tyrone led the pace and guided us in a straight line. I stared at his fins the whole time while trying my best to keep up. Though we moved a lot faster than our first bay swim, we weren't moving fast enough.

When we were a quarter of a mile from the turnaround buoy, I started to hear splashes and got excited! "We catching up, Ty . . . I hear the rest of the class!"

"No, man," Tyrone said with frustration, "They going in the other direction."

"What?" I asked.

"They already checked in at the halfway buoy, and they're heading back. We ain't passing nobody, man! We dead last!"

Let's just say that my excitement quickly departed.

When we finally got to the buoy, we checked in as instructed.

"Adeleke, Tyrone, swim pair ten," he said.

"Adeleke, Tyrone, swim pair ten," I echoed.

Instructor J, furious for having to wait for us again, yelled, "Yeah, we know! You're the only two left who haven't checked in! Tweedle Dee and Tweedle Dum, got it. Now go!" We took off back to the start.

About a mile and a quarter into every swim was when hypothermia began to creep up on me. Being a corpsman, I knew the onset signs. In order to keep warm, the human body reduces muscle contractions, the nervous system slows down, and the impulses that move one's body decrease. What did that mean for me? It meant that once hypothermia started, I couldn't move my arms and legs to the extent needed to propel me through the water. If I'd known how to swim with the fins properly, I still would have felt the effects because of my low body fat percentage, but they would have shown up around the end instead of at the 1.25-mile mark.

By that point I could barely move.

At this point Tyrone was pleading with me. "What are you doing? Please don't do this again!"

"I-I-I . . . I'm . . . t-t-t . . . trying," I said. Though my body was shutting down, I still had full brain function, so I kept talking to myself. *Pull, kick, pull, kick, pull, kick.* I used my mind to force my body to do something that biology said it couldn't do. Finally, about two hundred yards out, I could see the red buoy bobbing with the current. The instructors in the green safety boat were staring in our direction. I could tell they were looking to see if I was quitting so they could drive up and pull me out.

"Aw, man!" Tyrone yelled.

"Wh-wh-wh . . . What . . . What's . . . up?"

"Pick your head up, Adeleke!" I looked up to see Tyrone pointing to the spot on the beach where our initial swim brief had taken place.

"Look! They're beatin' the whole class because of us!"

When I focused, I could see the entire class still in their wet suits, some sprinting up and down the berm, others doing push-ups, and others bear crawling. I later found out that before the swim one of the instructors pulled the OIC aside and told him that the class would "pay the man" until I either quit or finished the swim, and knowing my swim history, that was going to be a while. I felt terrible!

I kicked myself into high gear and moved as hard as I could. By the time we got a few yards away from the check-in boat and buoy, I was so out of it that all I could do was doggy paddle.

I couldn't speak, so Tyrone checked in for me. "Adeleke, Tyrone, swim pair ten. Adeleke, Tyrone, swim pair ten. Time?"

"One hundred and eighteen minutes! Failllll! Get to the beach!" Instructor W yelled.

Tyrone grabbed me by the web belt and had to swim-drag me to the beach. When my feet touched solid ground, the class beatdown ceased. As usual, two guys ran to Tyrone to help carry me into the barracks shower.

I expected the class to hate me, but they didn't. My peer evals were always consistently good. My classmates knew that I crushed everything else, from log PT to boats on head, to the obstacle course and runs, but the swims were where I struggled.

• • •

Hell Week is by far the worst part of BUD/S: twenty-four hours of training a day for six straight days. It typically starts on Sunday evening and ends on Friday afternoon. The students get two hours of sleep on Wednesday—if they make it that far—and two hours of sleep on Thursday. All the other hours are filled with everything done during the first four weeks plus more: log PT, countless surf tortures, boats on heads, and an endless supply of mind games.

Due to the ferocity of Hell Week, we all had to go through a medical check to ensure our bodies were healthy enough for the torture. For most of us, our bodies were already ravaged and constantly trying to repair themselves. Our immune systems were not in the best shape, which made us susceptible to viruses, cellulitis, and other weird infections that I'd never heard of until then.

As I stood in line, I was extremely nervous, more nervous than I had been before any of the timed ocean swims. Why? Earlier that morning I had started coughing up blood.

Being a corpsman was a good thing at times, but it was also a bad thing. I say bad because I knew exactly what I was dealing with: swimmer-induced pulmonary edema, or SIPE.

SIPE is a serious and potentially fatal condition that occurs when the lungs fill with body fluids. It's often caused by submersion in cold water. The signs and symptoms include shortness of breath, crackle-like sounds in the lungs, and violent coughing that produces blood-tinged sputum. It was easy for me to put two and two together; two days earlier I was submerged for two hours in freezing cold water while Tyrone screamed at me to hurry up, and now I was coughing up blood.

The pre–Hell Week medical check was like a conveyer-belt operation. A staff corpsman scanned our medical records, a nurse handed us a disgusting concoction to drink, and three doctors did a quick exam.

Right before I stood in line, I snuck to the corner of medical to spit up another glob of blood-filled mucus. I had to make a decision. I could report my condition, which would lead to me getting a medical rollback and having to start BUD/S all over with Class 251. Or I could hide it, push through Hell Week, and have the following week to recover.

The decision was easy. There was no way I was going to report it. I mean, more than 130 guys had already quit. Guys who from the time they could say the word *SEAL* had wanted to be a SEAL. Guys who were stronger than me, faster than me, with more of an all-around advantage than me, had quit, and I was still standing. If those guys couldn't go through the last four weeks once, how the heck would I be able to go through it twice? I'd rather die in Hell Week than go through all that again.

When I stepped into the clinic, I held back my coughing as much as possible. This was when being a corpsman helped. I knew how to hide my condition, and if anyone raised questions, I knew how to explain it away as something else.

After downing the concoction I was handed, I stepped forward to Dr. Ryan. A few months earlier I had been assisting his wife, the other Dr. Ryan, on medical exams at Camp Pendleton, and now I was the patient.

"Hey, Dr. Ryan! I'm still here!" I said as I stood in my tri-shorts with my arms out.

"Adeleke! How you doing, bud?" he asked as he began the exam.

"Besides the normal aches and pains and a BUD/S-crud cough, I'm good," I replied.

He examined my eyes with his penlight. "You're doing great, man! I've been following your progress."

"Thank you, sir."

Then came the test that would potentially reveal my condition. Dr. Ryan placed his stethoscope's earplugs in his ears and put the diaphragm up against my chest.

"Deep breath. Deep breath," he requested.

I acted like I was breathing deep, but I was just making a shushing sound with my lips parted.

"Another deep breath."

I said to myself, *What am I thinking? This guy's a doctor. He's going to figure it out.* Anticipating that the gig was up, I started breathing normally, hoping that the crackles hadn't started yet.

When he pulled the diaphragm off my chest and took the stethoscope from his ears, he looked at me and said, "All the ladies at the clinic are happy for you. I've been sharing your progress with my wife, and she's been passing it on."

I replied nervously, still expecting him to send me for X-rays. "Yeah . . . that's cool. . . . Thank you, Doc. Please tell them I said hello."

"I'll pass along the greeting. Hey . . . good luck next week."

"Thank you."

I was gonna need it.

• • •

By Sunday morning my coughing was worse, but I didn't care. Over the last few weeks I had learned it's the mind that dictates to the body what must be done, not the other way around. So I convinced myself that my body would push through despite my illness.

That morning, we were all confined to the Howe Classroom. I sat with the other two African Americans in the class, Tyrone and Keller. One of our classmates brought the *Gladiator* DVD for us to watch, so toward the end of the day, we all focused our attention on the film, hoping to draw some extra motivation from it. As the score played throughout the scenes, I was reminded of all the hard work I had put in at Camp Pendleton while listening to the same score and many others. It was as though someone knew what I needed and used that film to remind me of all I'd done to get there. After it was over, *I was ready*. Sick as a dog, but ready!

At 5:00 p.m. an instructor entered the classroom and ordered us to make our way to the Hell Week tent. The large tent sat to the west of the grinder by the beach entrance. In the tents were the cots we would sleep on—*if* we made it to Wednesday. Once I found my cot, I got settled, lay down, and went to sleep.

About an hour later I was abruptly woken up by the sound of machine-gun fire and what sounded like explosions. *Clack, clack, clack, clack! Boom, clack, boom!*

Hell Week had officially started.

"Get out of the tents, you turds!" an instructor yelled.

I donned my hat and quickly made my way down the aisle between cots with my hand on the back of the guy in front of me. When I got out of the tent, there were instructors everywhere: instructors I had never seen before, instructors from other phases of training, even INDOC instructors.

"Get to the grinder now!" one of them yelled to the group of guys around me.

I ran through a cloud of smoke from a smoke grenade and made my way in the direction of the grinder. I couldn't see anything for a second and collided with another student who was also disoriented. When I got to the grinder, there were even more instructors.

One pointed in our direction and yelled, "Drop down!" The guys in my vicinity all dropped to the push-up position, and I followed suit. As we did push-ups I looked around for members of my boat crew. I knew at some point we were going to do logs or boats, and I wanted to be as close to my crew as possible when the command came.

It was mass chaos. Some students were on the beach, others by the tent, and some on the grinder.

"Bear crawl to the surf!" an instructor next to our group ordered.

Yikes, that's a long way! . . . You sure you want us to do that? I thought as I began my bear crawl with equal weight on both hands and feet.

When our group got halfway there, another instructor yelled, "Hit the surf!" So we got up and sprinted to the surf zone. As always, it was cold.

The back-and-forth exercises, machine-gun fire, and sim-bombs continued for another twenty minutes. Then suddenly it stopped.

Ding, ding, ding! Someone had quit. *Who was it?* I wondered. Because of how much we'd endured in the last four weeks, it was hard to imagine anyone quitting.

Master Chief got on the megaphone. "Everyone to the beach! Line up facing the ocean!"

I quickly made my way to the beach. When I arrived, I found a few members of my boat crew and squeezed into line next to them. The remaining members of the class stood at the waterline, awaiting our next orders.

Instructor H spoke through the megaphone. "Six days. This is just the beginning of a long week. And guess what? We've already had two quitters."

"Two? I only heard the bell ring once," I whispered as water dripped from my hat onto my face.

"Adeleke!" When Instructor H called my name, I was bemused. I hadn't quit, so why would he call my name? "Adeleke! Where's Adeleke?"

"Hooyah! I'm right here!" I yelled with my hand in the air.

"Oh, there you are. How could I miss you? Guess what? Your swim buddy . . . Tyrone? . . . Yeah . . . he quit."

My heart sank. I didn't want to believe it. Just three hours earlier we were in the classroom, joking and laughing together. I hadn't sensed any doubt in Ty. Why would he quit?

Instructor H asked, "You want to join him?"

"Negative, Instructor H. I'm good!"

"We'll see," he replied.

Master Chief started delivering familiar commands over the megaphone: "Forward . . . march." We marched into the dark, cold water. "Take seats."

By this point the adrenaline had worn off, so I began to feel all the effects of SIPE. My chest was tight, my breathing was labored, and it felt like I had spiderwebs in my lungs. *If I die, I die. I'm not quitting or going to medical.*

Ding, ding, ding! The cold water got to somebody else.

As I lay there in pain, sick and freezing, I did something I hadn't done since I was eight. I called out to my dad. I began to say, "Dad, help me. Help me. I can't do this on my own."

During INDOC, we were taught the four pillars of mental toughness: positive self-talk, visualization, goal setting, and arousal control. I had used positive self-talk a lot during the past four weeks, but now I was going to run it into the ground.

Okay, Remi, don't think about Friday. Your goal is to just make it to the next evolution, and once you get to that evolution, your new goal is to make it to the next one. Okay? Okay, got it.

After a full round of surf torture, we were commanded out. "Line up on your boats in boat crews!" Soaking wet, we dispersed from our line and ran to our boats. Each boat crew had seven guys.

Master Chief continued, "Prepare to up boat! Up boat!" With three guys on each side and one at the back, we lifted the boat, slid under it, and rested the boat on our heads. The guy in the back slid up to the center, and the other six held the perimeter.

Throughout First Phase we had experienced boats on heads many times, and it was painful. It felt like my neck was going to explode! Like surf torture, boats on heads had a way of breaking the strongest guys.

Master Chief gave us our first exercise with the boats. "Lunges! On my count, begin!"

On *one* we knelt on our right knees as a crew. On *two* we stood up, on *three* we knelt on our left knees, and on the overall count we stood back up.

Master Chief led the cadence on the megaphone, "One . . . two . . . three."

"ONE!" we all yelled.

"One . . . two . . . three!"

"TWO!"

"One . . . two . . . three!"

"THREE!"

Lunges were miserable, especially when the crew wasn't in sync. Before we got to five, I could hear other crews cussing and screaming at each other in anguish.

When the lunges ended, Instructor W led us on a long run south toward Imperial Beach with the boats on our heads. It was grueling. The entire time, I struggled to breathe, but I kept driving.

Three miles later we arrived at Silver Strand State Beach. We were given a one-minute water break and then ordered to stand by our boats. I looked right and left and saw that a few more guys were gone.

Instructor W yelled, "Hit the surf!" We all jumped in the ocean, then lined back up on our boats.

"Prepare to up boat! Up boat! We got a long run coming! If you're going to quit, you better do it now," Instructor W said.

Ding, ding, ding! A couple more guys quit.

"Prepare to down boat. Down boat! Get in a height line and count off by seven!" Due to the number of guys who had quit, we had to reorganize the boat crews to ensure that each one had six to seven men.

After the boat crews were reorganized, Instructor W repeated, "Prepare to up boat! Up boat!" I could hear the groans as the boats were repositioned on our heads. My neck was on fire, and my lungs were done. I could hear myself wheezing. I knew that wasn't good.

As we continued south, an instructor ran beside our boat. He was checking to make sure everyone was carrying their weight. Before Hell Week started, I had confided in my boat crew regarding my medical condition. Knowing how much it would suck to get rolled back to day one, my crew supported me.

About a mile into the second leg, I said, "Sorry, guys . . . I'm hurting bad. . . . Can we slow down for a quick second?" I just needed a second to catch my breath before I went hypoxic.

When the instructor running alongside our boat heard me, he went ballistic. "What did you just say? Slow down? No! Quit! You don't tell your boat crew to slow down!" A few other instructors heard the commotion and ran over. After the instructor who had been running alongside filled them in, they made our boat crew stop running, pulled me aside, and chewed me out. It was like I was in the midst of a cyclone. I was called every name in the book and told to quit. I wouldn't do it. I just couldn't, and I didn't want to tell them what was going on, or I'd have to start over.

"Adeleke, you know what a performance drop is, right?" the instructor who'd been running alongside said. He meant they'd declare my performance level unsalvageable, and I'd be cut from BUD/S for failing to keep up with the instructors' standards.

"Hooyah!" I replied.

He continued, "If anyone hears you say 'Slow down,' or sees your weak ass lagging, you will be performance dropped. Do you hear me?"

"Hooyah!" I replied.

"Now, get back on your boat!"

I scurried over to my boat crew, and we continued.

As the sun began to break on Monday morning, we arrived at our destination in Imperial Beach. After our breakfast and water break, we were sent into the ocean for another surf torture. The sun was coming out, but it didn't warm us up; it was the first week of March.

From one of the trucks, Instructor E spoke through a mounted megaphone. "Guess what? I'm sitting in this nice warm truck. I have the heat on full blast. Ooooh . . . what's this?" He lifted up a cup of coffee. "I have a nice hot coffee. And . . . I have blankets. Just quit, and you can get out of that cold water, dry off, and hang out in this *hot* truck! Any takers?" Ten minutes after his solicitation, a couple more guys got up and quit. *Ding, ding, ding!*

My plan to take Hell Week one evolution at a time was working. The more goals I achieved, the more empowered I felt. I made it through log PT, then more races with boats on heads, then lunch, then another surf torture, then a beatdown session, then dinner, then a three-mile log run back to the state beach, and then a boat paddle back to the other end of Coronado Island. Before I knew it, Monday was coming to a close, and we were about to hit 12:00 a.m. Tuesday.

Though I had gotten that far, I was on the instructors' hit list. It was impossible for me to give 100 percent. I knew why, but they didn't. So after repeated warnings, I expected to be performance dropped before the sun broke Tuesday morning. If I didn't quit, they were going to make me suffer for not quitting and then get rid of me. In my heart I had come to terms with that. If I was dropped, there would be no shame or regret on my part.

With boats on heads, we arrived at a steel pier after 1:00 a.m. Having watched BUD/S 234, I knew what was coming. And knowing the condition of my body, I knew this would be the evolution that would break me.

"Prepare to down boat! Down boat!" We all placed our boats on the ground. Hell Week had started out with about eighty students, and now there were only fifty left.

"Prepare to enter the water! Enter the water!" We all jumped into the water between the U-shaped docks. I don't know how deep it was, but deep enough that none of us could touch the bottom.

As I treaded the freezing cold water with my uniform and boots on, my head kept dipping under the surface. Between my lack of energy and my inability to breathe normally, I felt like I was drowning.

"Adeleke! Quit!" an instructor yelled.

That's all it took. The rest of the instructors in my vicinity were on me like piranhas.

"You can't swim to save your life! As a matter of fact, you suck at life!" Instructor H said.

"Hooyah," I tried to say while sucking down the disgusting bay water.

Instructor H continued, "We're not throwing you a life jacket! And guess what? Your swim buddy, Tyrone, ain't here to help you either!"

"Hooyah." In essence I was saying, "F*** you."

"You might as well quit! Or we can just performance drop you before the morning."

I guess that was his way of saying, "F*** you," back.

"Everyone out of the water!" Master Chief yelled.

Thank God, I thought as I swam to the dock and struggled to pull myself out.

When we were all out, he said, "Take off your shirts, pants, socks, and boots!"

I stripped down as fast as possible. As I did, an instructor walked behind me and said, "Hurry up, Adeleke!"

Instructor W blurted out, "Oh, it's *that* name again. No worries. He'll be gone soon."

I stood there shaking as if I were having a seizure. I tucked in my arms and held both hands over my crotch.

"Arms up!" We all lifted our arms.

I could feel the crisp cold wind cut through my skin, enervating the tissue in my body.

After ten minutes we were ordered to lie flat on our backs on the cold steel pier. Lying there, I could gradually feel all the heat getting sucked out of my body.

Ding, ding, ding! Two more guys quit.

"Feet!" We quickly trembled our way to our feet.

"Enter the water!" We all jumped back in.

Immediately I began to experience the same type of immobility that I felt at the 1.25-mile mark of every ocean swim. Movement in my arms and legs got slower and slower, and I began to spend more time under the water.

Though most of the instructors' eyes were on me, I had this fear that if I sank to the bottom, no one would be able to find my dark body in the darkness of the bay, so I reached out and grabbed the side of the dock. This sent the instructors into an even greater rage.

"Get your f***ing hand off the dock, Adeleke!"

All right. You said you'd rather die than quit or start over. Let's get ready to die, I said to myself before releasing my hand.

Due to the high risk of the evolution, Dr. Ryan and the entire medical team were standing by, observing. I felt so bad when I saw him. The instructors were eviscerating my performance, and he was right there watching.

Damn. Word is going to get back to Trotter that I didn't make it. I cared more about that than dying.

After minutes of treading water for the second time, I heard Master Chief yell, "Adeleke, get your dumb ass out of the water!"

This was it. I was about to get dropped. I climbed out of the bay and stumbled my way to Master Chief. "Hoo-hoo-hooyah," I stuttered.

"Go see medical!" he commanded.

Yes! I thought. Getting a medical roll would be better than being performance dropped. "Hoo-hoo-hooyah," I replied.

When I got to Dr. Ryan, he instructed the staff corpsman to take a rectal temp. It was humiliating. *Now I know how the sick babies at Camp Pendleton feel.*

"Eighty-eight-point-seven!" the corpsman said in shock.

"Get him in the Ambu now!" Dr. Ryan commanded. The corpsman loaded me in the Ambu, threw blankets over me, blasted the heat, flipped on the sirens, and rushed me to medical.

As we raced down Naval Amphibious Base (NAB), I could see the siren lights reflecting off of the glass. *Aw, I'm glad that's over. It's going to suck to have to start all over, but at least I won't be dropped,* I said to myself as I lay there.

When we got to medical, the staff went through their rewarming protocol. The now-damp blankets were pulled off me, prewarmed blankets were wrapped tightly around me, a wool hat was placed on my head and wool socks slid onto my feet, and I was eventually given an IV with prewarmed saline.

An hour after I'd arrived, Dr. Ryan approached me. "How are you feeling, Adeleke?"

"Like I been hit by a bus," I replied.

He grinned and said, "I can only imagine. Listen: your temperature is gradually getting back to normal. In about thirty minutes Chief Fortin will be here to pick you up."

Pick me up? I thought. "Sir . . . listen. I can't go back out there. I mean . . . I'm not quitting. I'm sick. I think I have SIPE—"

He tried to stop me. "Adeleke—"

"I need a medical roll. Can you give me a medical roll?" I said.

"Adeleke . . . look . . . I know we know each other outside of BUD/S, but I can't let our personal relationship affect this decision. I'm sorry." He stood there for a second, then slowly walked away.

I was so frustrated! *I just came out of hell, feeling like hell, and now I'm about to go right back into hell, feeling like hell!*

I had one last shot to prove I was serious. I grabbed a pinkish vomit basin that was on the table next to my bed. I sniffed and swallowed and sniffed to try to conjure up mucus. I was already coughing, so it wasn't hard at all. Within minutes I got a solid chunk of bloody mucus in my mouth, then spit it into the basin. When the corpsman came back around to check on me, I showed it to him. "Look, dude! I'm sick, man . . . I'm sick."

He looked down in the basin for a quick second, then proceeded to pull the IV out and blankets off. "Adeleke . . . sorry. It's not my call. You've got to go back."

At that moment Chief Fortin walked in with a sadistic smile. "Adeleke! You're still alive."

"Hooyah," I muttered.

He went right into a short brief. "Your fellow brethren are at CISM Field by the bay. They're getting surf tortured. Yeah, that again. You'd save yourself a drive if you quit now."

"Negative. . . . I don't want to quit," I replied.

"Roger that. . . . Well, get your clothes on and get in the truck."

The drive back was miserable. I sat in silence in the front passenger seat while Chief Fortin drove. The heat was blasting, and I knew that as soon as I got to CISM Field, I'd be thrown right back into the water.

We pulled up, dismounted, and made our way toward the class. I could hear them screaming from the bay, "HOOYAH!"

When we got to the shoreline, Chief Fortin stopped me and played good cop. "This is your last chance. Look at your class over there. It's cold, Adeleke. You've been warm for—what?—two, three hours? You're not built for this job. There's nothing wrong with that though. Only a fraction of the military is built for what we do." Pointing to the bell, which was now attached to an instructor's truck, he continued, "The bell is right over there. Go quit. Listen: I will personally give you a ride back to the barracks. Blast the heat, play some tunes."

I replied with confidence, "Negative, Chief! I'll join them in the water." Then I trotted my way to the filthy, cold bay.

After the CISM Field surf torture, we started base tour. Base tour consisted of nonstop races up and down NAB with the neck-breaking boats on our heads. My lungs were shot, so I knew there was no way I'd get through it. Despite that notion, I also decided that I was going to put everything I had left into it.

"Stand by! Bust 'em!" Instructor G commanded.

The remaining boat crews took off. *Drive, drive, drive, drive.* I repeated the mantra I had created during my Camp Pendleton hill runs. The short rest had helped. I wasn't feeling great by any means, but I was feeling good enough to manage.

About thirty minutes later, my lungs snapped out of their amnesia. I felt like I was breathing through a kiddie straw. I started to feel dizzy from the lack of oxygen, and before I knew it, I had fallen to the ground. I was still conscious, and the instructors were on me like blood-drunk hyenas.

"Get up, you quitter! There's nothing wrong with you," Instructor G said as I stumbled my way to my feet and began to stagger behind my boat crew. "Medical cleared you. . . . So stop faking and get under that boat."

I mustered the last ounce of strength in my body, and after about thirty seconds I caught up to my boat crew, stood erect with my head under the boat, and kept driving. Despite my being back in position, the instructors didn't care; they wanted me gone. Three instructors ran beside me, shouting all kinds of stuff.

"Drama queen!"

"Weak!"

"Loser!"

And then just like that, in the midst of the chaos, everything went blank. I can't tell you exactly what happened, but from what I was later told, every part of my body stopped moving at the same time. My arms fell down to my sides, and like a leaning tower that has passed its point of no return, I face-planted onto the concrete. One student described it like seeing a robot powered down in midflight.

The instructors flipped my motionless body over and tried to bring me back to consciousness. After two minutes, one of the instructors did a deep sternum rub, which led my nerves to shock me awake. When my eyes opened, everything seemed hazy. I could see instructors running to me and the Ambu pulling up. I remember coughing violently. It felt like my lungs were full of dust.

The medical team loaded me back into the Ambu and raced me back to medical. I kept going in and out of consciousness. I couldn't feel anything, hot, cold, or pain. *Am I dying?* I thought. *If I am, it's not as bad as I thought it would be.* It seemed like a peaceful slipping away.

Interestingly, I didn't feel any anger toward the medical staff or instructors. I understood why they had done what they did. They see malingerers all the time, guys who are absolutely fine but don't give 100 percent and won't quit. When the malingerers sense they're headed for a performance drop, all of a sudden, they've contracted the Ebola virus. The instructors believed I fell into that category.

As soon as we got to BUD/S medical, Dr. Ryan listened to my lungs. All he could say was, "Oh my . . . that's not good." A civilian ambulance was called, and I was rushed to Balboa Hospital with sirens and lights blazing.

My self-diagnosis turned out to be correct. X-rays showed that my lungs were filled with fluid. I was subsequently diagnosed with SIPE, pneumonia, and another potentially fatal condition, rhabdomyolysis. There was no way I could return to Hell Week. Instead, I spent two days in the ICU, then three more days in general recovery.

Like I told Instructor W, I'm hard, not dumb!

CHAPTER FIFTEEN

AFFIRMATION

The edge is a difficult place to explain.
The only ones who really know where it is
are the ones who have gone over it.[1]

"Yes, Ma . . . I'm fine," I said to my mom as I rode back to NAB in the BUD/S duty van. I had just been released from the hospital.

My mom, who was full of emotion, peppered me with questions. "Are you sure? Remi, tell me again, what happened? Wait . . . do I need to come out there?"

"No! Ma, listen. I'm good! Stop trippin'!"

"Don't talk to me like that, Remi! Luis called me from the side of your damn hospital bed! *You were in the ICU!* They almost killed you!"

As my mom yelled through the phone like a BUD/S instructor, I told the driver, "You can let me out right over here."

"What?" Mom asked, full of frustration.

"I'm not talking to you, Ma. I'm talking to the driver."

As we pulled up to the north gate of the BUD/S compound, I told the driver, "Right here is good." Then I redirected my attention to Mom. "Ma, I got to go. I'm not supposed to walk through the compound on the phone."

"Wait! Are you going to do it again?" she asked.

"Do what, Ma?"

"Your *crazy* training!" she replied.

"I don't know, Ma. I hope . . . I mean . . . no one said anything to me." During my entire stay at the hospital, I had been expecting some type of message confirming that I had been med rolled, but it never came. I thought for sure I would be rolled back to the next class, but the silence left me in a state of uncertainty. In my mind my fate could have gone either way: performance drop or med roll.

"Bye, Remi. I love you."

"Love you, too, Ma."

One of the worst parts of Hell Week was the chafing. The instructors kept us wet and sandy the entire time, and both elements got everywhere. Due to the perpetual running, by Monday night of Hell Week, large patches of skin on my inner thighs and belt line had been rubbed off, leaving bloody wounds. Every time I hit the salt water surf or bay, the pain was excruciating. So when I climbed out of the duty van and made my way through the compound entrance, I waddled in like a bowlegged cowboy.

After walking through the gate, I saw what was left of my old class—around thirty-eight guys. Full of jubilation, they proudly sported their new brown T-shirts and congregated between the medical building and their former barracks. Two major events signified graduation from Hell Week: moving out of the BUD/S-compound barracks and into the barracks by the surf mart and receiving a brown T-shirt to wear during training. Prior to graduating Hell Week, all students trained in white T-shirts.

Though my former classmates were still in recovery, the smiles and laughs seemed to outweigh the destruction done to their bodies. No more log PTs, no more surf torture, no more boats on heads or random beatdowns. They were all one major step closer to being a SEAL.

I was happy for them, but because I didn't make it, I was also dejected and embarrassed. I don't know how I did it, but I picked up my pace and sprint-waddled the best I could into the barracks. I didn't want them to see me and perhaps invite me over.

When I got into the building, it was totally silent, like a ghost town. I made my way into what was once my four-man room. Everyone's stuff but mine had been cleared out. Only one of my roommates had made it. The other two quit.

I could hear the waves crashing and receding as I sat on my bed, reflecting on the past five weeks. "If I wasn't sick, I would have made it. I know it!" I said out loud.

Then came a knock at the door.

"Adeleke! You in there?" From the sound of the voice, I could tell that it was Master Chief.

Expecting the worst, I said to myself, *Aw, damn. This is when I find out I've been dropped.*

"Hooyah!" I said as I ran to the door to open it.

When I opened the door, Master Chief and Chief Fortin made their way in. I stood at attention, anticipating another reprimand for my performance.

Master Chief gave me the command to relax, at which I broke from attention.

"Adeleke, on behalf of the instructor staff and medical team, we apologize. We didn't know that you were sick, especially that sick."

Trying to pacify the situation, I said, "Hooyah. It's okay, Master Chief. I understand."

Master Chief continued, "It's not *okay*, Adeleke. Part of being a SEAL is admitting when you screw up . . . and that we did. On a good note: we're so happy you didn't quit." I stood there in shock. Since being at BUD/S, I had never heard a student talked to by a superior in such an even-leveled manner. "You exhibited what we look for in a SEAL: a knuckle dragger that's half-dead, down and out, and in the midst of chaos but still says, *F*** it; let's go!*" Chief Fortin kept a laser focus on me as he nodded. "That's a SEAL mentality!"

Fully encouraged at this point, I said, "Hooyah!"

Chief Fortin said, "We've already made the decision to med roll you to 251."

"Hooyah!" I replied.

They both turned to walk out. I looked at them as they exited, hoping to get the piece of information that was most important to me—at what point would I join 251? The beginning of Hell Week? Perhaps the week before Hell Week?

As soon as they stepped into the hallway, Chief Fortin turned to me and sarcastically said with a smile, "Congratulations! You get to start all over again, day one."

Despite the revelation that I had to repeat *everything*, including the torture swims, I wasn't despondent in any way. As a matter of fact, I felt the complete opposite. I was as jubilant as the guys right outside who'd just made it through Hell Week!

In retrospect, I believe my attitude stemmed from the affirmation I had just received from these two warriors. Though I wasn't aware of it, I had always sought affirmation, whether from my peers in the Bronx or older male family members. I believe one of the main reasons I wanted to make it in the music industry was because I wanted the world to affirm me, tell me I was great, tell me I was somebody, tell me all those things my father never had the chance to tell me. And there I was, in that barracks, not looking for it, when it arrived in a way that changed my entire outlook on having to go through five weeks of hell, *again*. Affirmation. In that instant my SEAL instructors became my new fathers. And just like every little boy who wants to make his father happy, I wanted to do the same.

. . .

Three weeks later I started all over with Class 251. And I was *crushing* everything again—except for the ocean swims. I passed drownproofing, which consisted of swimming, bobbing, and floating with my hands tied behind my back and my feet tied together, but I failed week one's swim. I passed the fifty-meter underwater swim on one breath, along with the fifteen-foot underwater knot-tying tests, but I failed week two's swim. I passed all my four-mile timed runs and timed obstacle courses, but I failed week three's swim. I endured surf tortures, boats on heads, and became a master at the grinder and log PTs and uniform/room inspections, but I failed week four's swim. Again, I was one of three African Americans in the class, and between that and my well-known history, I stuck out to my instructors like a fly on a wedding cake. I couldn't get away with anything, so I had to be near-perfect when it came to *everything* outside of swims.

Just like my previous class, more than two hundred guys started the First Phase of 251, but by the time we got to pre–Hell Week med checks, we were down to double digits.

I was still standing.

"How are you doing, Adeleke?" Dr. Ryan asked as he started his exam.

"I am good to go! Really. This time I . . . am . . . *ready*!" I replied confidently.

He replied, "All right. Let me check those lungs of steel. Deep breath. Deep breath." I could tell he wasn't taking any chances. He spent more time listening to my lungs than he did during the first pre–Hell Week exam. It was as though he was on an excavation. "Again," Dr. Ryan said. I took a few more deep breaths.

"Everything sounds good. Look, Adeleke: I know we all said it a lot, but . . . we're sorry for what happened. We've changed some things around here, and it's not going to happen to you or anyone else again."

"Yes, sir. Thank you," I replied. I never confessed to him that I knew about my condition before the last pre–Hell Week med check. The way I look at it, if it hadn't happened as it did, it would have probably happened to someone else, and the outcome could have been worse. So I kept my mouth shut.

After his full exam he said, "Everyone here at medical is rooting for you. You're gonna do just fine."

"Thank you, sir. I'm ready," I replied.

• • • •

"Yeaaaaaah!!!! Come on, boys! We got this!" It was Tuesday morning of Hell Week around two thirty. The original leader of my boat crew had quit, so due to my rank, I was appointed to lead my seven-man team. "Keep driving, boys! We win this leg again and we get a short rest!" I yelled. We were in the midst of base tour with boats on heads, the same evolution that almost killed me two months earlier.

We had won the last two legs of base tour and were rewarded each time by the instructors. The award consisted of being allowed to sit on our boat while the rest of the class got punished. As we say in BUD/S, "It pays to be a winner!"

When it was time to start a new leg of the race, the instructors put our boat crew all the way in the back. This made it even more challenging for us to get back to the front. I didn't care that we had won the last two legs; despite our starting placement, I was bloodthirsty and wanted to win them all!

"F*** yeah, Adeleke!" an instructor yelled as he ran alongside our boat. The tone of the instructors was diametrically opposite that of my last Hell Week. It was like they were rooting for me along with the medical staff. Instructor E continued, "It pays to be a winner! Get your crew back to the front, Adeleke!"

"Hooyah!" I said to Instructor E. I refocused on my boat crew as I repeated in cadence, "Drive, drive, drive, drive!" Before I knew it, my crew was repeating it in unison with me, "DRIVE, DRIVE, DRIVE, DRIVE!" We passed one boat crew, then another, and another. I could see the demoralized looks on our opponents' faces. It was as though they were saying, "Aw, these guys again!"

Before we knew it, we were back to the front. I still didn't care; not only did I want to be in the front, but I wanted our margin of victory to be as wide as possible. "Drive, drive, drive, drive!" Within seconds of getting to the front, I could no longer hear the groans and pavement patting that the other boat crews made. It was just my team and the instructor who led the pace; we were alone.

After about five minutes Instructor G pointed to an empty parking lot and said, "Pull over and sit on your boat! Prepare to down boat! Down boat." We all placed our boat down, sat on it, and high-fived each other. Instructor G quickly redirected his attention to the other boat crews that were far off in the distance. "Hurry up!"

As soon as the rest of the class arrived, the beatdown commenced while we sat on our boat and sipped water that the brown-shirt rollbacks brought to us.

"You guys are doing great," my old friend Keller said. He was a brown-shirt now. He walked up to me and slapped me on the shoulder, "Good shit, Remi!"

Brown-shirt rollbacks are students who made it through Hell Week but are rolled out of their class for medical or performance reasons. Once that happens, they enter what's called "rollback land," where they work on their deficiencies, recover, and/or train for three hours a day. Once BUD/S medical or the rollback chief deems them ready to reenter training, the rollbacks pick up where they left off with the next class. The only students who could work Hell Week were the brown-shirts.

Keller was a medical rollback. After he graduated from 250's Hell Week, he began feeling extreme pains in both legs. Dr. Ryan sent Keller for X-rays, which revealed that he had multiple stress fractures in both legs.

As I sat on my boat with my crew, Keller pumped me up like a boxing corner man. "Just three and a half days left, dog. Come on, baby!" he said in his Alabama accent.

"Roger that," I said.

He looked at all of us and said, "Y'all got this! Three and a half!" After we were all fully hydrated, Keller ran to an instructor's beck and call.

Three minutes into our rest, something unexpected came over me. I wasn't feeling right. I was feeling woozy.

Instructor G pointed at my boat crew and said, "Prepare to up boat! Up boat!" We quickly mounted the boat back on our heads. Then Instructor G commanded, "Walk to the back. We're getting ready to start another leg."

My wooziness got worse. *Oh damn*, I thought. *What's going on? Am I sick again?* I stumbled as we started walking to the back toward the last boat crew. *Man . . . man . . . I . . . I . . . got to keep it together . . . dammit! Not again!*

I could hear Instructor G at the front of the starting line say, "Stand by! Bust 'em!" The whole class took off.

As I tried to motivate my boat crew, my words started slurring. I couldn't speak normally. I struggled to say, "Let's go!" After a few steps, I collapsed. Unlike my last collapse two months earlier, I was completely coherent. My brain functions were all there; I just felt weak. I rolled over on my back and tried to sit up, but I felt like I weighed a thousand pounds.

My guys yelled for a corpsman, and within seconds the instructor corpsman was over me.

"What's going on, Adeleke?"

I slowly slurred my response. "I dunno. . . . I was fine."

He reached for my hand. "Let me see your finger." As I lifted my hand, he grabbed hold, pricked my finger with a needle, then wiped the blood onto a strip.

Seconds later I heard him say to Master Chief, who had just walked up, "Low glucose."

I had drained so much energy pushing myself that my blood-sugar levels were extremely low. The instructor corpsman pulled out a few glucose gel packs and had me suck them all down. Like a vampire who'd just drained a victim, I immediately felt the effects. I sat up like a slingshot that had just been released, and I thought, *I'm baaacck!*

• • •

We were all lined up on the beach, facing the berm, when Master Chief commanded, "About face!" It was Friday afternoon of Hell Week, and I was still there. As usual, we were getting ready for another surf torture session.

Master Chief continued, "Lock arms!"

Damn! This thing ain't over yet? Thought Keller said we'd be done by Friday afternoon.

"Forward march!" The remaining members of our class began to make our way toward the water. Just when our feet were about to step into the first puddles the waves created, Master Chief yelled, "And halt!" We stopped as we wondered what was next. "About face!"

When we turned around, the entire instructor staff was lined up on the top of the berm. In the center was the American flag, which an instructor gradually lowered. That's when I knew it was over! I had made it through Hell Week!

"Bring it in!" Master Chief yelled. It was a funny scene. Chafed to the meat, we all waddled over to Master Chief and formed a circle around him. The instructors came down from the berm and stood behind us.

Master Chief gave a speech. "Only 25 percent of students who start Hell Week make it . . . and now you're part of that 25 percent. This is a defining moment for all of you—a moment that, in the unlikely event you make it through the rest of training, you will be able to look back on in times of adversity. Look around." Master Chief gestured as he pointed to the other instructors. "Those knuckle-dragging, pipe-hitters behind you all went through what you just went through, and because of that we respect what you accomplished today! Be proud of yourselves, boys. And be ready for training next week! Hell Week is secured!"

With raspy voices, we all let out our violent war chant, "HOOYAAAAAH!" Afterward, the commanding officer of BUD/S, Captain S, and the executive officer, Commander Ryan Zinke, gave their speeches.

When it was all said, we dispersed and made our way to the grinder to get our brown shirts. Right when I got to the gate that separates the compound from the beach, Captain S and Commander Zinke approached me. Knowing they were the kings of the compound, I snapped to attention.

"Adeleke," Commander Zinke said.

"Hooyah, sirs! Sorry . . . sir and sir." I replied.

"Congratulations for making it through Hell Week," Captain S said as he extended his hand to shake mine.

"Thank you, sir," I replied as I looked at him.

Then Commander Zinke looked at me with a smile and said, "Now we're going to teach you how to swim."

I turned my gaze to him, smiled as wide as I could, and said, "Hooyah!"

Chief's Lagoon City illustration

The family taking the boat out to see the Lagoon Development Project's progress

The family with one of Chief's business partners, outside our home in Ikoyi, Nigeria

Our family driver, Felix, Bayo, and I, hanging on Victoria Island, Lagos

Grandma, Bayo, and I,
hanging in Nigeria

Our sweet Aunt Dokey,
always serving others

Grandma, Ma, Bayo, and
me in front of the building
where I grew up

My first business
venture, 8th Wonder
Entertainment: the
8th Wonder team
keeping it 100

Back in my hustler
days—when I
thought I was tough

Navy boot camp graduation: still trying to be hard in a sailor outfit

Half dead, soaking wet, and cold during Hell Week

Day 1 BUD/S grinder PT: I can't hide.

The look when you realize the next few months are going to suck!

Surf torture was my kryptonite.

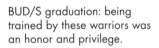

My boat crew and I, to the far right, putting our logs away: pays to be a winner!

At the top of the mountain during Mojave Viper marine training: great times with the Marines

BUD/S graduation: being trained by these warriors was an honor and privilege.

SQT Class graduation

Platoon getting ready to leave Camp
Mercury for a Direct Action Mission

Christian and I back
together again for
another deployment

Geared up and heading out on
a Direct Action Mission

Snowman, Raj the interpreter,
and I, getting ready for meeting
with informants

Grilling out with Bingo at a Camp
Mercury barbecue

Christian and me at the Camp Mercury church, where my speaking and teaching ministry started

Actress Jamarla Melancon and I, performing a scene from *Fences* at the Lee Strasberg Institute

Hooding ceremony, School of Business & Leadership, Graduate Program, University of Charleston, Charleston, West Virginia

With my family and professor John Lee for my bachelor's degree ceremony, University of Charleston, Naval Amphibious Base, Coronado, California

My brother, Bayo, and me at a San Diego Nigerian Banquet, November 2009

Our wedding photo in the rain, October 2012

© STANLEY TAKWANA TONGAI ATAGI

Aunt Dokey and I, riding in a limo, on our way to her 100th birthday party

Mom enjoying her time with her grandsons Cayden and Caleb

Jessica and I headed to the opening of an exhibit featuring my story at the Museum of the Bible

My second time working with Michael Bay, this time on the set of *6 Underground*

Sharing some words with Michael Bay at the premiere of *Transformers: The Last Knight*

I can't resist a little daddy time whenever my boys sneak into the office.

CHAPTER SIXTEEN

MY OWN WORST ENEMY

The same things that are good for
us can also be bad for us.

Yo!" Keller yelled at the oversize black bouncer, waving and trying to get his attention. Keller pointed at me first, then at Rasheed, and said, "He's with me! And he's with me! Them two right there!" It was Friday night, and we were outside Deco's, a hip-hop nightclub in the Gaslamp Quarter that sat between TGI Friday's and the Gaslamp 15, the theater I snuck off to when I was on duty more than a year earlier.

There was a long line outside the club, and along with Keller, a bunch of self-appointed shot callers were trying to reason with the bouncers to skip the line.

As Rasheed and I stood toward the back, I could hear the bass from Snoop Dogg and Pharrell's new song "Drop It Like It's Hot" as it spilled out of the club. Keller had already been inside doing what we called a "recon for girls."

"Come on! Y'all good!" Keller said as he waved us over. We got out of the line and made our way through the crowd. When we got to the front, the bouncer checked our IDs, pulled back the velvet rope, and let us right on in.

"I told you, Remi! We're good!" Keller said.

I slapped him five and jubilantly did my best Tommy from *Martin* impersonation: "We going out tonight, doooog! Yeaaah."

At the moment I was a brown-shirt rollback. Two weeks earlier I had failed the last swim of Class 251's First Phase, which was expected by everyone, including me. Instead of giving me a single class roll, the BUD/S leadership decided to double roll me in order to give me enough time to learn how to swim with fins. That meant I wouldn't class back up for three more months, when 253 graduated from Hell Week. With my schedule entailing only four hours of training in the morning Monday through Friday, and optional swim workouts on Saturday, I was on a brown-shirt rollback vacation.

Inside, we walked up the steps toward the club's dance floor and bar area. Keller led the way while Rasheed and I followed. Rasheed was one of the two other African Americans who started Class 251 with me. He had graduated from Hell Week and moved on to Second Phase, which was dive phase.

"How's it looking up there?" I asked Keller, referring to the girls.

He turned back and did his usual Spartan *300* impersonation, "The enemy outnumbers us a paltry three to one. We are good . . . to . . . go!" In other words, there were more women in the club than men.

Rasheed teased, "Stop acting like you're gonna do something, Remi!"

I rebutted swiftly, "I'll be the first to leave with a chick tonight! Watch me. Watch . . . me!"

Being in BUD/S made us all very competitive. We would often compete to see who would be the first to find a girl at a club and go home with her. "It pays to be a winner" applied to us as much outside of BUD/S as it did inside. The DJ spun Sean Paul's new reggae song "Get Busy" as we danced our way through the crowded club. Keller and I broke off from Rasheed and went straight to the bar while Rasheed went straight to the center of the dance floor and started his stripper dance routine.

"What you drinking?" Keller yelled over the noise.

"You know me . . . fire water!" I replied.

Keller laughed, then turned to the bartender. "I'll take two Hennesseys with Coke!"

"Look at that fool!" I yelled as I tapped Keller to get his attention. Rasheed, who was six three and shredded, was in the middle of the dance floor, dancing shirtless with two girls. "Minnesota, man! He's from Minnesota!"

"Cheers!" Keller said as we bumped glasses. "You see anything you like?"

"Yeah," I said with my eyes laser focused on an olive-skinned girl halfway down the bar. "This chick is lookin' at me like I'm . . . Jesus of Nazareth!"

"Yeah?" Keller asked.

I continued to stare at her as she stared back at me.

"Watchagonnado, Remi?" Keller egged me on.

"I'll see you later . . . later-later! Pays to be a winner, right?" I said before making my way over to her.

"What's up?" was my introduction.

"Hey," was her reply. I hated it when a girl gave me that type of response. It wasn't enough to play off of. And to me it was a sign that I was going to have to either come up with something synthetically charming or ask her to dance. I did neither. I softly took hold of her hand, threw it over my shoulder, and danced my way to the dance floor while she followed. My new interest and I danced seductively only a few feet from Rasheed and his entourage.

"What are you?" I asked.

"Human," she replied with a smile.

I chuckled and said, "I could see that. I mean, what's your background? Your complexion is . . . *wow* . . . you're beautiful!"

"Thank you. My dad's Italian, and my mom is half-Mexican and half-black."

Okay, now I want this girl even more, I thought. "That explains why you're so gorgeous. And listen, I'm not just saying that to get with you or anything. I'm just keeping it real. I mean . . . in reality, I'm already with you," I finished with a smile.

She cocked her head to the side and asked, "Are you?"

"Yeah, you followed me out here, right?"

She smiled, turned, and slowly danced away from me, with her head still turned in my direction as if to say, "Take that back."

I quickly grabbed her hand and, still smiling, said, "I'm sorry. I'm just playing."

"You better be. And if I'm already *with you* . . . what's my name?" she asked. We continued dancing.

"Hmm . . . that's a good question. Look . . . again . . . I'm not trying to kick game to you. And what I'm about to say ain't no corny one-liner either. You ready?" She nodded, and I continued, "You're so fine, you don't need a name. I mean . . . if I was your *daddy* . . . I would have just named you *Fine*."

She giggled and said, "That's a corny one-liner. And my *daddy* didn't name me Fine. He named me Candace!"

"Nice to meet you, Candace. I'm Remi."

She stopped dancing and looked at me suspiciously, then gave me a response I'd heard from women many times. "Come on. Remi? Seriously. What's your real name? Your *mama* didn't name you *Remi*."

"I'm serious. It's Remi. That's my name."

"Okay, Remi. Let me guess. You're a pilot who's only in town once a month . . . and you have a secret family somewhere. . . . I don't know . . . because you have an East Coast accent, maybe New York?"

I reached into my pocket, pulled out my ID, and held it up to her eyes. "See . . . Remi Adeleke!" Then I turned to walk away in the same playful way she had seconds earlier.

She reached out and grabbed my arm, and when she did, I knew I had her.

"You're cute. So what is it that you do, Remi?"

"You tell me first," I replied.

"I'm a federal agent. Now you?"

"Hmm . . . that's impressive. I'm a Navy SEAL." God forbid a BUD/S instructor found out what I'd just said! But I didn't care. I wanted her as much as all the other women who appealed to my eye. For some people, crack is their drug of choice. For others, it's alcohol, and for others, it's adrenaline. For me, it was women. Women were my crack, my weed, and my ecstasy all wrapped into one.

• • •

"Shit, shit, shit, shit," I repeated after looking at my clock.

Candace, still half-asleep in bed, whispered, "What's wrong? What happened?"

As I swiftly threw on my clothes, I told her, "I'm late!"

"Late? It's Saturday morning, Remi. Navy SEALs work on Saturdays?"

I replied, "Yeah . . . it's training." I gave her a kiss and said, "I'll call you after I'm done, okay? Maybe we can grab some dinner tonight?"

"Okay, I'd like that," she replied.

"All right, I'll see you later."

I raced out of Candace's apartment, jumped in my Mustang, and took off to base. Even though I didn't *have* to go to the optional weekend swim training, I wanted to go. I wanted to use every opportunity I had to improve my swim times.

I arrived at the combat training tank (CTT) on NAB an hour after training had already started. When I jumped out of my car and headed up the ramp that led into the CTT, I could hear Instructor E shouting instructions.

"Jason! No, after you pull with your dominant arm, you have to follow through with a slight roll!"

"Dammit . . . huh . . . what do I do?" I whispered. In the military we have a saying, "If you're not early, you're late." I figured it would be worse for me to show up late than for me not to show up at all, so I turned around and slowly walked back down the ramp toward my car.

As I sat in the driver's seat, I vowed that I would make it to every voluntary Saturday training event, but I didn't. Throughout my entire rollback, I made it to only two sessions. The reason for my absence was always the same: I was at the clubs, bars, or lounges every Friday and Saturday night. And as I got deeper into my time in rollback land, I added Wednesday and Thursday outings to my list as well. All the benefits I had at Camp Pendleton were gone now; there were way too many distractions in San Diego!

• • •

"All right, Adeleke. You pass this swim, and you'll get to class back up with 253 in two weeks." It was September 2004, and all the brown-shirt rollbacks were standing on the beach in swim gear. For the past three months, Instructor E had been working with me to finesse my swim. He was a great teacher and very patient.

Instructor E continued, "Crabtree, you're Adeleke's swim buddy for this one."

"Hooyah!" Crabtree replied. Crabtree had been rolled for runs but could swim like a dolphin. He could guide us in a straight line, so all I had to do was follow.

We rollbacks weren't the only ones on the swim. This would be 253's last swim before they entered Hell Week, so they stood in line with us, waiting for the First Phase instructors to arrive for the overall swim brief.

I'm ready. I'm confident. I can do this, I said to myself. I didn't feel my usual pre-swim anxiety. I felt good! Not only did Instructor E see my improvement, but I felt my improvement. I cut through the water faster, stroked cleaner, and exerted less energy in the process.

In the midst of my thoughts, the First Phase instructors arrived.

"Drop!" Instructor H yelled. The entire 253 class dropped to the push-up position and started pushing them out. We brown-shirts had the luxury of standing by and observing.

"Holy magnolia! Look who's here," Instructor H said as he looked in my direction.

"Hooyah, Instructor H!" I replied.

"Adeleke, drop down," Instructor H commanded. I immediately dropped to the push-up position. Then he walked up to me as my face stared into the sand, squatted, and said, "Adeleke, you'd better not fail this swim. You hear me?"

"Hooyah!"

Then he commanded, "Recover!" I immediately popped to my feet. His words gave me added motivation. The entire BUD/S staff had pretty much handed me a graduation slip. I couldn't let them down, or worse, cause them to regret their decision.

After we swam past the breakers and lined up, the command came that I had heard over a hundred times: "Stand by! Bust 'em!"

Crabtree and I took off. Our immediate goal was to break away from the chaotic pack. He got a little bit ahead of me, and I focused my attention on his fins. *Kick, pull, turn. Kick, pull, turn.* I repeated the swim sequence Instructor E had embedded in my brain.

I swam and swam and swam. Ten minutes passed, then fifteen, and guess what? I noticed a difference. I could hear and feel other students around me. Unlike my swims with Tyrone, Crabtree and I weren't alone anymore! I was among those who kept the standard! *Hooyah!* I thought.

Before that day, I would get upset when students who had already turned around bumped into me. But now, when students jostled me, I said to myself, *That's fine by me, as long as I'm still with ya!*

When we arrived at the one-mile turnaround point, we had to wait in line to check in.

Wow! This is what it feels like to keep up! Huh. I could get used to this, I thought. There were swim pairs all around us. When it was finally our turn, I proudly yelled in unison with Crabtree, "Adeleke, Crabtree, swim pair ten. Adeleke, Crabtree, swim pair ten!"

"Good job, Adeleke! Go counterclockwise around the buoy and head back!" Instructor W said.

"Hooyah!" we both replied at the same time.

As we made our way back, I couldn't help but think of Tyrone. *If only you could see me now, brother.*

I kept my mantra up the entire mile back. *Kick, pull, turn!*

Suddenly Crabtree stopped and yelled, "Adeleke! We're almost at the finish! Let's sprint!" During rollback training, Instructor E often had us do sprint drills, and they were torturous!

"I'm with you, dude! Let's do it!" I replied. I stroked, kicked, and turned with everything I had. My cadence got stronger. *Kick, pull, turn! Kick, pull, turn!*

Then suddenly in midstroke, I felt a tug on my fin. I popped my head up. "Who the—?" It was Crabtree.

When he saw that he had my attention, he pulled back his swim mask and with a gregarious laugh said, "Adeleke! Stop! You passed the check-in boat and buoy!" I was so in the zone that I didn't realize I'd finished!

When I kicked back to the check-in boat and screamed, "Time?" Instructor W delivered the news I'd been waiting nine months to hear: "Adeleke, Crabtree, eighty minutes! Pass!"

If I had been a Christian, I would have said, "Hallelujah!" But instead I said, "F*** yeah!"

* * *

After 253 graduated from Hell Week, which was the fifth week of First Phase, Keller and I classed up with them. This would be my third class in less than one year. In the three weeks left, I passed the next two timed ocean swims and graduated to Second Phase.

Along with my training transition, another transition was taking place in my life. The confidence I gained from making it through two First Phases and finally passing swims had gradually turned into full-on pride!

Though rollback land proved to be good for me, it also produced some bad habits. I got so used to the free time that when I classed back up, I couldn't stop partying or sleeping around. In my convoluted mind, I had already made it. I was a SEAL, though in reality I wasn't.

I failed my very first swim in Second Phase. The passing time had dropped from eighty-five minutes to eighty minutes, but still that was no excuse. I should have passed, and everyone knew it. A lot of people were upset about that failure, and just like that, I was out of the instructors' good graces and back in the hot seat.

During the second week of dive phase, I failed my second swim. And when it seemed things couldn't get any worse, the class entered pool week.

Pool week consists of a series of dive exams that test students' ability to operate under extreme pressure and still make good decisions. The first test of pool week is called ditch and don (Monday), in which students have to swim to the bottom of the nine-foot section of the CTT, procedurally take off their dive rig, stow it, resurface without the rig, then swim back down to procedurally don their rig. Then there's night ditch and don (Tuesday), which was the same test conducted with a blacked-out face mask. The third is called buddy gear exchange (Wednesday). In this test two students swim to the bottom of the nine-foot section with only one student wearing a dive rig. They have to buddy breathe while the testing student takes the dive rig off the other student, then dons it himself. The fourth test is called night buddy gear exchange (Thursday) and is done with both students wearing a blacked-out face mask.

Then there's the infamous tread. The tread is a five-minute water tread with twin-80 dive tanks (weighing in at about sixty pounds) on a student's back, plus a twenty-pound weight belt and fins. While treading, a student has to keep his hands above the water. If his hands touch the water, he fails. After five minutes of treading, the student swims twenty-five meters to one end of the pool on his stomach, then twenty-five meters on his back. Each student has one chance at the end of each day to pass the tread test. If a student doesn't pass by Thursday, that student is either performance dropped or performance rolled—*if* the student is lucky.

Now, after Hell Week it's highly unusual for a student to quit. The class numbers pretty much stay the same—until pool week, that is. Pool week is where classes can lose anywhere from four to twenty students due to performance drops and rolls. Due to the difficulty of pool week, not only do the instructors give extensive classes; they also offer up their personal time on the weekends to help prep students.

Because I was too busy being a player, I never showed up to any of the optional prep sessions.

• • •

On Monday of pool week Instructor C gave the command, "Prepare to enter the water! Enter the water!" The first group of students jumped into the CTT to start their tread test. The rest of us sat on the pool deck with our backs to the pool; we weren't allowed to watch. I along with the majority of the class had passed the first pool week test, ditch and don.

As I sat with my back to the pool, all I heard was splashing, moaning, groaning, and other sounds of great distress.

"Aweeee!"

"Ohua!"

"Haaaa!"

"Haww!"

With my head down, I turned to Keller and whispered, "*Damn* . . . What they doing to them boys? It sounds like they dying!"

Keller looked at me somberly and said, "I know, dog. And we're next!"

Chief G yelled at a student, "Get your f***ing hands off the side of the pool! I don't care if you failed! Keep going!"

"I can't . . . I can't breathe . . . I swallowed a lot of water, Chief!" the student said.

Chief replied, "You're talking to me, aren't you?"

"Hooyah!" the student said.

"Then do you know what that means? It means you can breathe! Get back in there, swallow some more, and when you really can't breathe, then maybe I'll give you some sympathy!"

I looked back at Keller and said, "Man . . . these dudes are Rick James, cold-blooded." Keller didn't respond this time. He just sat there with his head down.

After the five minutes were up, Chief G yelled, "Time! For those of you who passed, swim down and back. The rest of you shit birds, get out!"

When the first group finished their swim, the next group, which included Keller and me, were called up.

Instructor C pointed at me and said, "Aw, shit! It's the guy who can't swim! All right, I'm taking bets." He looked around at the other instructors. "I say he won't make it past two minutes."

Chief G chimed in, "Two? Wow, that's generous, I say . . . let's see . . . forty-five seconds."

"What do you say, Adeleke?" Instructor C sarcastically asked.

"Hooyah!" That was my way of saying, "I agree with you, but I don't want to admit it."

Chief G gave the command, "Prepare to enter the water!" If I didn't have bones in my chest, my heart would have beaten itself through my skin. "Enter the water!" I jumped in with my full-dive rig: twin-80s, weight belt, harness, and fins.

As soon as I hit the water, I shot my arms into the air. It was pure chaos. People were bumping into each other, water was splashing everywhere, and most of the instructors' eyes were on me.

I think I did fine the first minute or so, but after that, my legs were smoked! I could no longer keep my head above water—at least not consistently enough to breathe as needed. And when my head would dip under the surface, my situation became worse. Imagine doing a two-hundred-yard full-on sprint and having to hold your breath for seconds along the way while still maintaining the same sprint speed! This was like that, only worse.

After a minute and thirty seconds, I could barely keep my head out of the water; it was a fight just to breathe. Then I started swallowing water. It was like I was drowning. I had almost no body fat, which means no buoyancy, and about eighty pounds of gear wrapped around me. Bad combination. Now I had insight into what it felt like when the Mafia wrapped cement blocks around their victims and threw them in a river.

I kicked and kicked and kicked with all I had, but nothing helped. After my head was completely submerged, my biceps followed, then my elbows, forearms, and finally my hands. I disappeared into the abyss.

Once my hands were submerged, I knew I had failed, so I tried to do the natural thing, which was swim with all limbs back to the top, but I couldn't. At that point I knew I was near drowning.

Oh my God, I'm about to die. They gonna kill my black ass again, I thought.

Then something kicked in, and I said to myself, *I failed, but I'm not going out like this*. I kicked and pulled the way Instructor E had taught me. I pulled some more, and finally my lips broke the surface, and I sucked in as much oxygen as possible, along with some water.

"He's alive! He lives!" Instructor C yelled.

Hearing Instructor C's response threw me into a rage! I felt like I had almost died, and this instructor was joking about it. *Roger that! You want to disrespect me?* I swam to the side of the pool with all my might and held on. That Bronx attitude began to leak out of me. I didn't say anything, but as the instructors verbally filleted me, I looked at them while thinking, *Whatever. Y'all ain't about to kill me. I'm holding on right here while y'all talk all y'all shit. And if somebody touches me . . . real talk! I'm climbing outta this pool and knocking 'em out!*

When all the passing students finished their swim, Chief G yelled, "Adeleke! Faillllll!"

As soon as I heard that, I climbed out of the pool, walked to the fail corner with Keller, who had also failed, and sat down. I was not happy, but there was only one person I had the right to be mad at, and that was myself.

The next three days played out the same way. On Tuesday I passed my night ditch and don but failed the tread a second time. On Wednesday I passed my buddy gear exchange but failed the tread a third time. Keller was diagnosed with an arterial gas embolism, which is a dive-related injury, and was med rolled to 254. When 254 started pool week, Keller classed up with them, failed the tread four times, and was performance dropped.

Thursday, I passed my night buddy gear exchange but failed my tread a fourth time. At that point, I knew I would be kicked out of training.

• • • •

Friday, I stood before a command academic review board. The board took place in the conference room that was located on the same quarterdeck I'd entered exactly a year earlier when I first checked into BUD/S. Now, in that same place, I was about to be checked out.

There were six instructors in the room. They all sat at a long table facing the entrance. I stood outside on the quarterdeck in my starched cammies and shined boots, with my blue dive-phase helmet in my right hand.

"Adeleke, come in!" Commander O said.

I replied, "Hooyah," before stepping into the room and standing at attention.

Commander O asked, "Adeleke, you've been here for a year, haven't you?"

"Hooyah, sir," I replied.

He continued, "Well, because of your length of time here, I'm sure you understand what's about to happen."

"Hooyah," I replied again.

Then the command master chief chimed in, "Adeleke . . . listen: you've been rolled three times. Once for medical, and the command decided to give you a double roll for swims."

"Hooyah, Master Chief," I replied.

Looking down at my record, Master Chief continued, "After being *double* rolled for swims, you failed both of your swims in Second Phase. And one of those failing times didn't even meet the First Phase standard. You swam eighty-six minutes." After reading through my stats, he looked up at me for a response.

"Hooyah. No excuse, Master Chief. I failed," I said, trying to keep it short.

Then Lieutenant B read me my rights. "Because of your triple rolls, your failure to meet the swim standard, and this week's pool week failures, you've shown us that you don't have what it takes to be a SEAL. We hereby performance drop you from BUD/S. You must immediately turn in your training gear and report to X-Division. The command career counselor will talk with your detailer, and you will reenter the general Navy."

"Hooyah, sir," I replied respectfully.

The commander asked, "Do you have anything to say, Adeleke?"

"Yes, sir. I want to thank you all for the countless opportunities that you have given me to succeed. When I look at what has transpired over the last year, I can't blame anyone but myself." I made sure to scan the entire room as I delivered my parting words. "I showed up unprepared. And when I had the opportunity to get remediation on the weekends, I didn't show up. My goal moving forward is to learn from my mistakes and come back ten times better."

In retrospect, that was the first time in my adult life I remember taking responsibility for my actions. In the past, my failures were always somebody else's fault, but finally I took a stand and pointed the finger at my own chest.

Master Chief concluded, "Dismissed, Adeleke."

"Hooyah," I replied. Then I did an about face and walked out of the conference room, through the quarterdeck, and out to the grinder. As I walked across the grinder, I stared down the Be Someone Special sign, then made my way to the barracks to move out.

CHAPTER SEVENTEEN

EXACTLY WHERE I NEEDED TO BE

"For those who exalt themselves will be humbled."[1]

As expected, I received orders back to Camp Pendleton, but this time I would serve as an infantry corpsman at 1st Battalion, 4th Marines. That's right: in relation to SOF (special operations forces), I was with the bottom tier, the grunts. And what made my situation even worse was the fact that there were no guarantees I would get back to BUD/S.

At the time, 1st Marine Division leadership required that each medic serve a minimum of three years and/or do two deployments, and receive their Fleet Marine Force (FMF) qualification before requesting entry into BUD/S. Because the wars were hot and heavy and Marines were on the front lines, both Marines and Navy corpsmen experienced heavy casualties. I personally knew three former BUD/S students who desperately wanted to return to BUD/S but were either killed or permanently disabled by IED blasts in combat. That's why I say there were no guarantees I would make it back to BUD/S. It had nothing to do with acceptance; before my departure I received an "early return" recommendation from the BUD/S staff. The question was whether I'd be alive and in the proper physical condition to participate. And would I still have the drive and motivation in three years to start all over again?

There's an old Jewish proverb that says, "For those who exalt themselves will be humbled." During my first drive back up to Camp Pendleton, the truth of that proverb hit me. Once again, I'd tried to exalt myself by playing a SEAL, and once again I was being extremely humbled.

I pulled into the parking lot of the FMF school around noon on a Friday. The Field Medical Service School was where corpsmen were formally trained on marine infantry edicts and tactics. As with the other BUD/S dropouts, I had to complete FMF training before checking in to my battalion.

The parking lot was empty, which seemed odd to me. I got out of my car with my check-in envelope in hand and started walking to the main entrance, which led to the quarterdeck. When I got to the door, I realized I'd forgotten a small bag of trash from a burrito I'd eaten. I didn't want that thing stinking up my car, so I made my way back, grabbed my trash, then headed to the quarterdeck. It was as empty as the parking lot.

"Hello? Hello?" I said as I peeked around the L-shaped hallway.

I heard a sound from an open door behind the quarterdeck, so I made my way there. A female was sitting in uniform at her desk.

"Hello," I said again as I stood six feet from her. She didn't acknowledge me; she just kept typing away.

Come on. Is this how my stay's gonna start? I'm talking to you, I thought as I kept looking at her. Out of the corner of my right eye, I saw a garbage can. So, naturally, as a human being would do, I slowly bent down to place my burrito bag in the trash.

As soon as my bag hit the bottom of the can, she spun her chair in my direction, snapped up on her feet, walked directly to me, and barked, "Who the hell do you think you are? Coming into my office . . . interrupting me!" She pointed to her chest. "And then you have the nerve to put your trash in my trash can! Stand at attention!"

Already despondent over being dropped from BUD/S and sent back to Camp Pendleton, I slowly got in the attention position and said, "I'm sorry."

"Sorry who?" She gestured to her anchors, which indicated she was a chief.

While having flashbacks of my first encounter with HM3 Trotter, I replied, "Sorry, Chief."

Pointing at the door, she yelled, "Now go back out and try again!"

I walked out of the office into the hallway, turned around, walked back to the door, knocked, and said, "Respectfully request to enter the room, Chief."

Her demeanor changed as if she had a split personality. She said in a calm tone, "Permission granted. Now, who are you?"

"HN Adeleke, Chief." I already knew what her next question was going to be, and in light of our bad start, I wasn't looking forward to answering it.

Then she asked, "Where did you come from?"

With a deep sigh and a bit of a stutter, I said, "Um . . . huh . . . BUD/S, Chief."

She smiled from ear to ear and transformed back into Sergeant Slaughter. "Ohhhh, you're one of those BUD/S duds! That explains you walking in here like you own the place, huh? You quit what . . . one . . . two weeks of BUD/S, and now you think you're hot shit?"

"Negative," I replied.

"Negative what?" she asked.

"Negative, I didn't quit. I was dropped after—"

"You guys are all the same. BUD/S has an 80 percent attrition rate, yet for some reason I never met one of you quitters who was man enough to admit that he . . . well, actually quit! It's always, 'I was dropped for this' or 'I was dropped for that.' Huh. I'd have more luck running into a leprechaun." She did have a point, but I wasn't one of those guys. Regardless, it didn't matter. I had paraded as a SEAL at clubs, and now the SEAL gods were making me pay for it through this witch.

"Check-in docs!" she said as she snatched the envelope out of my hand. After she read through the documents, she said, "You start training Monday. Do you live off base, or will you be living in the barracks?"

"I live off base, Chief, in San Diego."

After Keller and I were dropped, he was stationed on a ship docked in San Diego. We decided to move into an upscale apartment complex not too far from his duty station. It was pricey, but for me it was worth it. The community boasted a twenty-five-meter lap pool that was heated throughout the year. Gone were the days when I had to run three miles to a pool and back. All I had to do was walk out of my apartment, go down a flight of stairs, walk across one of the parking lots, and there I was, poolside. I didn't know when or if I was going to get another shot at BUD/S, but if I was, I wanted to make sure I was more than prepared. And as it related to my daily commute, I didn't care. I wanted to be as far away from Camp Pendleton as I could during my off hours.

Chief replied, "San Diego? Well, that's dumb! You'd better be ready for training Monday. And if you're late more than once, I'll see to it that you go to captain's mast . . . *and* that you're confined to base! Dismissed!"

"Hooyah! I mean, yes, Chief."

I wasn't in Kansas anymore! I walked out of that office like a wet puppy on a winter night, having received the humbling I deserved. It would be an understatement to say that was a low point for me. Honestly, there is no combination of words that could describe how miserable that moment made me feel.

• • •

Two months after checking into FMF school, I graduated without incident. It was a walk in the park compared to BUD/S. I breezed through the academics and moonwalked through the physical conditioning. Our six-mile ruck hikes through the hills of Camp Pendleton were a struggle for most of the women and some of the guys in my class. I, on the other hand, was in such great shape from BUD/S that I would run to the back of the pack, have two physically drained female classmates hold on to my ruck straps, pull them uphill, then run back for two more classmates and do the same. Actions such as this earned me the nickname Supa Doc, which was one of many nicknames the marines would later call me.

In April 2005, I made my way to Camp Horno, which was located twenty miles northeast of Camp Pendleton's main gate. As I drove there for the first time, I became frustrated. *Damn! Where is this place? I thought the hospital was far, but this is in the boondocks! My gas bill for the month is going to end up more than my rent!*

About forty minutes after driving through the gate, I finally arrived at the 1/4 Battalion Aid Station (BAS). The aid station was a rallying point for the thirty corpsmen spread out among the five-hundred-member battalion. It also served as a home for the battalion's medical leadership.

I stepped out of my Mustang in my marine fatigues, with my check-in envelope in hand. This time I had made sure to bring a copy of my recommendation letter, which clearly stated, "HN Adeleke was performance dropped from Second Phase of BUD/S." I wasn't going to let anybody put me in the category of quitters again!

When I walked into the clinic for the first time, it was bustling. Sick call was under way, and marines were sprawled out all over the place, waiting to be seen by their platoon docs or the aid station physician.

"Doc! I'm burning, man!" a young marine joked as I made my way down the packed hallway. "I need you to punch my bore, check my goods." He laughed as he gestured to his groin area.

I grinned and said, "Yeah, maybe you should have checked the goods before you checked in the goods."

Another marine I passed jumped in. "That's a big doc," he said to the comedic marine, then continued, "I want to get switched to your platoon, Doc! What platoon you going to?"

"I don't know, brother," I replied.

"He's gonna be in my platoon!" the comedic marine said as he shoved his buddy.

Walking down the hall for the first time, I knew I didn't want to be there, but I learned within seconds that it might be a fun ride.

When I arrived at the leadership office of the BAS, I made sure to knock before I entered.

"HN Adeleke reporting for duty."

A short Filipino sailor looked in my direction and responded, "Come on in."

Okay, we're starting on a good note.

The sailor extended his hand for a handshake. "I'm HM2 Rosca. I'm the LPO for the BAS."

"Nice to meet you, HM2."

Then came the million-dollar question. "So . . . where did you come from?"

I pulled out my recommendation letter, which was neatly placed on top of my check-in papers, and handed them to him. "BUD/S, HM2. I was dropped in Second Phase." *Yeah, yeah, yeah, I ain't quit*, I said inwardly.

He looked at the letter and said, "Wow. You made it through Hell Week. That's impressive. What happened?"

"In short, I didn't do what I was supposed to do, acted like I already made it, and got humbled. Now I'm here."

He nodded, "Well, we can all use a little humbling sometimes. And I tell you what: there's no place that will humble you like this place."

I laughed inwardly. *Yes, I know. Trust me: I know.*

"So here's what I'm thinking," HM2 Rosca said. "You're obviously in shape, and the scout sniper platoon could use a secondary corpsman. Would you be okay with joining that platoon? If not, I know Alpha Company and 81s are also in need of an extra corpsmen."

As it relates to the Marines, scout snipers fall into a specialized category. They're not necessarily special forces, but very close to it, so I figured for the time being that would be the ideal place for me to land.

"I'm fine with scout snipers, HM2. Thank you."

• • •

Being with scout snipers was a great experience. Even though I was a corpsman, they didn't treat me like one. They allowed me to learn everything they knew, including long-range marksmanship, intelligence collection by means of surveillance, and the tedious art of stalking. I was able to keep my fitness up by participating in their mandatory long-distance timed runs, and I was even allowed to challenge my new brothers with workouts I created. In essence, in the platoon I was treated like one of the marines—and in some cases even better because doc was the one in charge of the meds.

Our platoon was a rambunctious bunch, always challenging each other and *always* partaking in some form of shenanigans.

"Doc! Doc! You good, man?" Lance Corporal Lanoie yelled from about fifteen feet ahead of me.

Our four-man recon element was hiking up Cleghorn Mountain in the Twentynine Palms desert. We were on a major training exercise known as Mojave Viper. Our mission was to get to the top of the mountain and laser a target for Apache helicopters to bomb.

I yelled back, "Yeah! I'm good." But under my breath I said, "Really . . . this sucks. Why did I do this to myself?"

What started out as a fitness challenge/bet had turned into a day of misery.

We all had a lot of gear to carry for the three-day mission, but I volunteered to carry both the upper and lower receiver of the M107 .50 caliber sniper rifle, a load often split between two marines, along with a load of .50 caliber rounds, my med bag, and a three-day supply of food and water.

"Hey, Doc Knockboots!" Lance Corporal Max yelled from about ten feet up.

"What?" I replied with a hint of frustration.

"What was Africa like?" he asked.

"Give me . . . a second!" It was hard enough to breathe, let alone hold a conversation, but my mouth had gotten me into this situation.

Max switched his attention to Corporal Stevens, who was a few feet ahead of him, and sarcastically said, "Hey, Corporal! I think Doc is fading! Looks like we're going to win the bet!"

I don't know why I agreed to it, but I made a dumb bet that I could hike up the mountain with all the gear I had committed to while holding a conversation the entire time.

When I heard Max's comment, my BUD/S instincts kicked in. I didn't want to lose. "It's hot!" I replied. I hoped my short answer would suffice.

"Hot like what? I need more of a description, Doc!"

Struggling to talk between breaths, I continued, "Hot . . . like . . . Mojave Viper hot!" *I won't lose this bet! I'll pass out before I lose.*

Max's job was to pepper me with questions in order to get me to give up.

"That's all you got to say? I thought we were supposed to be having a conversation, not a—"

"And . . . hot . . . like . . . like . . . your mom on her wedding night . . . after everyone was gone . . . and she changed out her dress for your daddy!"

"Oooooh, Doc got jokes!" Max said.

Trucking along with my head down, I continued, "I told y'all . . . I could keep talking . . . and do this! This is . . . nothing!"

"Okay, Doc! You ready for our next topic?" Max shouted.

Huffing and puffing, I yelled back confidently, "Yeah . . . let's go!"

"What was BUD/S like . . . before you quit?" Max joked.

I let out a loud laugh that echoed off the mountain. "It sucked bad! But at the same time . . . it was . . . the best place to be! It's not hard because it's necessarily physical. Every guy that shows up has what it takes to be there, physically; otherwise, they wouldn't be there! It's . . . the mental aspect that kills them! Like this: this here is not just physical; it's mental. Physically, I can do this . . . but my body tries to tell my mind it can't. So I have to push with the object that's . . . stronger than my body . . . and that's my mind!"

Before I knew it, I had belted out a whole monologue, and it didn't slow me down one bit. I guess that's how it was anytime I talked about being a SEAL or being at BUD/S. I still wanted it, and my passion to be a SEAL continuously proved that it could dissipate any pain, depression, or boredom that I encountered.

"Damn, Doc! That's poetic!" Max replied.

"Yeah!" *And at this point I'm winning, so please give me another BUD/S or SEAL question*, I thought.

"Hey, Doc!" Max yelled down.

"What up?" I replied.

"I'm glad you quit BUD/S! Because if you hadn't quit . . . you wouldn't be here with us!"

I replied with a smile as I stared at my next steps, "Thanks, Max! I'm glad . . . I quit too!"

Being out there in the wilderness with my marines was great for me. For the first time since my departure from BUD/S, I was finally learning to accept my place, my newfound brotherhood, and most importantly, my humbling. Back at Camp Pendleton was exactly where I needed to be.

CHAPTER EIGHTEEN

EVERYTHING WORKS OUT

"And those who humble themselves will be exalted."[1]

H ey, HM3," I heard a marine say as he walked up to me. I was sitting at a table aboard the USS *Peleliu* in the center of the ship's galley—or in layman's terms, cafeteria.

Now that I had been promoted into what the Marines considers a non-commissioned officer position, I stood up to greet him as peers would. "Good morning, Sergeant. Thank you for taking the time to meet with me."

"Yeah," Sergeant Sanchez continued with some harmless sarcasm and laughter. "I made sure to open my schedule. Like I have a lot to do on this ship anyway. You know, I've seen you around on the ship, and a lot in the gym, but we never had a chance to talk. It's good to finally meet you."

It was 2006, and I had been transferred from the sniper team to the 81mm mortar platoon. Instead of being sent to Iraq or Afghanistan, our battalion was selected to deploy as a marine expeditionary unit (MEU). In short, that meant we would be sailing around the Pacific. We had been under way for a month and a half but now sailed in the direction of the Middle East. Another battalion was taking heavy losses in the second battle of Ramadi and was in desperate need of reinforcements. Therefore, we were weeks away from off-loading our battalion into Kuwait to stand by for entry into Iraq.

Sergeant Sanchez was part of the Marines special operations command (MARSOC). Every time our ship sat off the coast of a country, Sanchez and another sergeant, named Haskell, both of whom spoke multiple languages, would depart on a helicopter in civilian clothes with an M4 and sidearm—or sometimes just a sidearm. After a few days I would see them back on the ship in their regular marine getup. I was curious about their work.

Sergeant Sanchez continued, "So I heard part of your story . . . you know . . . getting dropped from BUD/S, being a part of the scout snipers for a bit, and shifting over to 81s. Listen, our unit is always looking for guys like you—fit and smart with diverse skills. We're not the SEALs, but we do have similar capabilities."

"Yeah, I'm open to hearing more about your unit," I said. "But I have to be up front. I'm more interested in what you and Sergeant Haskell do. I already know what marine special forces do. I get it, but what you guys do is completely different, and that's not hard to see."

"Well, we do HUMINT for our unit. And now that I think about it, you seem like a great candidate for it."

"Roger, but what's human? I mean, I know what a human is, but what do you mean by that?"

He laughed and then said, "Let's grab the corner table."

Oh, this is going to be good if we got to change tables for this dude to fill me in. We got up and moved.

As soon as we sat down, he continued, "It's HUMINT, not *human*."

"Sorry. I misunderstood. So it's an acronym?"

He answered, "Not quite. It's an abbreviation of *human* and *intelligence*."

"Got it. So what is it that you do?" I asked.

"We talk to locals who have information. Simply put, it's a form of intelligence gathering. Nothing fancy. We're not out there running around like James Bond, defusing nukes and kissing dames. We're just talking to people."

"Interesting. What kind of people do you talk to?" I asked.

"Good people, sometimes bad people . . . and everyone in between."

"I'm sorry for all the questions, but—"

"No need to apologize." He leaned back in his chair, grinning. "Exactly what you're doing is what we do."

"Roger. So no offense or disrespect intended by my next question, but you're a five-foot-eight Mexican, and Haskell is a six-foot-tall white guy. How do you blend in to talk with these people? I mean, depending on what country you're in, they could spot you a mile away."

"First off, no offense taken. Second, my parents are Panamanian, not Mexican. And third, you'd be surprised. If you can learn how to observe and connect with people, I've found that what's on the outside will quickly disappear. Listen, HM3, this is not a job that requires certain looks; this is a job that requires a brain." He tapped the side of his head. "What we do in some cases allows the door kickers to kick doors." He smiled and continued, "And when we feel like it, we kick doors with them. Best of both worlds."

Oh, that's dope! I thought. "This might be far-fetched, but can I go out with you guys sometime? I can run med support . . . just in case."

He laughed. "I can tell you know how to connect with people, but it doesn't work like that. First you got to get through SOF selection, and if you make it, then there's still HUMINT training that you have to qualify for and graduate from." He stood up. "Listen, I have to go, but seriously, you should consider joining marine special operations as a corpsman."

I knew what I wanted, and no program would change my mind, so I gave him a neutral response. "Roger that."

Before he walked away he turned back and whispered, "And between me and you, our offload date got pushed up. We'll be boots on the ground in Kuwait by next week. I'll see you around."

"Roger that, Sergeant."

As he walked away, I couldn't help but think I'd be a good fit for a job like his. I'd always had the ability to talk my way in and out of anything; some would say it was the gift of gab. It's like my environment prepared me for it. Sheesh, I was able to talk Mr. K into giving me an opportunity to change my grade the day before graduation.

I was sure the SEAL Teams had some kind of HUMINT-type program, and if they did, I vowed to get in.

• • •

We arrived in Camp Buehring in Kuwait in the spring of 2006. It was hot as hell, but I wasn't complaining. Compared to the last two months on the "floating prison," Camp Buehring was a paradise. For starters, the base was the size of a small city, so I could walk around freely or ride the bus instead of being confined within the walls of a ship, breathing recirculated air. Second, the food on base far surpassed the "for prison or government consumption only" food prepared by junior sailors and marines who weren't too happy about having to prepare food. And I'll just leave it at that. And third, the amenities were amazing. There was a massive gym that had everything I needed and more, and a USO center filled with video games, books, pool tables, and movie rooms. The base even had fast-food restaurants and a shopping center.

What made my new living arrangements even better was the added benefit of having a lot of time on our hands. Our platoon had mandatory training about once a week. Other than that, our only mission was to sit and wait for the call to cross over into Iraq. I made sure to take advantage of all the free time. I created a daily schedule and stuck to it. My mornings started out with a light pre-sunrise jog with my fifty-man platoon. After that was breakfast, followed by cards in the hooch. Once my morning breakfast had settled, I tried my best to boogie to the gym before I needed to use the facilities. I say that because the Porta-Potty was never fun to sit in when the heat index reached 115 degrees Fahrenheit, and one of the only places with actual bathrooms was the air-conditioned gym. After a two-hour workout, I ran back to the tent, showered in the mobile shower, then spent the rest of the day and night at the USO. That was my daily routine.

One day, while making my way to the USO, I noticed the battalion aid station LPO, HM1 Rosca, sitting at the bus stop.

"HM1, what's up, man? It's been a while." Rosca had also been promoted since we first met back at Camp Pendleton. Because of his rank, he was now attached to the headquarters element, so we rarely saw each other.

"Hey, Adeleke. I'm doing well! Where you headed?" Rosca asked.

"The usual: USO, then dinner, then back to the USO."

"I'm heading to the USO too. Mind if I walk with you? By the time the bus comes, we'll probably be halfway there anyway."

"Not a problem at all," I said.

As we made our way down the hot sidewalk, HM1 asked, "How's 81s going for you?"

"It's good, definitely an adjustment going from twenty marines in scout snipers to fifty here, but I can't complain. How's everything on your end?"

"Same, same. Just waiting for the word, like you. All will work out in its natural timing," he said in a serene manner.

HM1 always had this peaceful, Zen-like demeanor, as if nothing bothered him. I had always been intrigued by it but never had the confidence to ask him about it. Knowing that at any moment we could cross over the border into the chaos of war, I figured that now was my chance, at least while it was just him and me walking through the Kuwaiti heat.

"You know, HM1, there's something different about you that has always intrigued me. With all due respect, what's your deal?"

He chuckled, then said, "Well, I'm spiritual, Adeleke. I believe that everything happens for a reason, and everything works out just as it should, so there's no reason to get stressed-out or worried. Just let the universe be what it is and do what it does."

His answer made me more curious. "So how is it that you achieve this—I don't know what to call it—mind-set? Are there specific spiritual books that you read?"

"Yes, I read. But reading can only get you so far. Meditation is what helps me find the peace within me and the peace within the world."

"Meditation, huh?" I replied.

"If you're open to learning, I could spend time teaching you. No pressure. Whenever you're ready."

Then I asked what to me was the most important question: "This has nothing to do with church or God or the Bible or any of that stuff, right?"

"Only if you want it to."

"I would prefer that it didn't," I replied. The way I saw it, Christianity was a show put on by hypocrites. I didn't like being told that the way I was living was wrong by people who couldn't seem to get it right either.

For the next few weeks I met up with Rosca to discuss spirituality and learn from him as much as I could. He taught me about meditation, the concepts of enlightenment, energy, breathing techniques, and the art of compassion. I would scribble notes from his books regarding light and darkness, patience, creating peace within, and controlling one's energies. Once again, I was all in! I wish my friends could have seen me, a six-two black guy in marine fatigues, meditating like no one's business. It was an enlightening experience (no pun intended), and, in all honesty, it was good for me. I say that because for a long time I had fluctuated between atheism and agnosticism, to the point that I would scoff at the very things I was beginning to dabble in. But seeing how Rosca always had a sense of peace and calm, my mind opened to the possibility of living a spiritual life completely outside the walls of religion, which I despised.

Within days of learning my lessons, I would quickly get the chance to put my new superpowers to the test.

One day our platoon drove out to a mortar range to practice speed setup drills. It's simple: a three-to-four-man team races to a position, sets up the mortar, dials it into a target, launches a few rounds, breaks down the mortar as fast as they can, then moves to another position to continue the sequence.

Due to the fact that I was the only corpsman on my side of the range, I couldn't participate. Why? If I was blown up by a mortar tube, there wouldn't be another corpsman in the vicinity to care for the injured. So I stood about twenty feet off the line and watched.

During the entire exercise, a few private first classes (PFCs) struggled with the setups. As the struggling got worse, the NCOs laid into them. I always had a hard time watching someone get yelled at or harshly punished for reasons that, in my opinion, didn't warrant it, especially after what I went through with Trotter. I'm not saying the NCOs were wrong, because according to military edicts, they weren't. I'm just saying I didn't like the way they went about doing what they did.

Now, prior to my meditation training with HM1 Rosca, I was known for popping off on NCOs when I would witness this kind of treatment. After one incident all the PFCs and lance corporals pulled me aside and said, "Doc, you can't keep doing that. I know you're trying to help us, but this is part of the marine way. Let it be." So I tried my best to do so.

As the punishment and yelling continued on the range that day, I meditated and relaxed and put myself somewhere else. The funny thing was, it was working.

The NCOs were relentless.

"You're an idiot, PFC!"

"You boot moron!"

"You're as dumb as this mortar tube!"

It went on and on and on, but I just meditated. Then they started making the guys do push-ups in their gear, and it was close to 110 degrees. I stayed calm, and, to my surprise, I politely said, "Excuse me, Sergeant. I don't have enough IVs to treat [I pointed to the PFCs] all them potential heat injuries. Respectfully request that you cease physical remediation."

The sergeant looked at me as if to say, "Wow! This is a new doc," then said to the PFCs, "Recover! You boots are lucky Doc cares about you! Now, get back on your tubes!"

After the marines were back on their tubes, I said to myself in a monk-like voice, *See, Remi? Just be calm; keep meditating; relax like Rosca. See how everything is working out? The high road, though it may seem weaker, is stronger . . . hmm, hmm, hmm.*

The day continued, and the verbal filleting came and went in cycles. At about eight we wrapped up night shoots, loaded up into our Humvees, and made our way back to Camp Buchring. I was so proud of myself for not losing it like I had many other times. Then something happened that would, let's say, pull me back to the dark side.

We were riding in a two-door pickup truck–type Humvee. There were long benches on each side of the flatbed. I was sitting at the top right corner of the bench, right behind the cab. Across from me was Corporal E, to my left was Sergeant G, and the rest of the occupants were PFCs, some of whom hadn't done too well on the range.

As we drove down the dusty, unpaved road, Corporal E cursed one of the PFCs. It was like Satan himself possessed the guy. I continued to sit there in my Zen state, staring at the corporal but not staring at him. Then Corporal E pulled off his Kevlar helmet, stood up, took two steps toward the PFC, and started smacking the top of the PFC's helmet with his own.

As I watched this scene unfold, I couldn't hold it together anymore. I broke from my meditative state and looked at the sergeant as if to say, "You gonna keep letting this go on?" As the seconds passed, I could slowly feel the meditative calm withdrawing from me, and when it did, I started to tremble.

The corporal hit the PFC again and again and again. Finally I lost it. I stood up and yelled, "I swear to God, Corporal . . ." When he heard me, he froze with his helmet in the air. "If you hit that kid one more time, I'm going to kick your ass right out of this truck while it's moving! Try me! I swear, you'd better sit your ass down!" I was seeing red; I really was. A small part of me wanted him to hit the PFC one last time so I could show this guy how serious I was.

With his helmet still extended in the air, he looked at me, then looked at the kid, then looked back at me, then made his way back to his seat. I stayed standing, so when he passed me, I hovered over him until he sat down. Once he was in his seat, I took mine and breathed my way back into my meditative state.

I guess there are some things no meditation can help.

. . .

After three months of waiting for the call that never came, the battlespace commanders decided to let us load back up onto the USS *Pelelui* and head home. A part of me was sad that I didn't get to Iraq and see combat, but another part of me knew that if I survived one more deployment, I could go back to BUD/S.

On August 15, 2006, we reached the San Diego harbor. Two days later, like clockwork, I was back in the pool, swim-finning away. And a week after that I received a phone call that would change the trajectory of my life.

"Remi!" HM1 Rosca said. I'd never heard my meditation instructor so excited.

"Hey, what's up, HM1?" I replied.

"You're not going to believe this! I just received orders to the medical head-quarters of 1st Marine Division!"

Knowing how great a leader he was, I replied, "Oh, that's awesome! Congratulations, HM1. You deserve it! What are you going to do there?"

"I'll be your new command career counselor!" Now, let me explain the odds of that happening. Each battalion has about thirty corpsmen, and there are four battalions in each regiment. In 1st Marine Division alone, there are four regiments and nine specialized battalions (marine special forces, tanks, headquarters, engineers, and so on). That's about 750 corpsmen in 1st Marine Division. HM1 went from being in charge of thirty corpsmen to overseeing the careers of 750, and I just so happened to work under HM1 for the last year and a half. There were only two career counselor positions, so the odds of my LPO getting that position were superslim to none.

Understanding what that meant, I yelled, "Are you serious?!"

"Yup. Hey, you still have that return recommendation letter from BUD/S?"

"Can a politician lie? Yeah, I got it!"

"All I need you to do is finish the requirements to get your FMF pin in the next few weeks. Once that's done, I'll walk your BUD/S package right to the command master chief. With your FMF pin, your BUD/S recommendation letter, and my explanation of your work ethic over the last year, you'll have no problem getting released to go back to BUD/S. As a matter of fact, you'll probably be able to start the first half of next year!"

That meant no second deployment! No three-year tour!

"Wow! Thank you, HM1. Thank you, thank you, thank you!"

"Like I told you, Remi, everything works out just as it should. Now, get to work on that FMF pin!"

"Roger that, HM1!" I replied. I was so emotional, I could've cried after I got off the phone with Rosca, but I didn't have time! I needed to get to work!

CHAPTER NINETEEN

A ONE-WOMAN MAN

A dream requires faith, and faith requires action.

Again! I said to myself before taking off for another fin sprint. It was April 2007, and I only had a month and a half left before I checked out of Camp Pendleton and checked back in to BUD/S. HM1 Rosca fulfilled his part of the bargain. As soon as I passed the written test and practical applications required for my FMF pin, he walked my package straight to the command master chief and got me released. The only caveat was I had to sign a contract called a Page 13, which stated, "If HM3 Remi Adeleke does not complete BUD/S for any reason, he must return to 1st Marine Division, and conduct two deployments, and remain for a minimum of three years." Because I was almost twenty-five, and the cutoff age for BUD/S is twenty-eight, this would most likely be my last shot to make it through.

"Again!" I yelled as I did another sprint. There was no way I was going to squander my last opportunity to become a Navy SEAL.

"Again, Remi!"

To ensure success, I created a grueling swim workout that I conducted at the end of my distance swim routine. I would flutter kick on my back while raising my fins out of the water to create more resistance and sprint twenty-five meters to the west wall of the pool. Right before arriving at the west end, I would extend my right arm out, grab the wall, spin myself around, and slowly kick the twenty-five meters back to the east end. As I got closer to the east wall, I would extend my arm again, grab the wall, spin around, and repeat the same sequence while yelling, "Again!" In short, for twenty-five meters I gave 150 percent, and for the other twenty-five meters I had a slight rest; twenty-five meters raw power, twenty-five meters slight rest; twenty-five meters extreme discomfort, twenty-five meters slight rest.

I yelled, "Again!" The purpose of the exercise was to build up my leg strength in such a way that no tread or swim could cause me to get dropped again. I kicked and kicked and kicked until I felt pain, and when I felt pain, I kicked even harder!

"Again!" My voice echoed through the pool area.

When I reached the east wall and got ready to start my next sprint, I felt a quick tap on my shoulder, which prompted me to look up. It was my neighbor Tom Cotter. He'd been yelling my name, but I couldn't hear his voice because I was so locked into the zone. Tommy was a forty-five-year-old triathlete and marathoner, a great guy from Boston. We sometimes swam together, and sometimes he just came around the pool to give me pointers.

In his Bostonian accent he said, "I see you're killing yourself again, Johnny." Johnny was another one of many nicknames I had acquired over the years.

Winded from my last sprint, I huffed and puffed between words, "Yeah . . . can never be . . . too sure! How's the old lady?"

"She's good . . . you know, traveling as usual."

"Good . . . tell her I said hello the next time you talk," I replied.

"I will. You gonna make it down to the restaurant this weekend?"

Tommy was a senior bartender at an upscale restaurant in the Gaslamp, called Blue Point. The past few months I had stayed away from the clubs, keeping my weekends light and easy. But when I did head downtown, I was right at Tommy's bar, sucking down tuna poke and Scottish salmon. It was a good replacement for me because I didn't drink alcohol. I just talked with Tommy or watched a game, and when it was all said and done, I was in bed by 10:00 p.m.

"Yeah . . . I think I'll try to make it," I replied.

"Good. Don't let me hold you up. Get back to your swim."

As I climbed out of the pool, I said, "No, no, I'm good. I was at the end anyway. My roommate is at work, and his girlfriend is at the apartment. Her friend is about to pick her up, so I need to head back so I can lock up before they leave."

"How is the new roommate situation anyway? You guys still running girls in and out of there like a revolving door?"

I chuckled as I dried off. "It's good. No differences. He's a solid guy, just like Keller. And yes, the revolving door is still functioning well."

My new roommate was also a doc at Battalion 1/4. After we got back from deployment, he was stationed at Balboa Hospital, which worked out perfectly, timing-wise, since Keller was on his way out. To my surprise, as well as to that of the rest of our friends, Keller decided to settle down and move in with his girlfriend. No one thought he would last in a committed relationship, but they're married to this day. The player days had finally ended for the old man. I, on the other hand, still struggled with the concept of committing to one woman.

Tom continued, "That's good, Johnny. I mean, the roommate situation. Well, I'll see you this weekend, huh?"

"Yeah, yeah. I'll see ya," I replied.

After Tommy departed, I finished drying off, threw on my shirt, collected my swim gear, and headed to the apartment. When I got to my door, I could hear what sounded like two female voices inside. *Nia's friend must have arrived*, I thought. I slowly made my way in. Upon entry I could see the back of a woman's head as she sat on the couch. Nia was on the other side of the kitchen island, talking to her.

"Hey, Remi," Nia said.

"Hey," I replied.

Nia said, "Cecilia, this is Remi."

Cecilia got up and turned to face me. "Hi, Remi."

I swear, when she spoke to me, it was like angels started playing harps, my ceiling opened up, and the sun came down and shined upon her. I was immediately attracted to her, to the point where I felt nervous. It wasn't a lustful type of attraction, where I wanted to rip off her clothes and have sex—no, I just wanted to be in her presence.

"H-Hi," I said nervously before stepping closer to shake her hand. She was beautiful: Filipino, golden brown skin, about five one, a bit tomboyish mixed with a lot of hipster and geek; clearly, she was different. She had a strong voice—not deep, just strong—not the type you would expect from a woman of her petite stature. She. Was. *Different!*

"You have a nice apartment. I like the way it's set up," she said.

"Thank you. Yeah, I try to keep it modern." Searching for words, I continued, "Organized . . . you know . . . Zen-like."

Nia jumped in. "Um . . . we should go. We got a lot of things to do." Looking intently at Cecilia, Nia added, "Remember?"

I wanted to ask Cecilia for her number, but I was so entranced that I didn't know how. "Um . . . yeah . . . so . . . have a good day. And . . . so nice to meet you. It's so nice to meet you."

She leaned in to hug me and said, "Nice to meet you, too, Remi."

Oh my goodness, hearing her say my name made my heart melt. Then just like that, they left. And when they did, the angels stopped playing their harps, the sun moved back into its usual position, and my ceiling closed up.

As soon as the door was shut, I ran through the apartment to find my cell phone. When I found it, I rolled through my contacts to find my roommate, Patrick, and hit Call. His phone just rang and rang. When his voicemail came on, I said, "Yo, Patrick, you have to give me a call ASAP! A-S-A-P! Call me!"

I put down my phone and paced. "That's the one! I will stay faithful to her! I will marry that girl. Come on, Patrick. Call me back, man!" I was preaching to my phone like it was Cecilia's dad.

About thirty minutes later my phone finally rang; it was Patrick. I didn't even say hello.

"Yo, Patrick, listen to me. Your girl was just over here with her friend Cecilia. I like that girl, man! I really like that girl! I need you to do me a favor and hit up Nia. Ask her if she would be cool with . . . I don't know . . . asking Cecilia if I can have her number."

"No need," he replied.

"What? She got a man or something?"

"No, her boyfriend broke up with her a month ago. No need because Nia called me fifteen minutes ago and asked if I would give Cecilia your number."

"What?!" I yelled through the phone.

"Yeah. Nia said Cecilia thinks you're cute . . . for whatever that's worth."

"Well, *yes*! Give . . . give her my number, okay? And get Cecilia's number so I can have hers too."

"Roger," he replied.

When we hung up, I said, "I'm *done*! I'm done with all the player stuff! Keller, baby, I'm right behind you, dog!"

• • •

Two days after meeting Cecilia, we went on our first date. There was a sushi place across the street from the apartment complex that was often empty in the daytime. So that's what I chose. I wanted to be somewhere where it could just be me and her, no distractions, no noise, just us.

It was probably the best date I had ever been on to that point in my life, because for the first time, I wasn't talking just to get into a woman's panties. I was talking because I genuinely wanted to get to know her.

"So you're beautiful, you're artsy, you're getting your MBA, and you're a web designer? Is there anything you can't do?" I asked.

She laughed and said, "Hmm . . . I'm trying to think. . . . Nope."

"I believe you," I said with a chuckle.

"I'm just kidding, Remi."

"Oh, and you're funny too."

"I can do push-ups," she said as she turned to the side to flex one of her triceps muscles.

"Dang! You're ripped too! Can you do more than me?" I asked.

"Yeah, dude. I grew up with two brothers and a dad who was in the Navy."

"Prove it!" I said. She turned out of her seat as if she was getting ready to get on the floor and do push-ups, but I quickly stopped her. "I'm just kidding, I'm just kidding."

"So . . . are you looking forward to going back to BUD/S?" she asked. We had been in the restaurant for more than an hour, and it wasn't until she asked the question that I realized how powerful her presence was to me. I had completely forgotten about BUD/S until she brought it up. In fact, I think I had forgotten about everything else too. The only thing that mattered to me for that period of time was her.

I answered, "Yeah . . . I am. I trained hard before I went the first time, but not as hard as I've trained this time. I know I'll be fine."

She looked me in the eye and said, "You're going to make it, Remi. I believe in you."

I love you, I thought, and then I paused and said, "I like you, Cecilia. . . . I really do. I don't ever open up to women like this, especially this quick. And I'm not saying what I'm about to say because I want something from you. . . . I'm saying it because I mean it. Since Friday I haven't been able to get you out of my mind."

"Remi, I like you too . . . but . . . I just got out of a relationship, and I still need time to heal."

"I totally understand. Take your time. We'll just hang out as friends. I'm fine with that. I just wanted you to know how I feel." In any other situation I would have pushed, but I saw her as delicate, and I was willing to wait however long I needed to wait to be with her.

"Thank you, Remi."

"You're welcome."

Probably sensing the need to change topics, she asked, "You go to church?"

"Church? Me, no. I'm not religious. But there's a meditation group I go to once a week in La Jolla. It's cool. We meditate, talk a little bit about spirituality, and encourage one another. Helps me stay calm, you know."

"That's cool. Well, I go to a great church, and it's really helped me a lot over the past few weeks. No pressure, but if you ever want to go, maybe we can go together."

My meditation group had helped shave off some of my rough edges as it related to being open about faith. So between that and my willingness—if necessary—to walk to hell and back with her, I said, "You know what? Wherever you go, I'll go."

"It's a date. So we'll go next Sunday."

Damn, this woman moves fast! "Uh . . . okay . . . I guess."

• • •

The next Sunday we pulled up to Cornerstone Church in my Infiniti G35 with personalized SUPA DOC plates. The building was under construction, so the members met in a large white tent. I felt so awkward walking in. The last time I was in church was for my grandmother's memorial service in 2002.

If God is real, I wouldn't be surprised if a bolt of lightning fell from the sky and lit me up, I said to myself as I shuffled in among the crowd.

"Where do you want to sit?" she asked.

"I don't care; you choose."

"All right." She walked us to a seat that was near the front.

Come on, girl. The front? I thought as I looked at her.

My face said it all. She replied, "You said pick."

As soon as the music started, everyone stood up and started clapping. I stood motionless, staring at those in front of me, inwardly mocking them. *Look at these idiots with their eyes closed and hands in the air. Who are they praying to? No imaginary god is going to come down and sprinkle success into your hands; you got to go out and get it yourself. You are all so weak-minded, so lazy, so gullible.* But when I turned to my right and saw Cecilia with her hands raised, eyes closed, and tears rolling down her cheeks—to me that was beautiful. To me that was real! For half a moment I thought, *Maybe one day*, but then a deacon came onstage and started asking for money, which quickly snapped me back to my senses.

After the service ended, she asked, "So what did you think?" I just looked at her and smiled. "Was it that bad?"

"No . . . it's just . . . it's just not my thing. But if you want me to come again, I'll come."

She punched me in the shoulder and said, "You're funny, Remi."

"Oh, is *that* what Jesus would do?" I replied sarcastically.

. . .

About a week before BUD/S started, Cecilia called me up in an unusual mood.

"What's wrong?" I asked her. "Everything okay?"

In a somber tone she said, "I like you, Remi, I really do, but I can't talk to you anymore."

"Did I do something wrong? I'm sorry if I did!" I was surprised. I hadn't even tried to have sex with her or anyone else. I was faithful to a friend!

"No, it's not you. . . . It's my ex, Grant. He wants to try to give it another shot. Listen, I can't throw that away, Remi. We've had five years together. . . . We own a condo together. Knowing how I feel about you . . . and how you feel about me . . . it wouldn't be fair to you *or* Grant if we kept hanging out. I'm not that type of girl."

"I respect that, Cecilia. And, hey, we're just friends anyway, right?"

"Yeah. I got to go, Remi. Take care of yourself. And kick ass in BUD/S, or I'm gonna kick your ass, all right?"

"Yeah, I will. Take care, Cecilia."

We had spent three weeks together. The girl even got me to go to church three weeks in a row, so I would be lying if I said I wasn't a bit hurt. I was. But the reality was, she was a loyal girl, and she had a valid point; five years is hard to give up for just a month. I really liked her, but I decided it was probably for the best. I couldn't focus on her. I had to let go and focus on what was in front of me—my last shot at BUD/S.

CHAPTER TWENTY

LAST CHANCE

A failure is only a failure if you don't learn from it.

If you lean on the f***ing log again, I'll kick your ass off! Do you hear me?!"

That wasn't a BUD/S instructor yelling at a student; it was me! Our class, 266, was on our second day of First Phase. The evolution at hand was circle of death by way of log PT. Circle of death consisted of each seven-man boat crew chest carrying a two-hundred-pound, twelve-foot log over the twelve-foot sand berm, then up the beach for about two hundred yards, back over the sand berm, and down the beach about two hundred yards. It was a nonstop circle, and it was painful for everyone. Now, seven men carrying two hundred pounds may not sound bad, but after already doing two hours of overhead holds, chest-carry lunges and squats, and eight-count body builders, just starting circle of death was enough to break the hardest man.

Ding, ding, ding! That was the sixth person gone since the start of log PT, and I was trying to get the seventh.

"You need to go quit, Jacks!" I yelled. He didn't respond; he just straightened his back a little and kept up the thousand-yard stare. I had seen that look many times before. I knew he wanted to quit, but he also didn't want to, and we were all suffering for it. Instead of carrying his portion of the weight, Jacks was leaning on the log for support.

Crabtree chimed in. "Go. Away. Jacks!" Like me, after passing his runs in rollback land, Crabtree classed up with 253, failed two runs, and was dropped. Fate would have it that we'd returned at the same time and ended up in the same boat crew. Crabtree continued, "You're worthless!"

Instructors had been observing Jacks's performance the entire evolution. He had already been given a glucose test, which he passed with flying colors, and it was too hot for him to be hypothermic. Having had the experience of being sick without the instructors' knowledge, I even asked him, "Are you sick? Is there something going on? If it is, I understand, and we'll carry your weight!"

"No . . . I'm fine," he muttered despondently.

Right before starting our twentieth ascent up the berm, Instructor M stopped us. "Prepare to down log! Down log!" We slowly placed the log down, not daring to commit the mortal sin of dropping it. Instructor M said, "Adeleke, walk with me." I followed him a few feet away from the log and my boat crew.

"You're the boat crew leader, right?"

"Hooyah!" I replied.

"What's going on with Jacks?" He already knew the answer, so I knew this was both an integrity and a leadership test.

I was so fired up, I responded, "He sucks! He barely had his hands on the log during our timed overhead drills. The only position I can keep him in is in the middle of the log because he can't hold the weight when he's on the ends. He keeps making the log heavier by leaning on it while we're at chest carry. He sucks, but he won't quit!"

Instructor M asked, "If I pull him off the log for this next lap, you think you and your boat crew can get to the front? You'll be a man down, but you think you can do it?"

"Hooyah! We can do it!" I replied confidently.

"All right. Once the class gets past you on this lap, I'll put you guys at the . . ." He paused to think about it. "You know what, I'll be fair. I'll put you ahead of the last two boat crews. Let's see what you can do minus Jacks."

"Hooyah!" I replied.

"Get back on your log."

As I ran back to my log, I heard Instructor M yell, "Jacks! You're sitting this one out! As a matter of fact, I want you to walk to the top of the berm and watch your boat crew do this entire next lap!"

"Hooyah!" Jacks replied as he scurried to the top of the berm.

I knew it was going to be a challenge. We had lost a good number of guys on the first day, but there were still eighteen boat crews left. That meant we would be starting in sixteenth place and would have to work our way around each crew.

When I got to my boat crew, I quickly briefed them on the plan. After the brief we picked up the log as smoothly and quickly as possible, held it to our chests, then eagerly stood by for Instructor M's command to start.

Like a caged lion about to be loosed on a sleeping gazelle, I said, "Come on, boys. We're going to crush this!"

Instructor M pointed at us and said, "Boat crew two! Stand by!" Then there was a three-second pause before he said, "Bust 'em!"

We took off up the berm. I had my boat crew recite my mantra the entire way up—"Drive, drive, drive, drive!" When we were on our way down the berm, we had already passed two boat crews. Then we turned left to head south. At this point we were all screaming different things to motivate each other.

Thirteenth place, twelfth place, eleventh place, tenth, ninth, eighth. By the time we got to the turn for the second berm, we were already in seventh. I yelled to the guys, "Go wide on the turn. Let's not get stuck behind anyone! Wide!" We did a wide turn with the log still at our chests, then jogged as fast as we could up the berm while the other boat crews walked. "Drive, drive, drive, drive!"

By the time we got down the other side of the berm and turned left to head north back to the starting point, we were in fifth place. "All right, boys! Let's run it in the rest of the way! On me . . . three, two, one . . . go!" My six-man team ran past the remaining boat crews, and before we knew it, we were in first place.

"HOOYAH!" we all yelled in unison after we crossed the finish line, which was where we started.

Instructor M didn't even have to say anything to Jacks. He just looked at the student for a second and shook his head. Jacks responded by dropping his head, then slowly walking to the bell as we watched. *Ding, ding, ding!* Just like that, he was gone. I guess it took him actually seeing how much he was hurting us for him to realize he needed to quit.

Instructor M yelled, "Adeleke!"

"Hooyah, Instructor M," I replied.

"It pays to be a winner, right?"

"Hooyah!"

"You guys are done with log PT for the day. Stow your log and get your boat crew off the beach."

Full of excitement, we all yelled, "HOOYAH!"

As we turned to walk to the log stowage area, Instructor M stopped us and said, "Boat crew two! Make sure you hydrate. The conditioning run is next!"

"HOOYAH!" we all said again.

As commanded, we stowed our log, ran off the beach, and waited by the medical benches for the rest of the class to finish circle of death.

That was the way it was for me during my third pass through BUD/S First Phase. I didn't just want to make it through; I wanted to absolutely obliterate anything and everything that crossed my path. For the next eight weeks, I passed everything again, except for . . . well, I'll get to that later. I passed knot tying, drownproofing, the fifty-meter underwater swim, lifesaving, timed runs, obstacle courses, and water works. I endured surf tortures, beatdowns, the seven stages of hell, grinder PTs, surf passage, and boats on heads. And just like my first two First Phases, I watched a plethora of guys quit while I still stood tall.

I'm sure if you have gotten this far in the book, your question is, "What about swims?" Well, here's my report: by the time I got to the last week of First Phase, I had passed *everything*, except for one . . . out of six swims. That's right; I had overcome my nemesis. I took all my swim failures from the past and turned them into lessons. And now those lessons were leading to successes.

When it came to my third Hell Week, I felt like a Viking! My only incident was, once again, a low-glucose collapse toward the end of base tour. I face-planted, got juiced up with glucose gel, then kept moving like the Terminator. And this time, when we got to Friday of Hell Week, I didn't have to wonder when it ended. I knew it was over when they told us to face the ocean and "lock arms!" When the command came, I stared off into the horizon with a smile and a thought: *I wish Cecilia was around to celebrate with me; but wherever she is, I hope she's happy.*

. . .

"Remi, you are crazy, dude!" Oscar said. Then pointing to a girl across the room, he asked, "Is that her?"

"Does it look like her?" I replied.

He shoved in around the other guys to get a closer look at the video playing on my phone. "No way; it is her! Dude, you're nuts!" he said.

The day 266 graduated from First Phase into Second Phase just happened to be my twenty-fifth birthday, so I threw a class party at my complex clubhouse. I invited Cecilia, but she never responded to my text. Oscar was referring to a different girl, a girl named Trish, who happened to be my neighbor and who didn't mind doing rather salacious things on camera.

Oscar tapped me and said, "Dude, she's looking over here!"

I replied, "So? She's not gonna do anything. Trust me: she's not ashamed; otherwise, she wouldn't have put it on camera." With Cecilia out of the picture, I was back to my hedonistic ways. Among other things, I was hooking up with girls and then discarding them or reusing them as I pleased. I was beginning to slip back out of control as I always did when things started going well.

Without me realizing it, Trish had made her way over to me. "Hi, Remi."

I responded nonchalantly without moving the phone. "Hey, Trish."

"What are you looking at?" she asked as if she already knew.

"Nothing, just going through some military photos."

"Really?" she asked.

"Yeah, really."

She responded as if she was convinced I was lying but couldn't do anything about it. "Okay!"

To add insult to injury, I said in front of the guys, "You know it's my birthday. . . . Imma see you later tonight, right?"

She rolled her eyes, stuck up her middle finger, then turned and walked away.

"Remi!" That was all Oscar could say. I didn't know if he felt bad for her or was impressed with me.

As I watched her walk away, I said, "Like I said, she's not going to do anything. Just like the rest of them, she knows how I am."

· · ·

Instructor C briefed us on the CTT pool deck.

"You will tread water with your *full* dive load for five minutes. At no time during the five minutes will your hands touch the water. If they do, you will fail!" I looked around and noticed some guys who were just as nervous as Keller and I had been when we first took the test. But I wasn't at all. I was so confident I would pass.

Instructor C, the only Second Phase instructor who'd been around during my first BUD/S stay, walked past me down the line. "After we call *time*, you will swim twenty-five meters to the north end on your stomach, touch the wall, then swim twenty-five meters back to the south end on your back. It is the only time when you can use your arms and hands. In the unlikely event that you make it back, you will have passed. Everyone passed ditch and don, so let's keep on the positive track! I don't want to hear any bitching or moaning . . . or any of those orgasmic sounds you clowns tend to make during this evolution!"

"HOOYAH!" we all said.

Then Senior Chief B asked, "Who wants to be in the first group that goes?"

Before anyone could answer, Instructor C ran back up the line and pointed at me. "Adeleke is going to go first!" he said with a smile and a laugh. "I want to see him fail again so he can go back to the regular Navy!"

I looked at him as if to say, "Seriously?"

He looked back at me and said, "Yes, I'm serious! Get jocked the f*** up and get ready to get in the water."

I said, "Roger that." But I continued to myself, *I can't believe this dude is trying to play me after all I went through . . . like imma come back here unprepared. Okay, imma show his ass.*

I put on my weight belt, pointed to a set of twin-80s for my dive buddy to pick up, and grabbed my fins. Because of the weight of the twin-80s, he held them up so the straps were at my shoulder level. I slipped my arms through, and he gently released the weight onto my shoulders.

I started working on my straps. Now, the strap settings are important. If the straps are too tight, it can make the tread harder. If the straps are too loose, the tanks will flop all over the place, adding extra discomfort or even separating from the diver.

I stood about eight feet from the pool and worked on my straps, trying to get them in the perfect position. While I was in the process of fixing my straps, Instructor C walked up to me and commanded, "Get up to the edge of the pool, Adeleke."

"Hooyah, just one second, I'm trying to fix my straps."

"I said now! Your time's up! What? . . . You're just scared because you're going to fail again, huh?"

"Negative. I'm good. . . . Imma pass . . ." As I kept working on the straps, I walked up to the edge of the pool with my fins. "I'm . . . I . . . just need to get these straps right."

As I stood at the edge still working on my straps, Instructor C completely ignored my request and yelled, "Prepare to enter the water!"

I cursed him under my breath.

"Enter the water!" I had no choice but to jump in.

As soon as I jumped in, the weight of the gear pulled me under. With my hands extended above my head, I kicked my way up. And as soon as my mouth broke the surface, I started my breathing rhythm.

Instructor C said, "I'll start the clock as soon as everyone's hands are out of the water!" Within seconds of the command, everyone's hands were in the air, and the clock started.

I did wide, slow flutter kicks. After two minutes passed, I felt exactly as I had the first five seconds; I wasn't winded or fatigued in any way. My sprint exercise that I created had worked! My hip and quad muscles were so strong that I didn't struggle at all. As a matter of fact, while I was kicking, I stared at Instructor C. *Now what you got to say? The worst thing you could have done was doubted me!* The surprised look on his face gave me even more motivation. It was almost as though he couldn't believe what he was seeing. Three minutes passed, then three minutes and thirty seconds. I was so happy because I knew I was going to pass, which meant to me that I was going to be a SEAL.

But then, as always in my life, something began to go wrong. Because I didn't get a chance to properly fix my straps, they started to come loose. Because of the space opening up between my back and the tanks, the tanks began to flop. It made the tread a bit harder, but I was still managing.

Instructor C yelled, "Time! Swim down on your stomachs!"

I had never gotten this far. Based on what I had experienced with the tread the last time, I expected the swim to be easy, but it wasn't. It was like swimming with a drunk fat kid on my back. To make matters worse, my right strap was starting to come off. *Come on, Remi; you can't fail this.*

Then, just like that, my right strap popped off and somehow—probably due to the commotion in the water—got wrapped around my neck. So now I was swim-dragging my tanks with one loose strap on my left shoulder and the other strap around my neck. But I didn't care, I was determined to get to the end.

As soon as I got to the wall, I slapped it in frustration, knowing that when I turned on my back, the weight from the tanks was probably going to cause the straps to come off completely. To my surprise, the strap around my neck fell off, but the strap around my shoulder stayed on.

Okay, you can still pass this! You just have to get back to the start. I kicked as hard as I could to get there as fast as I could, but when I was halfway back, my left strap came off, and my tanks slowly sank to the bottom of the pool. At that point I knew I had failed.

I swam to the edge where I started, then climbed out. I was furious!

"What happened, Adeleke?" Senior Chief said. "You passed . . . but technically, you didn't."

When I heard "you didn't," I looked in Instructor C's direction and lost it. "I told Instructor C I needed to fix my straps! I told his ass!"

"Whoa, whoa, Adeleke! Drop the f*** down! You don't talk to an instructor like that!" Senior Chief pointed to the ground.

I immediately got in the push-up position, which was the best position for me to be in at the moment. I stared at the ground, shook my head, and muttered, "I told him . . . I told him. This is my life, man, and this dude is playing with it like it's a game. This ain't no game."

Senior Chief squatted down beside me and said, "You need to calm down. If you can't keep your cool here, how can I trust you to keep your cool out on the battlefield? You'll get another chance tomorrow, Adeleke."

With water dripping from my head, I replied softly, "Hooyah."

Then Senior Chief commanded, "Recover." I stood back to my feet.

My luck didn't get any better the next day. After passing night ditch and don, I quickly geared up, ensuring I had enough time to properly fix my straps.

"Prepare to enter the water! Enter the water!"

I jumped in, confident that I was going to pass. I successfully treaded water for five minutes again, then made the swim down on my stomach. On my swim back, I was staring up in the sky as I passed the diving board at the center of the pool, then everything went black.

Due to an abnormal O_2 to CO_2 ratio in the blood that treading sometimes created, I had a shallow-water blackout. I later found out that it took three instructors to swim my dive gear and me back to the surface.

When I finally came to, Senior Chief stared down at me and said, "Adeleke! Good news, you're still alive. Bad news, you failed again."

Are you kidding me? I thought.

At the end of the day, all the students who failed the tread were ordered to the BUD/S quarterdeck conference room for a board. The last time I was in that room, I was performance dropped and sent back to Camp Pendleton. I knew that wasn't going to happen today, but still, I didn't want to be anywhere near that place.

The Second Phase OIC opened up the board. "So you're all here because you failed to meet the minimum standard for the tread . . . twice. This board is more of a warning than it is a final decision. If you fail the next two treads, you will stand before us in your dress uniform [he scanned all twenty of us] and we will determine whether you will be performance dropped or performance rolled. My advice to you . . . don't leave your fate in our hands. Go out there tomorrow and make the decision to continue with the rest of your class."

Then Senior Chief went down the row of students, asking each one of us if we had attended the optional weekend training.

When he got to me, I said, "Hooyah." That's right. This time my weekends weren't for partying, just for rest and any optional training offered. I had learned my lesson.

After all the instructors said their piece, all the students were dismissed, except for me.

Senior Chief said, "Adeleke, you've had some bad luck, haven't you?"

"Hooyah," I replied.

"Listen, dude: we know you can do this. You pretty much passed twice, okay? But pretty much is not the standard here, and we can't let you go on until you meet the standard. So just go out there tomorrow and get it over with so we can continue with training, okay?"

"Hooyah, Senior Chief," I replied.

"Dismissed!"

The next day I passed the buddy gear exchange test with ease. Afterward I went straight to the passing area, sat down, faced the fence, and focused on meditating and breathing. I had been so confident before the last two treads that I didn't do anything my spiritual teachers had taught me. I whispered to myself, "Calm, Remi. In and out, in and out." I cleared all the negativity and noise out of my mind. I searched for the peace within. When I found it, I stood up, had my dive buddy help me don my tanks, and waited for the evolution to start.

"Prepare to enter the water!" Senior Chief commanded.

You are one with the water. You are one with each inhale and each exhale. Peace among the chaos, I declare. I was in the zone, stone-cold focused, jaw clenched, and body still.

"Enter the water!"

As soon as I hit the water, I popped back to the top. I decided to keep my eyes closed this time to center my senses within.

Everything that I had been taught was working. The five-minute tread felt like two minutes.

"Time! Start your swim on your stomach!" Upon the command I opened my eyes and turned around with my hands still in the air. Once I saw my target, I slowly dipped my hands in the water to begin the swim.

Even though I was past the hardest part of the test, I didn't let go of my meditative state. I breathed in cadence with my mantra, "Peace . . . peace . . . peace." I made it to the wall, spun around, kicked off, and started my flutter kick on my back.

As I stared into the sky, I couldn't help but think of my pool-sprint workouts. I did those workouts when it was cold, when it was raining, when the pool area was packed, and when it was empty. I did it when I didn't want to do it, and I did it after long drives back from Camp Pendleton. I was staring at the same sky I had stared at on so many days and nights. It was a full-circle event, and for the first time since starting BUD/S, I finally felt gratitude to the universe for all that I had to go through to get back to this point. *Thank you for making me do this tread three times. Now I understand why. I wouldn't have appreciated my journey if I had passed this the first time. Thank you.*

When I touched the starting wall, I peacefully climbed out of the pool as if nothing had happened. The calm that I had derived from my meditation was still lingering.

Senior Chief yelled, "Adeleke! Pass! It's about damn time! Now drop down for taking so long to pass the tread!"

"Hooyah!" With the tanks still on my back, I dropped to the push-up position.

This time, as I stared at the ground with water dripping from my body, I knew it was over. I knew that despite having six more weeks of dive training and eight weeks of Third Phase (land navigation, weapons, demolition, and tactics), nothing was going to stop me. I was going to graduate!

"Recover, Adeleke!"

CHAPTER TWENTY-ONE

LOVE AND CHAOS

There's always *something*.

After Master Chief finished his speech, the command officer (CO) of BUD/S walked up to the podium to deliver what would be our final address as students.

"Class 267. You have run 806 miles. You have swum 77 miles. You have paddled a boat for more than 19 hours. You have run the obstacle course 29 times. You have spent 35 hours diving underwater. You have done 126 hours of physical training. You have shot 3,000 rounds of ammunition. You have treaded water for 5 minutes with all your dive gear. You have held your breath for 50 meters underwater, and you have completed the most demanding training week in the United States military, Hell Week. If you're standing here today, that means you have met the requirements I just listed, and the many other requirements necessary to graduate BUD/S."

If you're wondering why he referred to Class 267, it's because I was rolled out of 266 at the end of Third Phase. But that was irrelevant at that point. I was there, at the private ceremony for instructors and students only. The big ceremony with family and friends would take place after we checked the boxes on the following qualifications: static line jump school, skydiving, SERE (survival, evasion, resistance, and escape) training, cold-weather survival, CQC (close-quarters combat), land warfare, and advanced diving. At these schools we would be treated like SEALs and no longer like tadpoles. When finished, we would check in to our respective SEAL Teams.

As the graduating members of Class 267 stood on the BUD/S grinder, the CO continued his speech. "This is a feat only a fraction of Navy sailors ever achieve. I want you all to be proud of yourselves . . . but remember to always keep a healthy measure of humility." Then he nodded in a way to elicit a response from us.

We snapped to attention and said "HOOYAH!" in unison, then snapped back to parade rest.

"When I hand you your certificates, you will no longer be referred to as students but as your new Navy rates: SO, special operators. This is the only rate that Navy SEALs now wear, so wear it with pride, boys. And welcome to the brotherhood!"

As I stood in the same place where I had faced adversity many times, I couldn't help but be filled with pride. Many people had told me I wouldn't make it; many people had scoffed behind my back because I couldn't swim or didn't have the academic scores, or because I was performance dropped the first time; but there I was, defying the odds once again.

The CO continued, "When I call your names, make your way up, grab your certificate, and then"—he pointed to the instructors lined up on the south side of the grinder—"I want you to shake the hand of each one of those men, who molded you all into what you are today."

Again we snapped to attention and said, "HOOYAH!" But this time we stayed at attention.

As usual my name was called first. "SO3 Adeleke!"

I marched forward in a straight line. After nine feet I did a military left-face turn, walked in front of the CO, then stopped, did a military right-face turn to face him, then rendered a salute with my right hand. The CO rendered a salute back. I dropped my right hand and shook his while he placed my graduation certificate in my left hand, "Congratulations, SO3 Adeleke. Job well done."

I replied, "Thank you, sir," then marched to the line of instructors and shook each one of their hands.

The icing on the cake was when I made my way back to my starting position. Staring right at me was the sign that read, Be Someone Special.

I did it, Aunt Dokey . . . I did it. Not only did I become someone special, but now "Special" is part of my name: Special Operator 3rd Class Remi Adeleke.

• • •

When life couldn't get any better for me, guess what? It did! One night, while I was sitting on my couch watching TV, Patrick walked out of his bedroom with his phone in his hand and said, "It's Nia. She said she needs to talk to you."

I scooted up on the couch, took the phone out of Pat's hand, and said, "What's up, Nia? Everything okay?"

"Remi, I need you to listen to me. Cecilia is my friend . . . she's a good friend . . . and I just want the best for her."

"O . . . kay . . . What did I do? I didn't do anything," I replied.

"I'm not saying you did anything. I'm just trying to prepare you." Nia sighed and said, "Grant broke up with her again."

Yes! I thought. "When?" I said.

"A month ago, but that's not why I'm calling you. I need you to understand something. She never stopped loving you, Remi." *She loved me*, I thought. "She went back and forth in her mind, but she stayed with Grant because that's just who she is. It's hard for her to give up on people even when they've already given up on her."

As Nia continued, I said to myself, *O . . . kay . . . and why am I getting preached at right now?* "So what is it you want me to do, Nia? Or . . . what are you asking me?"

"Cecilia loves you so much, Remi!" I could hear the intensity in her voice. "So when she calls you tonight . . . and asks you if you want to go to dinner tomorrow night . . . and you say yes . . . and after dinner, when weeks have passed and you two are in a relationship . . . I'm asking you . . . please don't break her heart like it's been broken before!"

I sat there, silent, and scratched my head. I knew I loved Cecilia, but I just needed a second to process everything.

"Remi! Did you hear what I said?" Nia asked.

I replied softly, "I love her, Nia. And I promise I won't break her heart."

"Thank you. You can expect a call from her in the next hour. Good night, Remi."

I replied, "Good night, Nia," then slowly handed Patrick his phone.

• • •

The next night—just as Nia had predicted—Cecilia and I were sitting across from each other at a dinner table. We immediately reconnected. It felt like our last seven months apart were cut out of time, and that night was sewn together with our last meeting.

"Then . . . what . . . happened?" She was laughing so hard she almost couldn't ask the question.

"That's not funny!" I said. "I thought my feet were going to have to get amputated. I couldn't feel them! I'm serious! So I woke up the classmate closest to me—who was also covered in snow, by the way—and I begged him to rub my right foot while I rubbed the other one."

She was still laughing. "And you're admitting that to me? I wish I could have seen that!"

"Listen, there's no shame in my game. It was the middle of the night, we were on the side of a dang hill . . . in the freakin' . . . Laguna Mountains, and I was freezing! I bet you would have done the same thing!"

"Hmm, I don't know about that." She chuckled, looked down for a second, then looked back up at me and softly said, "I thought about you a lot the last seven months, Remi."

"I thought about you a lot, too, Cecilia . . . a lot."

"I'm sorry I jumped into your life and then out of it like that. I should have—"

"No . . . you don't need to apologize to me. It was a crazy time for both of us. Everything worked out just the way it should've. Look at us now. We're here . . . together."

She replied, "You know, you always knew the right thing to say at just the right time."

I could see she was getting a little emotional, so I thought it would be the right time to reassure her of how I felt. "I love you, Cecilia. I've loved you since I first saw you."

She moved her hand across the table, grabbed my hand, and said, "I love you, too, Remi."

We didn't need to ask, "So are we in a relationship now?" That moment said it all. I was her man, and she was my girl. And as any smart woman who just entered a relationship would do, she started laying down the law.

"I need you to know something. I know you've had a hard life, Remi . . .

and I know the journey ahead won't be easy, but I accept that. And I will support you through all the difficulties you'll face. I got your back." Then the tears begin to well up in her eyes as she said, "I've been hurt a lot in the past. You don't know this, but my relationship with Grant almost destroyed me. Remi, I just need you to provide security for me, for my heart. You understand?"

I nodded and said, "I understand. Your heart is safe with me."

"And one last thing, Remi, please. If you ever feel the urge to cheat on me or come close to cheating on me, leave me before you do it; just leave me. And then after you've left me, then you can go do whatever it is you're going to do. But if you cheat on me and I find out, I will never look you in the face again."

"Cecilia, I would never do that."

• • •

We spent all of our available time together. She and her dog, Brutus, practically moved in with me. As promised, I treated her like a queen, and she treated me like her king. Her friends became my friends, and my friends became her friends. And if anyone tried to get between us for any reason, we dealt with it immediately. She had a friend of many years who wasn't too happy about her dating an African American. Let's just say that when that revelation came to light, *friends* was no longer a term Cecilia used between them. And anytime we were at a club together and she was hit on, all she had to do was turn around and point me out. The culprit would see me, then sheepishly tiptoe away.

It was a pristine time in our lives. We both had great careers, and we were both so happy with each other. We didn't even argue once during the first four months of our relationship.

• • •

With her arms wide out and her joker-like smile, Cecilia jumped into the living room and said, "How do I look?" She was wearing my old SEAL training sweater and my First Phase BUD/S helmet.

I lowered my cottage cheese cup and said, "You look like you're ready for training. But there's only one thing missing!"

"What?" she replied.

"Stand at attention!" I said in an authoritative tone. She quickly snapped to attention. I put my breakfast down, walked around the kitchen island, and stood right in front of her.

Referring to her stance, she asked, "Is this what I was missing?"

I replied, "No, this," then leaned down to her five-one frame and gave her a kiss.

In her typical nerdy-comedic tone, she replied, "Hoo . . . yah." She kissed me again, then asked, "Did I say it right?"

I smiled and said, "Hooyah, yeah, you said it right."

"Are you ready for today?" she asked. "It's gonna be your *first* time jumping out of a *plaaaane*."

I grabbed my backpack, gave her one last kiss, then said, "Good to go. Oh, and just in case I die . . . I love you."

I tried to close the door before she could respond, but I heard her say, "Don't say that, Remi!"

It was the last Thursday in February 2008, and I was on my way to static line jump school. For the last three days, our jump class had gone through all the classroom and mock-up training required.

Static line jumping is a simple concept. A jumper stands at the door of a plane with a parachute on his back. One end of a line is attached to the parachute by way of a release hook, and the other end of the line is attached to the plane. After a jumper exits the plane—typically at fifteen hundred feet— gravity takes control and the hook pulls open the parachute, then releases.

Now, before I get to the tricky part, let me touch on a major difference between a free-fall parachute and a static line parachute. When a free-fall parachute opens, there's a right toggle and a left toggle. When a parachutist pulls down on the right toggle, the parachute responds immediately and turns right; when a parachutist pulls down on the left toggle, the parachute immediately turns left. Pulling down on both toggles at the same time serves as a braking mechanism, and the parachutist's descent slows. When a static line parachute is open, there are also two toggles, but a parachutist can pull as hard as possible on either toggle, and the parachute will barely respond. Oh, and there are no brakes. So, in essence, a free-fall parachute has more control than a static line parachute.

Because a static line chute is so difficult to control, our jump instructors taught us a landing technique called parachute landing fall, or PLF. The technique is used to displace the energy of the body when it contacts the earth at high speeds. When executed properly, a PLF allows a parachutist to survive uninjured at landing speeds that would otherwise cause severe injury or even death.

At the school's hangar, Ozzy, a pro skydiver with more than twenty thousand free-fall and static line jumps, briefed us.

"All right, guys, you were briefed yesterday, so I'm going to keep it short. The doors to the plane will open at fifteen hundred feet. You will be in your assigned sticks of four. Heaviest guys to the front of the plane, lighter guys to the back. Once you exit the plane, look up to ensure that you have a full canopy. If you are not sure, you have about . . . fifteen seconds to figure it out."

Everyone looked at each other and laughed.

"When you land, you will *run* to the drop zone [DZ] medic, Rachel, and check in. Once she's checked you in, load the bus and stand by for movement back to this hangar. When everyone has completed four jumps, you've met the graduation requirement. And listen, we have the airbus scheduled for the entire day. Which means we're going to try to get everyone qualified *today*. If we can do that by COB tonight, Frogman Friday will be in effect."

I whispered to myself, "That's what I'm talking about. Let's get this done and over with."

Ozzy continued, "Immediately check in with the medic after I finish my brief. Then I want each of you to line up behind the PLF box. We're going to run some practice landings. Once the jump instructors are satisfied with your PLFs, we'll load up the first group of jumpers. Blue skies!"

As instructed, after the DZ medic checked me out, I lined up behind the PLF box with the other operators. When it was my turn, I successfully completed two PLFs off of a five-foot box, then got cleared by a jump instructor to don my parachute.

"You ready for this, Adeleke?" Dill, a fellow SO, asked.

"Absolutely!" I replied.

"You think you might shit yourself?"

Again, I said, "Absolutely!" Come on. I had never jumped out of a plane in my life. I would be lying if I said I had zero trepidation.

Within thirty minutes of donning my parachute, we were in the air. I was the second man from the door in the first stick, which meant once the green light flashed on, our group would be the first out. When we arrived at fifteen hundred feet, the back doors opened up, and the sound of rushing wind filled the plane.

"Uh-oh! It's . . . about . . . to go . . . down," I said with my eyes wide open.

The jumpmaster screamed over the wind, "First stick . . . on your feet!" We all stood up in unison.

"Right face!" We turned right to face the exit of the plane.

"Step to the edge!" We all carefully shuffled to the edge of the exit. It's funny how a person's heart rate can get up to 150 beats per minute even while he's completely still. My heart was moving like I was treading water with four tanks.

"Go, go, go, go!" the jumpmaster yelled.

"Oh, damn!" I said.

I rushed out of the plane with a guy in front of me and two guys behind me. As soon as my feet left the ramp, I started my five-second count: "One one thousand, two one thousand . . ." If our parachute wasn't fully open at "five one thousand," we were to look up to check for errors in our canopy. If there were errors, we were to utilize our backup parachute, which rested on our stomachs.

". . . three one thousand . . ."

On three, I felt my velocity slow down rapidly. I looked up to see if I had a full canopy, which I did. Then I pulled down as hard as I could on the right toggle to inch myself into the wind. Being into the wind is important because it helps slow the rate of descent. Having the wind at your back can be dangerous.

From my elevation, I could see the mountains, the ocean, the fields, and the curve of the horizon. It was a beautiful experience, one that could only be clearly seen from where I was descending. And in that moment I learned a lesson: sometimes you have to go through the chaos to get to the beauty. And that lesson was so timely because it related to what I went through with Cecilia.

"Feet, thigh, hip, back . . . feet, thigh, hip, back." As I got closer to the ground, I repeated the PLF sequence. "Here it comes, here it comes," I said right before hitting the ground, then *boom*. It was a hard fall, harder than expected, but I followed the sequence, and from what I could feel it worked.

After a moment on my back, I rolled to my right to ensure I hadn't broken anything; then I rolled to my left to do the same. Afterward I turned my neck and lifted my legs and arms. Everything checked out, so I popped to my feet, gathered my parachute, and ran to Rachel, the DZ medic.

"SO3 Adeleke, checking in."

Rachel asked, "How was your fall?" Static line jumps are notorious for producing injuries. The jump instructors make us run to the medic because if a person is injured, he won't be able to run. So the run is something of an initial medical check.

"Good," I replied.

"Any injuries to report?" she asked.

"Negative. I'm good to go."

She pointed to the bus and said, "All right. Make your way to the bus."

One down, three to go, I thought.

When we arrived back at the hangar, Ozzy brought us in for a short debrief and update. "Everybody made it back alive, I see. Any questions before you load up for the next jump?"

We all shook our heads. It was pretty straightforward: jump out of the plane, check the chute, PLF, check in, and do it again.

"All right . . . good. Quick update: the winds have picked up, so make sure your PLFs are as good as they can be. Also make sure the volume on your walkie-talkies is at max. The drop zone operator [DZO] will call your individual number if he sees you need correction. Remember: the first guy in the stick is number one, second guy two, and so on and so forth."

About an hour later we were back in the air.

"Step to the edge!" the jumpmaster commanded.

My nerves had completely dissipated. I was ready!

"Go, go, go, go!" The first guy jumped, then I jumped, followed by the last two.

"One one thousand, two one thousand, three one thousand . . ."

I went through my checks. "Parachute okay, toggles." I pulled hard on my right toggle, then pulled hard on my left.

About a minute after my parachute opened, the DZO started speaking over the radio. "Number two guy, you need to turn into the wind."

I was the number two guy, but I was already into the wind. It was blowing right in my face, so I figured he was talking to someone else.

Ten seconds later the DZO said in an elevated tone, "Number two, you need to turn into the wind now!"

Come on, dude! What's going on? I'm into the wind. Both of my hands were on my toggles, and the radio was pinned right below my chest. I looked around to see if he was talking to someone else, but I couldn't see anyone around me.

Then I heard him scream over the radio, "Number two guy, I said turn into the wind, right now!"

At this point I figured maybe the commander knew something I didn't know. It was only my second jump, after all. So with the wind already in my face, I pulled down as hard as I could on my right toggle.

As my parachute gradually turned, I began to feel the wind shift from my face—which was not good—to my left side, and then a gust blew my parachute over to the point where the wind was at my back.

"This is not good! I knew I was into the wind! Why did I listen to that dude?"

I later found out that because of the slight difference in my weight, I had fallen past the number one guy, and so, from the ground perspective, I was number one, and the original number one guy became number two. That's who the DZO was talking to, but neither of us in the air understood that.

With the wind now at my back, my speed rapidly increased. What made my situation worse was the fact that, with the weak toggles, I didn't have enough time to fully turn back into the wind. If I tried, there was a high chance I would land sideways, and with the wind being as strong as it was, that could lead to life-threatening injuries or even death.

Seconds away from the ground and with the wind still obnoxiously at my back, I said, "I'm so sorry, Cecilia. I shouldn't have joked with you like that before I left. Damn. Here we go again." I knew I probably wouldn't die, but I also knew that I would definitely break something!

"Here it comes, here it comes!"

Snap, crackle, and *pop!* Those were the exact sounds I heard, in that order. I severed my medial malleolus, which is the bone of stability, in my right ankle. It felt like someone had put a .45 to my ankle and pulled the trigger.

"Aw! Damn! Ooooooh!" My whole body got hot. I lay in the shrubs for a minute, cursing a streak, expecting someone to run to my aid, but no one came.

As I lay there, the wheels began to turn in my head. *My ankle is already broken. All I have is two jumps left today. I can try to conceal my injury, do these last two jumps, get my certificate, then go to the hospital. Or I can go to the hospital now, wait six months to start static line all over, and risk breaking it again on another jump.*

I made my decision. Though it was a crazy idea, I decided I would go for it.

Imma do these last two jumps on a broken ankle.

I picked myself up off the ground and slowly stood up. When I took my first step, I felt the severed part of my bone slip, which caused me to collapse again.

"Daaaaaamn! Oh . . . Oh!" The pain was excruciating! *Come on, Remi. You've been through worse. Pick yourself up. . . . PICK YOURSELF UP!*

"Okay, okay," I said before standing back up. When I got to my feet, I gathered my parachute and started walking and cursing my way to the check-in station. With each step the bone slipped in every direction. Then my boot got tight from the swelling, which helped mask a bit of the pain.

As I got closer to the station, I said to myself, *All right, Remi. You have to act, boy! Shut down that pain and come up with something quick.*

Rachel yelled out, "SO3! Why aren't you running?"

"I'll tell you in a second." *Come on, Remi. Think, think, think!*

She met me halfway and said, "Why are you limping? What happened?"

Being a medic and knowing that if she pulled off my right boot, the gig would be up, I said, "I think I sprained my left ankle."

"Okay, take off your boot so I can see what's going on."

Okay, this is working. I sat on the ground and slipped off my left boot. *Please don't ask me to take off my right to compare.*

As she examined my ankle, I said, "It's funny; I'm a corpsman . . . and I see these all the time. Now I'm the clown having to get treated for one."

As she continued the examination, she asked, "You're a corpsman?"

"Yeah. I think I sprained it. The pain isn't that bad. I'm sure I can finish the last two jumps."

She finished her exam, looked at me, and said, "Yeah, you're right. It's not that bad, just a little swelling. Are you sure you can do the last two jumps?" Her assessment was hilarious! I say that because there was absolutely no swelling.

"Yeah, I'm positive. After we finish today, I'll go to medical and get an ACE bandage or something."

"Okay, doc. You can go get on the bus," she replied.

"Thank you," I said.

Part of me said, *Yes!* But the other part of me said, *Damn. Now you're committed. No turning back.*

As soon as I got on the bus, I told my fellow operators, "Hey dudes. My ankle is so f***ed!"

They said, "Aw, no! That sucks!"

"Listen. I need you guys to help me hide this until we finish these last two jumps."

Dill said, "We got you covered, Remi." He ordered a few guys to grab all my gear.

I tried to meditate on the bus, but I couldn't. The pain was too distracting, so I just kept saying, "Just two more, Remi; then you can go to the hospital."

When we got off the bus, Ozzy was right there waiting to debrief us. "I heard somebody got injured," he said.

"It was me. Sprained ankle. But Rachel cleared me. I'm good to go."

"Great, but good news . . ." Ozzy's next words were a dagger to my heart. "You'll have the rest of the day and night to rest up. The winds are way too high now. It's too dangerous to let jumpers out. We're going to wrap up training for the day, and we'll see you all bright and early in the morning."

Noooooo! That meant I would have to wait a whole extra day to go to the hospital. The guys tried their best not to look at me.

After I finally got to my car, the drive home was really awkward. It was too painful to use my right foot, so I had to drive with my left foot.

My new roommate, Gavin (who was also an SO), helped me up the stairs. As soon as I walked across the threshold of our apartment, I collapsed. There was no way I could walk anymore. I had to crawl everywhere: to the bathroom, to the kitchen, to my bedroom. When it was finally time for me to go to sleep, I made the mistake of lying in my bed. When I lay flat on my back, gravity pulled the severed bone down. The same thing happened when I lay on either side. So I crawled out of the bed, crawled to the living room, and fell asleep sitting on the couch. That was the only position that allowed me to sleep semi-comfortably.

The next morning Gavin drove us back to the flight hangar. Cecilia had stayed at her parents' home the night before, so she met me behind the hangar, handed me some food, gave me a kiss, and said, "I'm so proud of you, Remi. You're crazy, but I'm proud of you. Go kick ass today, and I'm going to take care of you after this is done, okay?"

"Okay, babe. . . . I love you."

"I love you too," she said.

I stepped back into the hangar and limped my way to the parachutes, but right before I lifted up my chute, Ozzy, said, "Bring it in!" I stood up and made what felt like a six-mile walk to the center of the hangar. "Good morning, guys. The winds are going to be light in the morning, but they may pick up in the afternoon, so just to make sure everyone's good, we're going to run some practice PLFs on the five-foot box. Once everyone is clear, we'll load you guys up for your first runs."

If I wasn't a knuckle-dragging, pipe-swinging *frogman*, I would have fainted. But I just stood there and thought, *Okay, I'm up for the challenge. Let's do this.*

At first my buddies tried to hide me in the back, but there was no way to hide me. I was one of two black guys in a class of fifty-four. I walked up the steps of the box, looked down to the ground, and jumped! When I hit the floor, I felt my severed bone slip and slide. *Aw, man, man, man!* I said inside.

There was no way I could land flat on both feet or bend my knees. Due to my improper landings, Ozzy said, "SO3, I'm going to need to see you do that again. I can't have you jumping if you can't do a proper PLF."

"Roger. I understand. . . . It's just that . . . I sprained my ankle yesterday."

"Are you good to jump?" he asked.

"Yeah," I replied.

"Okay, let me see another PLF."

I went back to the box, made the excruciating climb up the steps, and jumped again, *Oh my, my, MY!* I don't know how I did it, but I managed to keep a straight face with each jump.

"Again, SO3," Ozzy commanded.

I must have jumped off that box six times before Rachel came running up. "Stop!" she said. "You can't make him do PLFs like that. He's fine to jump, but we need to rest his sprained ankle as much as we can. Save the impacts for the actual jumps."

I looked at her like, *Where were you five minutes ago?*

Before I knew it, I was back up in the air.

"Step to the edge!" the jumpmaster commanded. The first time I walked to the edge in fear, the second time, confidence, and this time in agony. "Go, go, go, go!"

I didn't even count. I didn't care if my parachute didn't open. If it didn't, I'd be put out of my misery.

As I descended, I tuned out everything the DZO said on the radio. I did not want to hear a word from that guy.

When I got closer to the ground, I made the decision not to take the full impact on my feet. I planned to strike with my heels, then immediately roll onto my back. It turned out to be a bad idea. I struck the ground right on my tailbone! That's right, added pain. I moaned for a few seconds, then rolled side to side to get enough momentum to roll onto my stomach. When I did, I just lay there facedown and kept talking to myself. *You just have to do one more jump, Remi! I know you're hurting. I know your ankle is obliterated, but one more. Get up!* With that I pushed myself up, gathered my parachute, checked in with Rachel again, loaded the bus, and headed back to the hangar.

I was a complete mess when I got back on the plane for my last jump. I was in so much pain. And then depression began to creep in. *First you get rolled out of Hell Week in 250; then you get rolled for swims in 251; then you get dropped from BUD/S in 253; then you get rolled in Third Phase in 266; now this.* Just as I had during my other classes, I had grown close to this group of guys, and I knew that after this jump, they would move on to their other qualifications and then their SEAL Teams. Once again, I would be left behind.

As I sat with my head down, I felt a slap on the top of my helmet, which prompted me to look up.

"Get your head up, Adeleke!" It was Dill. I lifted my head and stared at him as he continued, "Look, I know your ankle is jacked up. I know your body is a mess. But listen: this is who we are. This is what we do! We do the hard things. We do the things that no one can do, and we do them with a smile. So I want you to pick your head up, stop feeling sorry for yourself, and jump out of the plane like the frogman that you are!"

I tell you what: that speech motivated me. He gave me exactly what I needed: a reminder of who I was!

"Thank you, Dill. I'll see you on the ground."

As soon as we got to fifteen hundred feet, the doors of that plane opened, the wind rushed in, and I heard that buzzing of the door. I stood up like a new man, a man who knew exactly who he was. No more feeling sorry for myself, and no more limping out of the plane. I walked to the edge, and when the command came, *I jumped*!

CHAPTER TWENTY-TWO

THE WILDERNESS

Through everything God made, they can
clearly see his invisible qualities.[1]

Bayo asked me, "So how's your recovery coming along?"

"It's good. Doctor said after another month of physical therapy, I should be able to start jogging." It was a little under three months after my accident, and Cecilia and I were driving down the 15 South while I spoke with Bayo on the phone.

"Everybody in my prayer group is praying for you," he said.

I sneered, "You can tell them I don't need their prayers. I'll be fine." Cecilia looked at me with shock. "Look, I got to go. I'll talk to you later."

Before he could finish saying, "I love you," I hung up.

"Remi, don't be like that toward your brother. He's just trying to be nice!"

I looked at her sternly and said, "You need to mind your own business, Cecilia!"

She had kept her part of the bargain through and through. I couldn't walk for three months after breaking my ankle, but during that time, she showered me with love and selfless service. The girl cooked for me, cleaned my apartment, ran my errands, and helped me to the bathroom. The superiors in charge of SEAL Qualification Training (SQT) allowed me to stay home throughout my recovery, so some days she would race to the apartment to spend her lunch with me, then race back to work. The woman even left her one-year-old Yorkie, Brutus, with me to keep me company throughout the day.

About two months after my injury, I, on the other hand, began to treat her like my worst enemy. There are no excuses that can justify what I put her through, but in retrospect there is an explanation. I was mad—at the world, at myself, at the DZO, at being stuck at home all day for months, and at anyone whose God would allow me to go through all the hell that I had gone through in my life. Unfortunately, Cecilia was the person closest to me, and I irresponsibly released my anger and bitterness onto her.

As I drove down the highway, she said, "And I guess you think it's also none of my business that you just stood there and let that girl flirt with you a minute ago . . . right in front of me, Remi!"

"You don't know what you're talking about," I replied.

"I don't know what I'm talking about? According to you, I never know what I'm talking about." She shook both hands by her head and sarcastically said, "I'm crazy!"

I didn't respond, just stared at the road.

Cecilia continued, "While we're on the topic of my *ignorance*, I'm going to ask you *again*, Remi. Whose . . ." She paused and snapped her fingers to get my undivided attention. "Look at me!"

I already knew the question she was about to ask, and I didn't want to answer it. So I said, "I can't look at you. I'm driving! You want me to get us both killed?"

She took a deep breath. "Whose earrings were those under your bed?"

A week earlier, Cecilia was cleaning my apartment when she found a pair of earrings another woman had conveniently placed under my bed. I was caught so off guard when she confronted me that I foolishly said they were hers. Like she wouldn't know what her earrings looked like!

"I don't know . . . maybe some chick I messed with before we got together."

"*Remi*, that was the fourth time I cleaned under your damn bed! There were never any earrings there before that!" As she started fighting back tears, she said, "I love you, Remi!"

I gave her the response I would often give her when I was in a bad mood. "I know you do!"

The tears started rolling down her cheeks, and she pleaded, "Please . . . just tell me the truth! Did you cheat on me, Remi? Did you?"

I took my eyes off the road for a second and responded in the same way I responded when my grandmother confronted me about my mother's engagement ring. "No. I didn't cheat on you."

. . .

Two weeks later, around May 10, I was released from my walking boot! Now that I was free, it was time to set someone else free: Cecilia.

I had been trying to find a reason to break up with her, and when I couldn't, I made one up. I took a disagreement we had and manipulated it into what I considered a valid reason to leave her. I'll never forget that day, despite it being one of those days I wish I *could* forget.

With her back against my coat closet door she said, "Remi! How could you do this to me?"

"I just think it's best we go our separate ways," I said.

Tears had been streaming down her face from the moment we started the conversation.

"I've given up so much for you. . . . I've done so much for you!" she said. She slowly slid to the floor. "Why, Remi?"

"It's just not working out."

As she continued sobbing, she said, "I told you when we got together . . . to guard my heart . . . and you just broke my heart!"

I looked at her as if to say, "Okay, so when are you going to leave my apartment?" When she didn't get up, I turned, walked into the living room, and sat on the couch. About five minutes later, I heard her get up, pack up a few things, then open and close my apartment door.

She did absolutely nothing to warrant me breaking up with her, and I knew that, but at the time I didn't care. I wanted to be with other women and not do it behind her back. It was all about me, me, me, me, me! I was so blinded by my sexual urges.

I need you to understand: she didn't look like a troll, and she wasn't dumb. The woman was gorgeous, she had her MBA at this point, she was accomplished, and she served me like I was a god. Guys were lining up waiting for her to break up with me. So for me to throw her away, let alone treat her the way I did, made absolutely no logical sense.

• • •

At the beginning of June 2008, exactly six years after I heard a voice tell me to join the military, I was lying in bed when I heard that same voice again. I'm telling you, it was real! I wasn't hungover, and I definitely wasn't high. I was in my right mind. And just as that voice softly spoke years earlier, saying, "*You need to join the military*," I heard the voice say, "*You need to take her back. You need to take her back.*"

I was resting on my left side, facing the window, so I pushed myself up and turned to look into my room. There was no one there, and as usual my door was closed, so I lay back down. Again I heard, "*You need to take her back.*"

Dammit! It was like the voice planted a little seed in my mind, and I wanted to dig it up before it took root. *I have money, I have this beautiful apartment, I'm about to go to my SEAL Team soon, and I have freedom to be with whoever I want whenever I want. Why would I take her back? No! I'm not good for her. She deserves better!*

My desk was in the corner of the room, to the right of the window. Right on top of my desk was a pair of tickets to a concert with the Roots and Erykah Badu. I placed them there two days earlier after purchasing them. One of the girls I was seeing was a huge fan of the Roots and Erykah Badu, and I had committed to taking her as a birthday gift.

"Okay, okay! I'll make something up," I yelled into the room. "And I'll take Cecilia, but after that, that's it!"

Feeling disgruntled, I picked up my cell to call Cecilia.

She answered in a somber mood. "Hi, Remi."

"Hey, how are you doing?" I replied.

"I'm doing okay."

"Listen . . . I'm sorry about last month. I was in a bad place."

"I know," she replied.

"Do you want to try to meet up? I have tickets to a concert. I thought about you when I bought them. I figured it would be a good way to hang out again." Of course, I was lying.

"Sure. When is it?" she asked.

"Next week." I gave her the details.

"Okay, I look forward to seeing you, Remi."

"I look forward to seeing you too," I replied.

I felt so bad, like I was pulling her back into my mess. But I wasn't doing it for me; I was doing it for whoever that voice was, whether my subconscious, intuition, the universe . . . or maybe even God.

. . .

The next week I stood near the entrance of Humphrey's Concerts by the bay, waiting for Cecilia. I could spot her walk a mile away. She was dressed to the nines in an off-white sundress, tan heels that matched her complexion, and sunglasses. Also, her hair was a lot shorter than it had been.

As I watched her stroll up, I got a flashback of our first encounter. *Come on, Remi. What are you doing? Look at her; you know she's the one for you. Stop it with all the games.*

"Wow, Cecilia . . . you're beautiful," I said when she approached.

She replied, "You always knew . . ."

We finished the statement together. ". . . the right thing to say at the right time."

I took her hand and led her through the jam-packed crowd toward our seats. When we found our spot, I put my arm around her, and we both just let the music wash away our problems.

Not only was the concert timely, but it was also—somewhat—providential. I say that because in so many ways the song selections spoke to our situation and directly to my heart. We nodded in sync when the Roots and Erykah Badu performed their duet "You Got Me." When "Coming to Break You Off" was played, I danced behind Cecilia while I whispered the lyrics in her ear.

But the song that spoke to me the most and actually threw me into a conflict was Erykah Badu's "Next Lifetime." She sang, *"The first time that I saw you boy, it was a warm and a sunny day/ All I know is I wanted you. I really hoped you looked my way/ Then you smiled at me so warm and sweet/ I could not speak/ You made me feel like a little bitty girl what did you do to me/ Now what am I supposed to do when I want you in my world/ But how could I want you for myself when I'm already someone's girl/ I guess I'll see you next lifetime/ Maybe we'll be butterflies/ I guess I'll see you next lifetime/ That sounds so divine/ I guess I'll see you next lifetime/ You don't have to cry no more."*[2]

The first part of those lyrics clearly described our first meeting, and the second half somewhat described my battle. I so wanted her in my world, but I already belonged to a few entities—and by that I mean pride, sexual addiction, and anger. I was set into a conflict because I so wanted to be with her, but I didn't want to keep putting her through the garbage I was putting her through.

After the concert we walked out into the parking lot, holding hands. When we got to her car, she asked me, "What are we going to do, Remi?"

I told her, "I don't know. I love you, but I'm not ready to be with you again." I thought, *It's not you, Cecilia. You're wonderful. It's me!* I wish I would have just said that out loud, but my pride wouldn't let me. I wanted her to believe it was partly her fault that we weren't together—just in case I needed to pull that card in the future.

• • •

A few weeks after the concert, I received a rather shocking call from my mother.

"Hey, Ma, how you doing?"

She said, "Hi, Remi," then got straight to the point. "You know I love you, Remi."

"Yeah, Ma. You tell me all the time."

"Well, part of loving someone is telling them when they're showing their ass!"

I replied with a little attitude, "What's up, Ma?"

"I spent all day yesterday with Cecilia!"

Aw, man! "Where? How?" I frantically asked.

"She's been out here for a week for work. We went shopping; we went to dinner; she came to the apartment. So you know what that means? We had a lot of time to talk!" Then my mom calmed down and went into

I'm-your-mama-and-I-want-the-best-for-you mode. "Remi . . . when have I ever gotten involved in any of your relationships?"

"Never, Ma."

"So you know if I'm getting involved now, it's important?"

"Yes, Ma, I know, I know."

"Okay, before I say what I have to say, I need to ask you—because you're my son and I want to hear your side—did she do something wrong to you?"

"No, Ma. You know how she treated me when I couldn't walk. She's great. She didn't do anything wrong."

"Okay, so now I know how to approach this." There was a long pause, then a deep sigh. "Remi . . . she's a sweet girl. She loves you. Now, I don't know if all them injuries you got in SEAL training affected your thinking, but if it did, I'm here to remind you: I didn't raise you to treat a woman the way you're treating Cecilia. So you need to fix this, or you're going to lose her, and you're going to regret it."

"Yes, ma'am." I couldn't be mad at Cecilia or my mom. Cecilia loved me, so she was right for going to the only person who could talk sense into me. And my mom was . . . well, she's my mom, she's awesome—*and* she was spot-on!

"I love you, Remi."

"I love you, too, Ma."

Let's just say that by the next day, Cecilia and I were back together.

. . .

On August 30, 2008, I stood by the entrance of the San Diego Naval Air Station airport. I was waiting for Cecilia. My new group of classmates and I were on our way to Kodiak, Alaska, for cold-weather survival training. When she dropped me off, I realized that I had forgotten some cold-weather snacks at the apartment, so Cecilia made the thirty-minute drive back to get them.

Things were going well. I had graduated from Freefall and SERE training without incident. As it related to Cecilia and me, I was still doing some things I probably shouldn't have been doing, but for the most part I was a lot better.

When she pulled up, she jumped out of the car and ran to me.

"I wasn't too late, right?" she asked.

"No, babe. I think we have another five minutes before we load up. You're just in time. Thank you." Out of the corner of my eye, I could see a few of my classmates looking in our direction.

She bashfully said, "Okay . . . so have a great trip." Then she leaned in to kiss me. I backed away and looked at her like, *What are you doing in front of my boys? Don't do that.*

I could see the tears well up in her eyes. She quickly said, "Bye," then walked to her car.

As she walked away, a buddy of mine, Todd, who was close enough to witness what just happened, approached me and said, "What are you doing? There's nothing cool about what you just did! Why are you treating that girl like that? She loves you."

Deep, deep, deep, deep, deep down inside, I agreed with him, and a part of me wanted to chase her down for that last kiss. But my pride caused me to look at Todd and say, "She's not going anywhere."

• • •

Later that evening we arrived at a small military outpost in Alaska. For the next month we were relegated to living quarters with minimal amenities. On the second floor of the building was an open barracks with two-man bunks. Because we would spend most of our days and nights out in the wilderness, we wouldn't use the bunks much. On the first floor was a common area where we would have our meals, but again, only when we weren't out in the open.

Along with limited amenities, our outside communication was somewhat limited as well. Similar to my drive up to Camp Pendleton for the first time, I quickly discovered that I had zero cell phone reception. There was a computer room, but the two computers in there operated on very slow landlines. And the only phone, which was also located in the computer room, would be shared among the thirty of us—if we had time to use it. If I could sum up that time period for me in one phrase, it would be: *desperately needed isolation from the world.*

• • •

"All right, fellas. This will be your fourth day of land navigation. Your packs should be filled with enough sustainable goods for three days, your warming gear, and camping supplies." Grizz, who was an active SEAL, continued his brief as he pointed to a map. "We tried to keep all your points for today within this six-mile radius. So with the individual points we gave you, and the number of guys in your class, your chances of running into each other are slim. But if you do, you're not to discuss whereabouts of stakes or give pointers."

We all nodded.

Grizz continued, "Again, once you find your stake, pull out your locator sheet, place it over the dog tags on the stake, and use your pencil to shade the imprint. All right, guys. This is the starting point, so go have fun. Hopefully we'll see you back at base camp tonight."

I had done an in-depth map study and plotted my points on the hour-long bus ride to the forest, so as soon as Grizz gave the word, I donned my rucksack and took off.

As I walked through the wilderness, it was so hard not to stop to admire the beauty. The snow hadn't started to fall yet, so everything was bright green. And the trees were massive; some shot up two hundred feet into the sky. Being from the Bronx, I had never seen a place like this, and never in a million years did I ever think I would end up in a place like this. *Remi*, I said to myself as I stood in awe at my first stake, *you have come a long way*. "Wow, this is so beautiful. I wish Cecilia could see this."

As I continued my walk, I noticed that one of the most serene aspects of the Kodiak forest was the silence. There were times when I would hear an occasional chirping from a bird or the rustling of trees when the wind blew, but for the most part, it was quiet. I was truly alone.

Something miraculous began to happen while I continued through the wilderness. In the silence and the beauty, I began to really reflect on my life—who I was and how I treated people. It was as though someone or something was holding up a mirror and showing me what I had become. And the more I walked and reflected, the more I didn't like what I saw. I saw a kid who stole an engagement ring from his mom and never confessed to her. I saw a person who treated his own brother like he was worthless. I saw a person who had integrity when it was convenient for him but didn't when it wasn't. I saw a prideful person whose favorite song had become "You Can't Tell Me

Nothing!" I saw a man who treated women like meat. And what hurt me the most was that I saw a man who treated a woman who truly loved him with constant contempt.

As the memories replayed in my mind, I began to be depressed, and then my depression led to anger. And my anger led to questions. *You did that? How could you do that to a person? What are you thinking? What is wrong with you?* It was as though I had been outside of my body on vacation for twenty-six years, and when I came back home and saw the mess someone had made, I was in shock.

At that time of year in Kodiak, daylight was from 7:00 a.m. to 9:00 p.m. So when I got to the last stake at 8:00 p.m., it was still bright. In the brightness of the night, I made a vow: "That's it. I'm going to fix me! I'm not going to be the same person I was anymore. I'm going to meditate more, and I'm going to spend more time with my spiritual group. I'm going to buy a ring and propose to Cecilia, and I'm going to be the man to her that I need to be. No more of this garbage. No more . . . no more!"

. . .

While I was having my epiphany, Cecilia was having an awakening of her own, forty-one hundred miles away from the Alaskan wilderness. The time apart from me helped her to reflect on our relationship: *I'm not special to him anymore. He's not keeping his commitment to guard my heart. I don't feel safe. I've sacrificed so much for him, and he just treats me like any other girl and not the person who was holding him up and supporting him when he was down. It would be better for us to be apart. . . . I don't want to hurt anymore.*

Unbeknownst to each of us, we were both making life-changing decisions. I was too late, and she was right on time.

Her tipping point came a week after my departure, when Cecilia went to a party and fortuitously met a SEAL's wife, Penelope.

After introductions were made, Penelope jumped right in, "So I hear you're dating a Team Guy. How's it going?" *Team Guy* is another term for Navy SEAL.

"Hmm . . . I don't know. Not the way it should be going."

"Look: I've been married to a SEAL for almost twenty years. I know the community well, and I've talked to many wives and girlfriends. SEALs are hard guys to be with, so my advice to you is simple: if things are not going well for you now, you're in for a hell of a ride—and I don't mean that in a good way." Cecilia just stared at her intently as she continued, "Look at yourself. You're young; you're beautiful. Jasmine tells me you have a great career. If you're not feeling right, you need to leave him. Trust me."

Cecilia nodded and thanked her for the advice. After that, her decision was somewhat made. That conversation instilled a fear in her that made it easier for her to leave me.

. . .

Back in Alaska, I was seriously taking the time to work on myself. I was meditating during my hikes. I even started following my brother's advice by praying before I went to sleep. I didn't know whom I was praying to, but I just prayed. Though I really couldn't tell much of a difference, I was feeling good, feeling confident. I felt so good that I was eager and excited to call Cecilia to tell her the good news. But that would have to wait until our first full day off on September 14.

. . .

It felt like it took forever for the fourteenth to arrive. That morning I got up extra early and crept down the steps toward the computer room. I wanted to make sure I was the first person to the phone. When I peeked in, I could see that the phone was free and clear. I ran in, picked up the phone, and dialed Cecilia's number.

"Hello?" She sounded like she was still half-asleep.

"Cecilia! It's Remi!" I said, full of excitement.

"What time is it?" she asked.

"It's about six fifteen here." I jumped right in. "Hey, I got to tell you something! I've had a lot of time to think out here. And I've come to realize that I've been a jerk to you. Heck, I've been a jerk to a lot of people. But I'm changing, Cecilia. When I come back home, I promise, I'm going to be a better man to you! And I'm going to marry you, Cecilia!"

She was dead silent on the phone.

"Hello? . . . Hello? Cecilia, you there?" I asked.

In a somber tone she finally said, "Yeah, I'm here."

"Did you hear what I just said? Isn't that great?" I was so excited, I expected her to be excited. But she didn't seem the same; something was wrong.

She continued in a somber tone, "Yeah."

"Are you okay? Are you sick or something?" Cecilia was always a ball of energy, so when she responded reticently, I thought she had the flu or a cold.

"I'm sorry, Remi. I wanted to wait to tell you when you got home."

I seriously thought, *Oh my God. She must have been diagnosed with cancer or something worse.* "Tell me what? Are you okay?"

Then she delivered the news. "I don't want to be with you anymore, Remi. You've hurt me too much, and . . . I've had enough. It's over."

When I heard that, I felt like I was in the *Twilight Zone*—literally. I had a total out-of-body experience. *First, I have this epiphany that I need to change, then I start to change on my own without anyone telling me to, and now she's leaving me!* "Wait, wait, wait. Did you hear what I said? I *know* I'm a dirtbag. No—I *was* a dirtbag, but I'm different now."

"Remi, it's too late. You've tortured me, and I don't want *this* for my future."

I went into negotiation mode. "Wait. Let's not do this now. Just . . . wait till I get back home, and let's see each other, and then we'll make a decision."

She wasn't hearing it. She simply said, "I'll be by your apartment to pick up my stuff when you get back. I'm sorry. I have to go, Remi. Goodbye."

"All right. I'll see you when I get home," I said.

I was in such shock when we hung up that all I could say was, "What . . . the f*** . . . just happened?"

I walked back to my bunk with that same thousand-yard stare I had seen on the faces of hundreds of BUD/S dropouts. I climbed to my top bunk and just lay there, staring at the ceiling. All kinds of thoughts came rushing in. *This is that karma thing Rosca talked to you about. All the stuff you did to all those people over all those years is coming back to you. The cell phone scams, the drug dealing, the speeding down the highway while ignoring your friends' pleas to slow down . . . lying to your mom and Cecilia over and over again.* In that moment I felt so guilty about everything, not just Cecilia, but everything. And my guilt quickly turned into a level of depression I had never experienced. *I need to get home so I can make things right with her and everyone else.*

In the weeks that followed, I upped my praying and meditation. Years earlier my brother had told me, "If you ever find yourself in a bad situation, and you've tried everything to fix it, and nothing has worked, just cry out to Jesus, Remi." So, there in Alaska, my prayer became simple: "Jesus, help me! Help me to release this guilt and shame and regret. Please make things right."

I don't know how I got through all the cold-weather training with the mental war that was going on in my head. And I *hate* the cold, but I did it all: hiked up a snow-capped mountain in the midst of a storm; sat in a freezing-cold Alaskan river for five minutes and then performed rewarming drills; swam with full gear from winterized boats to deserted Alaskan islands, and froze my butt off in my one-man tent. The whole time I just kept repeating, *I need to get home.*

• • •

On September 28, I finally returned from Alaska. The first thing I did was call Cecilia. She held the same stance; she wasn't taking me back. So, for the time being, I gave up pleading with her and just set up a time for her to pick up her belongings from my apartment. I figured that if she saw me in person, all her feelings would rush back, but I was wrong. When she arrived the next day, she simply picked up her stuff and left. She was as cold as I had been the day I left her crying on the floor months earlier. I tried not to choke while tasting my own medicine.

A few days later, on Saturday night, October 4, I was lying in my bed, just a mess about everything. And as I lay in my bed, dejected and tired, I was suddenly overcome by a deep darkness that seemed to completely swallow me. I'm not making this up; this was a darkness that I could feel, touch, and see. I had never experienced anything like it. And like the two times I heard the voice, I wasn't dreaming. I was wide-awake.

Whatever this thing was, it made my inner being feel sick. Of course, I'd been physically sick before, but I had never felt sick in my spirit (my inner being), and I didn't know what was going on. I didn't know what to do. It was too late at night to call Rosca or my other spiritual teacher, so I called Cecilia.

Now, here's how twisted my mind was: for some strange reason, I figured that if Cecilia took me back, that would fix my guilt, that would fix my pain, that would discard the darkness that was overshadowing me, and through that event all my wrongs would be made right.

When she answered the phone, I just began to beg her to take me back. Over and over again I begged her. "Please take me back, please. I need you to help release me from my anguish. I'm different now!"

And over and over again she said, "No! I won't take you back!"

Finally—and I don't know where the words came from, but they just spilled out of my mouth—I said, "Okay, if you won't take me back, can you please just take me to church?"

I'm sure she was taken aback because she paused, then replied, "Okay. I won't take you back, but I'll take you to church . . . tomorrow! But that's it!"

Here's the crazy thing: once she said that, the darkness that was anguishing my spirit dissipated, and I immediately felt a sense of peace.

The next morning, I got up, threw on a red collared shirt and jeans, and jumped in my Infiniti. Honestly, a part of me was going to see Cecilia, but another part of me was hoping to encounter something supernatural that would free me from myself, my guilt, my past—just everything.

. . .

Back to Cornerstone Church I went. The church was now out of their tent and in their newly renovated building. Cecilia met me outside and walked me to seats right at the front of the church, again. I could tell she was being extra careful in how she interacted with me. She didn't want to send any mixed signals about where she stood. I respected her for that.

I thought, *Wow. I can't believe I'm here . . . in a church, hoping that a God I can't see will do something for me.*

The last time I was there, I mocked the congregants' admiration of what I considered at the time to be an imaginary god. Now I had a somewhat better understanding of why they cried joyfully, sang vociferously, and raised their hands submissively. Perhaps at some point in their life, they were in my position, believing that something bigger than them would drag them out of their agony and give them a second chance.

Despite being up front, I can't tell you anything about Pastor Sergio's message that day. What I can tell you is that it made me reflect on my life in the same way I had reflected as I walked through the Alaskan wilderness. I could clearly see all my sexual escapades, my lies, my verbal vulgarity, my greed, my abuse, my anger, my hate, my guilt, and the effect that it had on me and others. *Could it have been God who was speaking to me out there? Showing me what I had become for the purpose of leading me right here?*

Cecilia sat directly behind me as I sat motionless with my eyes laser focused on the pulpit, not daring to turn to the right or to the left.

At the end of the message, Sergio delivered a short speech that I guess was meant to challenge anyone seeking a fresh start at life. That's what I do remember, and that's what brought me to tears—a so-called big bad tough guy who had gone through the hardest military training known to man—twice.

He said, "Would you please stand with me?" Upon his request the entire congregation stood up. He continued, "I believe today that God is speaking to someone about surrendering their life to Him, someone who needs to experience the power of His forgiveness."

That's me, man . . . that's me, I thought as I nodded.

He continued, as he scanned the crowd, "Will you say yes to Jesus so you can begin the journey that He's been wanting you to be on? Will you believe that when He rose on the third day, He was actually thinking about you rising up from your situation? It all starts when you begin to let go of your fear, and you say, 'Okay, God, things haven't been right. I want to make things right.' Listen to me. There are no accidents. He's drawn you here by His love, and He's saying, 'Son, daughter, I love you. I see your pain, and I see your hurt, and I see your sorrow.'"

Everything he was saying was spot-on! It was as though I was the only person in that 1,050-capacity auditorium, but I wasn't.

Sergio continued, "If that's you today, I want to pray with you the prayer that changed the trajectory of my life and that I know will change yours as well. Quickly hold up your hand so I can see those with whom I'm praying."

I felt no shame. My hand immediately shot up into the sky, like a first grader eager to answer a teacher's question.

When Pastor Sergio saw my hand in the air, he pointed to me and said, "God bless," then continued around the room as others raised their hands.

Then he instructed, "I want you to keep your hands up. By keeping your hands up, you're telling God you're all in. Now, for those with your hands up, repeat after me: Dear God . . ." I could hear the echoes of the crowd as my voice joined with theirs.

"I stand before You . . . with my hand held high . . . saying yes to You. I've been wrong . . . but today I want to get right. I ask for Your forgiveness. I believe by faith . . . Jesus, You died on the cross . . . and You rose on the third day . . . to give me the hope of heaven . . . and to give me hope now. Holy Spirit . . . fill me now . . . with the power of Your presence. . . . Transform me from the inside out. . . . Today I boldly declare . . . I am born again . . . ready to serve Jesus . . . with all of my heart . . . all of my mind . . . and all of my strength."

I would be lying if I said I felt electricity surge up and down my body or that I fell to the floor in convulsions. That didn't happen, but what did happen was I felt an instant peace. A peace that softly spoke these words: *You are forgiven, and everything will be okay.*

CHAPTER TWENTY-THREE

THE ULTIMATE TRANSFORMATION

"One thing I do know. I was blind but now I see!"[1]

In the four-month period after I committed my life to Jesus, my faith grew exponentially. It was like I had been placed on a rocket ship and shot into a new dimension. Day after day I would experience miraculous events. I began to feel God's presence; I began to encounter Him in a tangible way, and I had so many dramatic encounters with God that all I wanted to do—day in and day out—was be with Him, and do for Him, and forsake the life I used to live so I could live this new life with Him.

The Bible says, "If anyone is in Christ, he [she] is a new creation; old things have passed away; behold, all things have become new."[2] That scripture became my life. I confessed to my mom about her engagement ring. I went back and asked for forgiveness from people I had hurt. My language changed. The way I viewed people changed. And even more miraculously, after twelve years of watching pornography and/or having sex, I completely gave it up and committed to a life of celibacy. Talk about a divine miracle! Not only was it a transformative time in my life, but it was also a rather hilarious time. I say that because all my friends who knew me and how I used to be were in shock!

They couldn't believe the changes in me. Some guys were so concerned about my sudden lifestyle switch that they questioned me.

"Are you okay, Remi?"

"What's going on with you?"

"What's up with you going to church all the time?"

"You mean we're not going to the club tonight?"

All I could say was, "I don't have all the answers . . . and I honestly can't explain it all to you right now, but all I can say is Jesus happened to me, man. Jesus happened to me."

It was interesting because my friends gradually became curious about God, partly because of the miraculous transformation they witnessed in my life. As a matter of fact, I'll never forget an event that took place right before I checked into my SEAL Team.

• • •

"Hi, Remi," a female said over the phone.

"Hey, Kiera. How are you? It's been a while," I replied.

"Yeah . . . look, Remi . . . I'm sorry for what happened a while back." Kiera and I had dated between the time when Cecilia went back to Grant and I graduated Hell Week. I can't remember why, but I decided to give Kiera a key to my apartment so she could be there when I completed Hell Week. As was typical of me at the time, I was cheating on her. During Wednesday of Hell Week, unbeknownst to me, she went into my apartment and discovered, let's just say, substantial evidence that I was cheating. When I got home the Saturday after Hell Week, she was gone, but she'd made it very clear that I had been caught.

She continued, "I'm sorry for the way I yelled at you afterward."

I said, "No, you're fine. We were both in different places at the time. So no worries."

"Thank you, Remi. Listen. I was thinking about you, and I'm going to be in your area in a few hours. Do you mind if I come over to hang out?"

"Not at all. That would be great! It'll be so good to see you. Would you like me to make some dinner?" I asked.

"No, I'll bring dinner. Can't wait to see you," she said before hanging up.

I tidied up a bit, then sat back on the couch to watch TV. As I was sitting there, a thought hit me. *Remi! She doesn't know who you are now. When you were with her, what did a call out of the blue like that mean? It didn't mean she was just coming over to hang out; it meant that she was coming to have sex!*

I jumped off the couch and said aloud, "Uh-oh. I need to call her and tell her not to come!" But then I felt a supernatural peace that simply said, *It's okay. You'll be fine. Put the phone down.*

Two hours later my doorbell rang. As I walked to the door, I whispered to myself, "Please, I hope she looks unattractive. I hope her hair is messed up. I hope she's wearing obnoxious house clothes. Please don't let her look the way I remember."

As I slowly swung the door open from right to left, I could see that she was gazing down. She slowly looked up and said in a soft tone, "Hi, Remi." My hopes were dashed. Not only was she as fine as I remembered, but the girl must have lied to me because she sure didn't look like she just happened to be in my area. She looked like she was heading to a music video shoot. The woman had on tight jeans, her hair and nails were done, and her makeup was tastefully applied. She was stunning. Oh, and her perfume smelled like luscious phero-mones. She knew what she was doing.

"Hey-lo, Kiera," I said nervously. "Come in."

She knew she had me. After I took the bags of take-out food from her, Kiera walked past me toward the couch with a seductive smile and sat down. As I took the food to the kitchen, I tried my best not to stare at her backside, and I prayed inwardly: *Lord! I'm really going to need Your help on this one. It's been three months since I had sex, and this girl is giving me every reason to justify why it might be okay. So I need Your help.*

When I got back to the couch, I made sure to sit on the opposite end.

She asked, "So . . . how's the Navy SEAL life?"

"So far it's been great. I check into my SEAL Team on Friday, so I'll get the full experience then."

Having served with Kiera in the Navy, I asked, "How about you? Where are you stationed now?"

"Oh, I'm over at Balboa Hospital. You know . . . doing the nursing thing."

"Cool . . . cool," I replied.

We sat in awkward silence for ten seconds. Then, sensing my hesitation to make the first move, she slid closer and asked, "Are you seeing someone?"

Help me, Jesus, I thought. "No, what about you?"

Her mood changed a bit, and with her head down she said, "I just found out that the guy I was dating is married. Yeah . . . wife, kids, house. I was a side chick the whole time and never knew it."

"Oh, man, sorry to hear that," I said sympathetically.

She quickly switched back to me. "I can't believe you're single . . . Navy SEAL." Then she said sarcastically, "You're still not bad looking. You carry yourself well. And I know you, so I know you're not hiding a wife under your bed."

I chuckled and said, "Yeah, I'm single. I had a life-changing experience a few months ago, and I think imma stay away from all relationships for a while."

"What? You? . . . Remi Adeleke." She pointed to the door. "Hold up. Did I walk into the wrong apartment?"

I laughed and said, "Nah, you're in the right place."

"Okay, I need to know what happened to you!" She paused, mentally backed up for a second, then said, "Oh no. You didn't get HIV, did you?"

I let out a huge laugh and said, "No, thank God! Though I probably should have, the way I was living."

She probed again, "So tell me what happened to Remi Adeleke."

"You really want to know?" I asked.

"Yes. I have to know!" she said.

"Well . . ." I explained everything to her: how I put my hope and trust in Jesus, how He had changed my heart, how I now viewed women as gifts that should be honored and cherished and not used like meat. I also told her I wanted to honor God by living celibate until I got married so I wouldn't confuse lust for love and end up with the wrong person. I told her *everything*.

Before I was halfway through, she was bawling. I mean, the girl couldn't stop crying.

Fighting through all the tears, she said, "You're so right! I've . . . been giving myself to all these . . . *men*! And time and time again . . . I get used . . . I get hurt. I'm in this never-ending cycle . . . and I don't want to live like this anymore. You know, Remi . . . I grew up in the church, but I got away from it. And that's what I need right now. I don't need another man right now. I need what you have. This might sound crazy, but can you please pray with me?"

The only word that came to my mind was *wow*! That was definitely not how I expected the night to go. It could have easily gone another way, the old-Remi way, but it didn't. We ate dinner, I prayed with her, gave her a big hug, and when she was ready, I walked her to the door.

I told her, "Kiera . . . I love you, and I want the best for you. Listen: If you ever need anything or if you ever just want to talk, call me, okay?" It's interesting because when I said, "I love you," it felt genuine. It didn't feel like a boyfriend-girlfriend-type *I love you*. It felt like, *You're special. I recognize that, and I care about you, and I don't want anything in return. You are loved.*

She replied, "I will, Remi. Thank you so much. Your talk is exactly what I needed . . . gave me a lot to think about. I'll see you around."

. . .

Another major event that took place was the end of my relationship with Cecilia. Though we had broken up months earlier, we still had feelings for each other and would still profess our love for each other. Sometimes we would meet in person, and sometimes we would talk on the phone for hours. She even came with my family to my SEAL Qualification graduation.

When she started a new relationship, the mutual feelings we had for each other led us into an odd and confusing situation; we both didn't know how to handle it or how to let go of each other. One thing led to another, and her boyfriend and I ended up having a respectful conversation. Cecilia and I weren't sleeping together or doing things that couples do, so I didn't feel the need to lie to the guy. Even if we had been doing those things, I would have told him the truth.

But thirty minutes after my call with the new guy, I got a call from Cecilia.

"You just ruined everything!" she shouted at me. "I never want to talk to you ever again!"

A few days later, after I figured she'd had enough time to calm down, I called her to apologize. And the very next day I got a call from her brother, Marc.

"What's up, man?" I said when I answered the phone.

"Look, Remi, Cecilia wanted me to ask you to never contact her again. It's just . . . that's just the best thing. No hard feelings on my end."

"I understand, Marc, and I won't."

"I wish you the best."

"Thanks, man. God bless."

A sad chapter in my life had just ended, right when an exciting chapter was beginning.

. . .

Around noon on a Friday, I pulled into the Naval Special Warfare Center. Having finished all my SEAL qualification courses, I was now wearing the gold-colored trident insignia and jump wings on my dress blue uniform, along with my military ribbons and new rank, SO2.

My perspective when I drove onto the base this time was totally different from the perspective I had when I first came to BUD/S in 2004. Back then, when I passed the surf mart, I pointed out guys I assumed were SEALs. This time I knew who they were.

"Adeleke! You have arrived, dude!" Neal—who had been in 266 with me—shouted as he crossed the street in front of my car with a group of SEALs.

"Yessir!" I replied.

Neal walked up to my window and asked, "You coming to 5, dude?"

I replied, "Nah, bro. I got orders to SEAL Team 3."

Neal said, "Dude! There are a lot of guys from 266 over there. They just got back from deployment, man! I hear it's a great place to be!"

I replied, "Looking forward to getting after it. Hey, bro . . . I'll see you around. Tell the 266 boys at Team 5 I said hello."

I pulled out of the surf mart and turned onto Trident Way, passing the BUD/S compound, where I had spent many days and nights. As I drove by, I could see a class getting hammered by a group of BUD/S instructors.

Better them than me. I wouldn't want to go through that again, I said to myself.

I pulled into the SEAL Team 1 and SEAL Team 3 compound, parked, grabbed my check-in envelope, stepped out of my Infiniti, took a look at my reflection in my car window to make sure there were no wrinkles in my uniform, then made my way to the Team 3 building.

When I entered, I got goose bumps. The walls were lined with pictures of platoons, past battles, and training operations. *Man . . . I'm here!*

I made my way into the first office, which was the operations office.

I peered in and saw a SEAL master chief sitting at a desk.

"Good afternoon, Master Chief," I said.

"Hey . . . are you one of the new check-ins?" he replied.

I handed him my check-in envelope and said, "Yes, Master Chief. SO2 Adeleke."

"Great! We look forward to having you." Master Chief pulled out my orders to inspect them. After looking through my documents, he turned to look at a sheet on his desk. From what I could see, it was a list of names. As he looked down the list, he continued, "I'm not . . . hmm . . . I'm not seeing your name on my list."

"Yes, Master Chief, I think I know why. I was supposed to go to the Special Operations Medical Course after graduating SQT, but I requested that I forgo the school and go straight to a team. I've had a long road trying to get here, and I just wanted to get to work. The detailer changed my orders at the last minute."

He replied, "Okay. That makes sense. Well, we weren't expecting you, so you weren't assigned to a platoon. As you'll soon find out, the guys are gone the majority of the year for training or deployment, so when they're here, they usually cut out early on Friday."

I smiled and said, "Frogman Friday."

"Yeah, you got it. I tell you what . . . follow me. I'll see if there's any platoon leadership around. Maybe I'll be able to find a platoon that will hold you until we finalize your location."

"Roger that, Master Chief."

I followed him down the empty hallway. First we checked the Alpha and Bravo Platoon offices. The doors were open, but no one was in either office, so we walked farther down the hall and knocked on the Charlie and Delta office doors. They were locked, and no one answered, so we continued to the last platoon offices, Echo and Foxtrot. Right before we were about to knock on the door, we heard the Delta office door open, so we turned to look. A tall, burly guy stepped out of the office and asked, "Were you knocking, Master Chief?"

"Yeah. This is SO2 Adeleke. He had his orders switched at the last minute, and the team wasn't expecting him. You mind holding him in your platoon until we figure out which one he's going to?"

He said, "No problem at all." The guy reached out his hand to shake mine and said, "I'm Ivica Hudika, platoon chief for Delta Platoon, but everybody calls me Hooty."

"SO2 Remi Adeleke," I replied.

Master Chief looked at me, said, "Welcome aboard," and made his way back to the ops office.

"I'll give you a quick tour," Hooty said as we walked through the hallway. "Where are you from? That's the intel office to the right."

"Well, I was born in Africa. . . . My father was Nigerian, and grew I up in the Bronx."

"Holy shit! That's a first!" We continued down the hall as he pointed out the various offices. "That's the medical department. I never met a Nigerian SEAL who was from the Bronx. You said *was*—what happened to your father? That's admin. On Monday they'll square away your will and power of attorney."

"He died when I was five," I said.

Hooty replied, "Sorry to hear that. My son Eric died last year."

"Man, sorry for your loss, Chief."

"Thank you. . . . Yeah . . . it changed my whole perspective on life. Let's head outside, I'll walk you over to the platoon spaces. So what specialties are you interested in?"

"Specialties?" I asked with a bit of bemusement.

"Yeah . . . as in sniper, medic, breacher—what are you interested in?" Hooty clarified.

"Well, I've been a corpsman my whole career, so naturally that seems like a good fit. But my primary interest is in HUMINT. I learned about it on my last deployment with the Marines, and we had a brief intro to it in SQT. I feel like that's right up my alley."

"Hmm, most Team Guys try to avoid that," Hooty said.

I understood why they would. Every encounter with locals required extensive report writing; every single detail of a meeting had to be documented. Guys would rather spend their off-time downrange, doing other things. Because I was so used to the writing assignments Mom had given me in my youth, I replied, "I wouldn't mind it."

"Usually the HUMINT program doesn't accept new SEALs. You'll have to do a deployment, then try to apply when you get back."

"Roger that. I totally understand."

We made our way outside. As we walked to the building that housed the cages (large lockers) and platoon spaces, Chief pointed out the indoor shooting range and armory. "On Monday make sure to check in with GM1 Pierce. He'll get you issued a weapons loadout, primary M4, secondary, optics, and suppressor."

"Roger that, Chief."

When we entered the platoon building, I could hear Chief's words echo up the long stairwell. "Also, if you're not early, you're late. Be at every platoon muster five minutes early." He was talking to me as if I was already part of his platoon. "Always check, check, and recheck your gear. If we're out on an op or training and you run out of anything—I don't care what it is, batteries or whatever it is you needed—that's on you. Check that shit multiple times before you go out the door."

"Roger that, Chief."

Hooty continued, "Don't take anything personal, and if you f*** up, own it. This is the big-boy club, no excuses." We exited the stairwell and made our way down the platoon space hallway.

When we got to the Delta Platoon space door, I noticed the legendary Punisher skull emblem on the door. That was the emblem worn by SEAL Team 3's Task Unit 2, which was made up of two platoons, Charlie and Delta. Many legends wore the skull patch, some of whom I was with in BUD/S 250 and 251—Ryan Job, Michael Monsoor, and Marc Lee. Other legendary members included Jocko Willink (who would later run my platoon through tactics training), Leif Babin, Kevin Lacz, JP Dinnel, Charlie Keating, Patrick Feeks, Brandon Looney, David Warsen, and someone I was about to meet on the other side of the door, called the Legend.

"One last thing. You're a new guy, so you know what that means?"

I replied quickly, "I'm the first to volunteer for everything."

"You got it," Chief replied.

Hooty opened the door to the platoon space. Sitting right in middle of the space was Chris Kyle, the most lethal sniper in American history. That moment really made me appreciate how far I'd come, and it made me appreciate the caliber of people I had earned the right to work alongside.

"Who's the new guy?" Chris asked.

Hooty answered, "SO2 [and then he pronounced my name a little like HM3 Trotter had] A-day-lay-kay. He's from the Bronx."

. . .

Months after checking in to SEAL Team 3, I was still in Delta Platoon. I never got switched, but it worked out perfectly. There was a total of eighteen SEALs in the platoon; eight of them were guys with whom I'd gone through BUD/S or SQT. It was like a reunion. The boys were back together! And like I promised Hooty on my first day, I kept my mouth shut, showed up early, and did what I was told.

As the months passed, our platoon moved through our unit-level training, which was required of every platoon before deploying. We did nine weeks of CQC and tactical movement in the California desert; five weeks of skydiving, closed-circuit diving, and boating in San Diego; six weeks of mobility and urban tactics on an island off the coast of California; five weeks of mountaineering and surveillance and reconnaissance in the mountains of Utah; and other training around the country. I was home one week, gone three weeks, home two weeks, gone four weeks. In essence, gone a lot, home a little. But regardless of all that was going on, I maintained my faith. And as I grew in my skills as a SEAL, I also grew in my relationship with God. It was a fun time. Everything was perfect in my life. I had the job of my dreams, and for the first time, I had an extended period of peace.

. . .

Toward the end of unit-level training, our platoon had a celebration party on the NSW beach. It was a simple gathering just for platoon mates, wives, girl-friends, and kids. Being one of the new guys, I got there early to help set up.

About thirty minutes after we got the party prepped, our platoon leadership—Hooty, our LPO, the OIC, and the AOIC (assistant officer in charge)—showed up. When Hooty walked up, I heard him say, "I don't know what's wrong with my wife. She won't get out of the car." I didn't pay it much attention as I tended to the grill.

About five minutes later I saw Hooty walk back to the car and try to convince his wife to get out. I thought, *Mind your own business, Remi. Just focus on the grill. Whatever's going on has nothing to do with you.* Hooty walked back to all of us and said again, "I don't know what's wrong with my wife. She's scared to come out of the car for some reason."

Finally, after thirty minutes of sitting in the car, this five-foot-two Filipino woman got out of the passenger seat and started walking toward us. Hooty yelled, "Finally!"

The woman didn't pay any attention to her husband. Instead, she walked directly up to me and in front of the entire platoon said, "I know you!"

Everyone looked at me with suspicion. Hooty said, "How do you know my wife, Remi?"

I looked at her, then him, and said, "I don't know your wife! I've never seen her in my life!" *Come on, lady. Why you trying to put me in a bad spot with my platoon?* I thought.

Then the lady said, "She loved you so much!"

"Who?" I asked.

Her answer shocked me to my core. "Cecilia. I met her when you were in Alaska . . . and talked to her. My name is Penelope."

I felt like I was back in the *Twilight Zone*. "So . . . you're married to him?" I pointed at Hooty. "And . . . you are the one who convinced Cecilia to dump me?"

"Yes. She was struggling with what to do, and I told her if she wasn't happy, then she needed to make the best decision for herself."

That was a *wow* moment for me. I mean, just to put this into perspective, the SEAL Teams are composed of about sixty platoons. Each platoon has one chief. And out of all the platoon chiefs I could have had, I was left in a platoon with a chief whose wife had played a role in my girlfriend leaving me, which subsequently played a role in me surrendering to Christ.

That revelation clearly showed me that God had always been with me— during the good times, during the bad times, and even during the times when I mocked and rejected Him. He had been orchestrating my life! It was His voice that woke me up and led me to the one recruiter who was willing to sneak me into the Navy. It was His voice that encouraged me to take Cecilia back. It was Him who connected me with the one guy who not only would get me back to SEAL training early but also would soften my heart as it related to spirituality. It was the Lord who played a role in my various transformations: from hustler to Navy boy, from a skinny kid who couldn't swim to a muscle-bound aquatic pro, from what the world would consider a failure to a great success. I gave up being a heathen and now desired to mimic Jesus in every way—my ultimate transformation. I already believed in the power of God, but Penelope and Hooty's connection to my journey took my faith to a whole new level.

CHAPTER TWENTY-FOUR

THE CHAMELEON

None of life's experiences are wasted.

Dear Special Operator 2nd Class Remi Adeleke,

Being selected as Sailor/SEAL of the Year in the Naval Special Warfare Community is an impressive achievement and honor. It speaks volumes about your accomplishments, dedication, and potential. The Officers and Directors of the Naval Special Warfare Foundation are delighted to recognize you for this career milestone.

We are honored to present you with this award in recognition of being the Sailor/SEAL of the year. We know the men and women of NSW are the best in the world, and to be selected number one in the command is truly special in a special community. Congratulations!

With Best Regards,

NSW Foundation President and CEO

• • •

As I read that letter, I couldn't help but think about my entry into the Navy. Because military regulations prohibited anyone with anything on their record (big or small) from joining, Petty Officer Reyes had to sneak me in. It was as though they were saying, "Because of your past, we deem you as a threat; therefore, you are part of the 80 percent who will not be let in."

Did some of my negative attributes manifest during my time in service? Absolutely! I snuck away while on duty three times—one of which you know about (the hospital story), and two other times (during corpsman school and BUD/S). There were times when my anger got the best of me, and I argued with marine superiors. And there were times early in my career when I did some things I should probably never mention. But all in all, I rose above my past. I rose above my mistakes. I conformed to what was expected of me, and in the process of conformity, I became an asset to the military. The content of the NSW president's letter proved that. I became *truly special in a special community.* And to think that it almost didn't happen because of some mistakes I made in my youth! Like Reyes alluded to before the judges: "Though people make mistakes, that doesn't mean that they don't have potential."

I was scheduled to receive the award in front of the entire SEAL Team 3 Command at the command Christmas party, but there was good news and bad news as it related to the presentation. The bad news was I couldn't be there in person to receive it. The good news was the reason why I couldn't be there: long story short, our upcoming deployment would entail locating, tracking, and capturing high-value targets (HVTs). This meant our platoon needed an extra HUMINT operative. The command wrote a waiver letter, I passed the arduous screening—which was a series of mental tests—and I was accepted into the school on my first try. That's right. I didn't have to wait until after a deployment to get in. I wouldn't be able to be at the presentation of my award because I was in the last week of HUMINT school.

• • •

After graduating from HUMINT, I was assigned a third platoon specialty, one I never in a million years thought I'd be offered.

Chief approached me as I was reading through predeployment intel reports. "What's up, Remi?"

"Hey, Chief," I said as I kept my gaze on the computer screen.

"Find anything good?" Hooty asked.

"Yeah . . . looks like we're going to have a large pool of informants to vet when we get boots on the ground. From what I'm reading, there's some ambiguity regarding who can and can't be trusted. Some guys may be in it for the money, some for patriotism, some just to get close enough to an American to beg for a visa, and maybe one or two ready to get close to an American so they can push the button on their suicide vest. I'll get a better sense when I'm face-to-face with some of these guys."

"Seems like you're on it," Hooty said.

I spun around in my chair to face him. "Yessir."

He continued, "So I just spoke to the platoon chief of the platoon we're replacing. He confirmed that nothing is going to change on the FOB when we get there." We would be stationed at a forward operating base (FOB) called Camp Mercury. "It's going to remain a self-sustained base. No cooks, so we'll do our own cooking. You and Christian Corey will be the primary medical team, and no chaplain services."

"Roger that, Chief."

"Listen, . . . We don't know what's going to happen to guys out there. And being far away from home, it might help to have some religious services," he said.

I replied nonchalantly, "Oh yeah. That would be cool. I can bring some video sermons to keep on hand if guys want to watch."

Hooty continued, "That's not what I'm thinking, Remi. I want you and Christian to be the platoon . . . pastors. I don't know—is that the right term?"

"I'm not a pastor, but I'm tracking. Are you sure? I mean . . . I've never been to Bible college or seminary."

"I've seen you reading your Bible on trips and, you know . . . answering guys' questions without shoving the Bible down our throats. So I thought if you're open to it, you can do it. Nothing crazy, just church service for guys who want it and a Bible reading here and there."

"You mean a Bible study, Chief?"

"Yeah . . . Bible study. That," Hooty replied.

I replied with a mixture of excitement and hesitation, "Absolutely! Thanks for thinking of me. I'll figure it out!"

He handed me a form and said, "No problem. Have your pastor sign this. Once you get it back, I'll run it up the chain of command, and we should have your lay certificate before we leave next week."

"Roger that, Chief."

The following weekend I drove to the local bookstore and loaded up on biblical study books: Greek and Hebrew translations, apologetics guides, eschatology books, Josh McDowell's *The New Evidence That Demands a Verdict* and Lee Strobel's *The Case for a Creator*. I was all set and ready to go. As I checked out at the bookstore, I thought, *If only all my old girlfriends could see me now: Remi Adeleke, from player to pastor!*

. . .

Two weeks later we landed in country. As I stepped off the plane in my civilian clothes and thick facial hair, I could see a succession of tracer fire fly through the night sky.

I had arrived as part of our early-arrival ADVON team,[1] which consisted of key leadership and two other HUMINT operatives. We made our way across the tarmac to a row of armored vehicles waiting for us. The rest of Delta Platoon would meet us in a couple of weeks.

As we sped through the massive military base, I couldn't help but stare out the window. From what I could see, the base resembled Camp Buehring in Kuwait. And just like at Buehring, there was a calm in the air, but this calm was deceptive. I didn't hear any explosions or screams, but I knew that beyond the walls of the base was a war-torn country full of guys on my capture list. And my personal goal was to get as many of them as possible.

After about a five-minute drive, we pulled up to our first bed-down location, where we would be briefed. In a short time we were huddled around a table in the briefing room. I could see the stone-cold looks on the faces of the SEALs around me. Inside I was jubilant, but on the outside I mimicked them. *Stay cool, Remi. Act like you been here before.*

The SEAL battlespace commander had been anticipating our arrival, so he had a PowerPoint brief loaded on the start page. Looking at his staff and pointing to us, he said, "I want to formally welcome Delta Platoon. They'll be replacing Team 1's platoon at Camp Mercury." As he spoke, I scanned the room in amazement. There were intel analysts sitting at multiple computers. There were multiple digital clocks at the head of the room that represented the major time zones. And there were multiple big screens that played live drone feeds from target locations or actual operations.

The commander continued, "In the past forty-eight hours, there have been a little over thirty DA (direct action) missions in the region. The raids resulted in the capture or death of these fourteen individuals [he pointed at the PowerPoint screen, which had pictures of each of the men] along with six suicide vests and two carloads of bomb-making materials."

HUMINT school taught me how to quickly memorize, process, and retain what was necessary and discard what was irrelevant; so that's what I did. Every piece of relevant information that I could retain—especially faces, names, atmospherics, and terrorist groups—would make it easier for me to connect with and question my informants.

I nodded as he continued. "We've updated your HVT list. As you'll see, there's still a lot of work to get done out here. You'll have two days to acclimatize; then you'll make movement to your FOB. Any questions?"

"What about rules of engagement?" Hooty asked.

"Ideally we want these guys alive. You can't pull intel out of a dead guy. But ROEs are standard. Follow the escalation-of-force protocol, and if you feel that your life is in immediate danger in any way . . . better them than you. You're warriors. You know what to do. Anything else?" the commander asked.

We all looked around and shook our heads.

"All right. Happy hunting, boys."

As we all shuffled out, an older SEAL abruptly stopped me. He sported a long beard and looked like he was in his midfifties. He pointed to the other two HUMINT operatives, Snowman and Brad, and told me, "Hey, stop those two."

I got their attention; then we all turned back toward the older gentleman.

"I'm Senior Chief Joe Kuhns. I'll be the lead chief for all the HUMINT guys in the region."

"Nice to meet you," I said.

"Because I won't be with you at Camp Mercury, I have three quick things to cover. One, I'm the first one that screens your reports. And then I have to send them up to region intel so they can package and present them to the battlespace commander. That means there are a lot of important people inside the military and *outside* who will be reading what you're writing . . . you know what I'm saying?" he said, referring to other federal agencies as *outside*. We nodded.

"Please. I have a lot of reports to read, and one of my biggest pet peeves is receiving shoddy writing. It makes my job harder, and then I'll have to go and make you do rewrites, and I don't want to do that. So just do your job right the first time, and that way you and your boys can get out the door to snatch up savages, then quickly get back to collecting more intel."

"Roger that," we all said.

"Second, remember your tradecraft at all times. If one of your informants gets exposed or killed, it's not going to be a good thing for you, especially if it's your fault."

"Roger," we said.

"Third, and this may go a bit against my second rule, but trust your instincts. If something deep down is telling you, *It's time to go*, leave. If something is telling you, *I need to say something*, say it. If something is telling you, *He's probably working for the opposition to plant bad intel*, figure out a way to work it against him or cut him loose. In relation to the amount of time you've been on this earth, you've only been doing this for a short period of time, but your instinct has been with you since you were conceived, so trust it."

I looked Joe straight in the eyes and said, "Roger that."

• • •

There we were, two weeks later, my interpreter, Brad, and me, standing at the inner entrance to an abandoned building in the middle of the night while we waited for a local informant to arrive. There was a light sandstorm passing through, which was perfect because it helped to mask both our movements as well as the local's.

As usual I was sporting a regular shirt, pants, and Nike sneakers. I had my M4 with suppressor, laser, and scope, and my SIG tucked into the back of my pants. We had already conducted several meetings to screen which informants we would keep and which to cut loose. This meeting would help us finalize our roster.

I looked at my interpreter and said, "Hey, Raj, he should have been here by now. Call him back and find out where he is."

Raj replied in his Lebanese accent, "You got it, boss." Raj was about sixty. He had emigrated from Lebanon to the United States in his thirties. Due to his ability to speak multiple languages, he was hired as a contractor for SOF units, and the Middle East became his home once again. The guy was as skinny as a toothpick, had nerves of steel, and was as funny as any comedian out there.

As I peered out the door, I could hear Raj talking in Arabic.

He pulled the phone away from his head and said, "He's pulling up now. The sandstorm held him up. Should I head outside?"

I replied, "Yeah . . . but same thing, I'll stand at the door with my M4 at the ready. Stay at least ten feet away from him. Have him lift up his shirt, undo his pockets, then spin around. If you see wires or a detonator—anything you shouldn't see—sprint in my direction, and if I have to, I'll light him up. If he clears the visual inspection, move in for a pat down; then have him pop the trunk, and check the entire vehicle. I'll cover you until you make your way in; then Brad will pick up the cover while I head to the meeting room."

Though Raj had been in the game for a long time, I made sure to re-establish my protocol before every meeting. I didn't want anyone's death on my hands, especially not a new friend's. Like Hooty always said, "Check, check, and recheck."

As Raj ran out of the building, I turned to Brad and said, "I'll take lead on this while you run security. Cool?"

"Cool," he replied.

When the car pulled up, I stared at it intently with my M4 at the low ready. As soon as the local stepped out, I began to whisper the details to Brad. "One guy . . . I don't see any passengers. White top . . . sand-colored pants . . . sandals. Looks clear from here. . . . Raj is moving in for pat down." After Raj finished and gave his typical I'm-your-boy-now hug, he conducted the vehicle inspection. Once that was done, Brad picked up the cover with his M4 while I ran to the meeting room to get prepped.

When I got there, I put my M4 on the floor to the side of my chair, moved my pistol to the front of my pants, set out the refreshments, and sat back as if I was in a lounge.

Within seconds Raj and the local, Abdullah, made entry. I stood up, stretched out my arms, and went into my best Martin Lawrence impersonation. "What's up, what's up, what's up, man!!!" It may sound stupid, but I had found that was the best way to break the ice and lighten the mood. During my time in Kuwait years earlier, I observed the local base workers in the shopping area watching African American comedies with Arabic subtitles. They would fall out in laughter at the comedies. What I found even funnier was that they knew about all the black entertainers—Will Smith, Wesley Snipes, Eddie Murphy, Martin Lawrence, and many others.

Some locals near Camp Mercury also watched dubbed American films. Knowing that I was probably one of the first African Americans some of these guys had encountered so closely, I knew if I could pull off the act, they would feel as if they were sitting in the room with one of their favorite actors, not some American who was trying to get information from them. Whatever it takes, right?

Abdullah didn't understand a word I said, but he smiled from ear to ear, then started laughing, so I continued with my act. "How you doing? I got beverages, nice couch. You know what? I'm so rude . . . have a seat."

Raj was laughing through his interpretation as well.

Abdullah finally said something in Arabic.

"What'd he say?" I asked with a smile.

Still laughing through his words, Raj said, "He said you remind him of Chris Tucker!"

"Chris Tucker! That's my boy!" I said, and then I tried to mimic Chris Tucker to the best of my ability.

Raj continued to translate as Abdullah babbled on: "He just said, 'I like this guy . . .'" Then Raj paused to get the rest of the translation: "He's different than the others."

I got him, I thought.

As the meeting continued, I stayed in character but turned down the energy a tad. I didn't want to ask about any bad guys; I just wanted to get to know him—find out about his family, his upbringing, his job—all information that would help me develop a profile I could later use for questioning purposes.

The meeting went on for about an hour, and by the end I had him asking me, "What can I do to help you?"

I told him, "Nothing right now. I just want to get to know you . . . you know . . . make some new friends. We can talk business another time."

Then Abdullah said, "I can find Umar. Everyone knows the Americans are looking for him."

My ears perked up. Umar Zahid was one of the top terrorist leaders in the region. His group was known for plotting or carrying out terror attacks on Western and even Muslim assets. He was also known for recruiting kids to become suicide bombers. For years American and local forces had tried to capture him, but due to the fact that he struck fear in the hearts of most locals and even had government officials in his pocket, it was like chasing a ghost. I wanted to wrap up a lot of guys, but my ultimate goal for that deployment was to catch Umar Zahid, dead or alive. For motivation, I even kept a picture of Umar in my trailer.

Without breaking character, I said, "Thank you, but it's okay. Maybe we'll talk about him another time."

He replied through Raj, "I didn't even get your name."

I replied, "Oh! Forgive me! People out here call me Abu Kareem."

He smiled and asked, "You're Muslim?" I didn't need the interpreter to translate; my Arabic was good enough to figure it out. But to stall I looked at Raj and acted like I needed a translation.

I knew the true answer was probably not what he wanted to hear. My training had taught me to never get involved in religious talk, so I started to give a neutral answer. "I do—"

Before I could finish, Raj cut me off and yelled at Abdullah in Arabic. He was scolding Abdullah for asking me such personal questions so soon. It was a good move; he was playing bad cop for a minute in order to deflect the question and maintain all the hard work I had done over the last hour.

When I felt it was appropriate, I jumped back in as good cop, grabbed Raj, and said, "Hey, man! Calm down. Easy." Raj looked at me, nodded his head, then began to lead Abdullah out. I grabbed my M4 off the floor and followed.

As we walked out, Abdullah carried on a conversation with Raj.

Raj turned to me and said, "He said his wife cooks very, very good! He wants to bring you food next time."

I looked at Raj as if to say, "I don't know about that. I'll take a bullet out here, but I ain't trying to die of food poisoning."

Raj reassured me, "It's okay, Kareem."

So I replied, "Yes, tell him I said I would love that!"

Before we stepped out of the building, Abdullah turned toward me for a departure hug. I gave him a New York dab and hug; then he said something to me in Arabic.

Raj translated, "He said he never met a black American before. And he appreciates you leaving your home to come here to help."

I laughed and said, "Tell him I said no problem, it's my pleasure." Then I looked him in the eye and said in Arabic, *"Ma'a salama."*

That was the way the majority of my meetings went. And I don't mean the Chris Tucker act; I mean fostering connections. I felt like I was somehow able to empathize with the locals: their struggle, their constant adversity, and their desire for a better life. Now, I'm in no way comparing my life to theirs. Weekly suicide bombings do a lot more damage to the human psyche than drive-by shootings like the one I experienced as a kid. But because of my upbringing in the Bronx and the many hardships I faced throughout my life, I had a good sense of what they were feeling. It was like I knew exactly what hat I needed to put on to make them forget about their problems and enter a new and fresh world for however long we met.

On the other end of the spectrum, the street smarts I gained from the Bronx helped me to quickly identify when a local was trying to play me for money; or worse, when a local was actually a terrorist in sheep's clothing. My HUMINT training made me good, but my instincts, sparked in my childhood and developed throughout my life, gave me an edge that made men like Abdullah trust me.

CHAPTER TWENTY-FIVE

WARRIOR PRINCE

Great men are forged in fire. It is the
privilege of lesser men to light the flame.
—THE WAR DOCTOR[1]

Raj yelled over the wind, "Abdullah is adamant that Umar's brother will be there tonight!" We had just got out of a meeting with Abdullah and were racing in a two-seater dune buggy to the Camp Mercury TOC (tactical operations center).

"I'm not doubting him. I'm just concerned that if we capture the brother, Umar will leave town again!"

"Do we have approval for the op?" Raj shouted.

"Yeah! After I vetted Abdullah's information against Hazzan's yesterday, we ran the intel package to Joe and the battlespace commander!" Hazzan was another one of our informants. "The op is a go if Mr. E says yes!"

I pulled up to the TOC, hopped out of the driver's seat, and began to make my way in. Raj stayed outside.

One of my platoon mates, Eli, yelled at me right before I opened the door. "Remi!"

I turned to look at him and said, "What's up, brother?"

As he ran up, he asked, "What's up for tonight? Are we getting out?" My intel gathering had led to a significant number of ops in the first three months. So many, in fact, that platoon mates would sometimes ask me if we were going on ops. Even Hooty would ask me some nights.

"I just got confirmation on where Umar's brother is bedding down tonight. If Mr. E gives us the thumbs-up, we're in it to win it. It's looking good."

Eli headed off to tell the others while I made my way into the TOC and went straight to Mr. E's desk. Mr. E was our platoon OIC.

I approached and said, "Sir, I just got out of a meeting with Abdullah. He confirmed again that Umar's brother Yasin is still at the wailing house location."

Mr. E leaned back in his chair and said, "Really?"

As I continued, Hooty, our assigned DIA agent, Paul, and our ScanEagle drone pilot, Kettner, walked up. "If we wait till one . . . maybe two a.m., we can sneak in and wrap him up before he knows what hit him. But . . . my only concern is—"

Mr. E finished my sentence. "If we capture Yasin, Umar will leave town."

"Yes, sir," I replied.

Mr. E looked at Paul and asked, "What are your thoughts?"

Paul was a fast-talking brainiac. The guy knew *everything* about almost every terrorist group in the world: names, locations, family connections, financing, religious affiliations. It was crazy. If I ever asked him a question about a person, ten minutes later he would still be giving me the answer. He didn't just give an appetizer of information; he gave the full-course meal.

Paul said, "Yasin may be worth it. He's the punk older brother who got stepped over by his younger brother. Some even say that's the reason behind their well-documented public disputes. He funds 30 percent of Umar's endeavors, plus he has a wealth of knowledge on other terror networks. Because all the attention is focused on Umar, Yasin tends to roll with little to no security. That means he may be an easy grab for you guys. But, yeah, chances are, if you capture him, Umar will disappear for a couple of weeks, maybe even two, three months." Paul took a long breath, as he usually did before giving his final assessment. "My conclusion: capturing him alive and getting him into a room with a master interrogator would be worth it."

Mr. E looked at Kettner and asked, "Can you get the drone over Yasin's location in two hours?"

"I already requested it for standby. I can have it up whenever you want," Kettner replied.

"There may be one small issue, sir," I said.

"What you got?" Mr. E asked.

"The only pictures we have of Yasin show him sporting an oversize beard. Both Abdullah and Hazzan separately confirmed that he shaved it down significantly. About two, three weeks' worth of growth . . . heavy stubble, maybe. Anyway, that's a significant change to his features. Might be best to bring Abdullah to make a positive ID. We can follow the same protocol we did with Hazzan. Keep him in the truck. We capture Yasin, take a picture, then bring the camera to the truck to show Abdullah."

"Do you think you'll be able to talk Abdullah into going?" Hooty asked.

"I'm sure I can talk him into it. Worst-case scenario, I'll have to throw in some cash to make it worth his while. But I'll make it happen."

Mr. E said, "All right. I'll jump on a call with the higher-ups to brief them." Then Mr. E looked at Chief and said, "Hooty, get the boys prepped. The op is a go."

Yes, I thought. I ran outside and told Raj, "Call Abdullah right now." Raj immediately pulled out his phone as I continued, "Tell him to turn around and meet you at the pickup point. If he asks why . . . just tell him it's an emergency."

"Let me guess: he's going on the op?" Raj asked.

"Yes, but don't tell him that! Once you grab him and bring him back to Camp Mercury, I'll figure out a way to tell him in person."

"Got it, boss," Raj replied.

As I drove to my trailer, I could see the bustling of the platoon. Guys were changing out of their lounge clothes into op cammies, weapons were being inspected, vehicles were getting started, and our point men had a map sprawled out on a table as they discussed the best routes in and out of Yasin's neighborhood. We were all individuals, but we operated as one well-oiled machine; everybody had a role to play, and each man did it with excellence.

I pulled up to the row of trailers, hopped out, and made my way into mine. As soon as I got to my room, I changed out of my civilian clothes and donned my op cammies and MOLLE vest,[2] which housed my ballistic plates and held my magazines, grenades, knife, radio, and other gear. I checked my

M4 and pistol, then tested my laser, night vision goggles, and red-lens head-lamp that I wore around my neck.

Once my gear was settled, I sat down for my pre-op devotional. "Though I walk through the valley of the shadow of death, I will fear no evil, for You are with me," I prayed. "Forgive me for my sins that I am aware of and unaware of. I pray for supernatural wisdom and understanding. . . . Lord, help us make the right decisions. I pray for supernatural protection upon the platoon. And I release my spirit into Your arms if it is Your will that I perish. In Jesus' name I pray, amen." After that I sat in my chair and played Lecrae's gospel rap album while I waited for Abdullah's arrival.

An hour later I met Raj and Abdullah on the other side of Camp Mercury, away from the trailers. When I walked up to Abdullah, I could tell he was surprised to see me dressed the way I was. He had never seen me in my operational gear. To him I had transformed.

I placed my right hand over my chest and said, "*As-salaam-alaikum.*"

He responded nervously while his eyes darted between me and Raj. "*Wa-alaikum-salaam.*"

I looked at Raj and said, "Tell him it's okay." Upon Raj's translation, Abdullah nodded. I continued, "I need your help, Abdullah. You're the only one who can point out Yasin for me. Can you please come with us to catch him?"

After Raj translated, Abdullah responded frantically in Arabic.

Raj said, "He says no. He will not go! If he is discovered with Americans, he and his whole family will be killed."

I replied, "Tell him I said yes, he's right. If he's discovered, he and his entire family will be killed. But ask him if I've ever put him or his family in danger."

They went back and forth in Arabic before Raj delivered his translation. "He said no, you haven't, but this is different!"

"Tell him he will not be seen. See that truck over there?" I pointed to the side of a large RG-33 MRAP as Raj translated. "Do you see any people in there?" On each side of the MRAP were two twelve-by-twelve-inch windows, with a third window that was smaller. The windows were made of thick ballistic glass. We operated only at night, so between the size of the windows, the thickness of the glass, and the cover of night, it was virtually impossible to make out the number of people in the vehicle, let alone their identities.

Abdullah took about thirty seconds to examine the truck, which was about seventy feet away. Then he looked at Raj and said in Arabic, "I don't know. I can't see whether anybody is in there or not."

After Raj translated Abdullah's response, I said, "Exactly. You're going to be in there the entire time. If we capture Yasin, I'll take a picture on my camera, then run to show it to you. If you say it's him, we'll take him with us. If we capture him, he'll be blindfolded and put into a separate vehicle. When we get back to base, we'll move him blindfolded to our detention center, and once he's there, we'll take you out of the truck and get you safely home. I know that's a lot, but do you see that you'll be protected?" I could see from Abdullah's demeanor that he was bending in my favor, but before he could answer, I wanted to make sure I sealed the deal. While staring at Abdullah intently, I said to Raj, "Tell him . . . 'You came here three weeks ago with tears streaming down your eyes. Why was that?'"

Abdullah responded through Raj, "Because of the kids."

Three weeks earlier Umar had ordered a hit on a government official who was a major catalyst for stabilization in the region. He didn't just want the official dead; he wanted everyone connected to him dead too. As usual, the coward Umar wouldn't do the job himself, so he tasked an illiterate suicide bomber who was brainwashed into being a martyr. The bomber drove a car full of explosives into the building he thought was the government official's. It wasn't; the guy was so uneducated that he couldn't read the Arabic directions he was given. Instead of hitting the government building, he ran the car into an educational building that was filled with kids.

Minutes after the explosion Abdullah showed up to help pull bodies out of the rubble. He personally carried three dead kids from the rubble to the morgue. It scarred his mind. When he showed up to our meeting, he was a mess—blood all over his clothes, dust and debris on his hair and face. I wanted to pray for him, but I knew the rules, so I stuck to them.

"That's right," I said to Abdullah. "Innocent kids were murdered for what? Nothing! Now, if we can catch Yasin . . . we'll slow Umar down for a while and may be able to get information as to how we can catch Umar in the future. But we can't catch the man responsible for what happened to those kids without his brother and without you."

Abdullah looked at me, smiled, then said in Arabic, "Okay, my friend. I will go."

I replied, "*Shukran*," which is "Thank You" in Arabic. Then I turned to Raj and said, "Place him in the holding room. If he wants, he can take a nap. We're rolling out at one a.m."

"Okay, Kareem," Raj replied.

• • •

"Five minutes out from insert!" Snowman yelled from the front of the vehicle. I pulled off my helmet, pulled on the black ski mask that I wore on every op, then put my helmet back on. Abdullah was sitting across from me. The surprise on his face when he saw me in my uniform was nothing compared to his look after I donned my mask. It was as though he was saying, *Who is this guy? And what the hell have I gotten myself into?* I smiled, but he couldn't see through my mask, so I just nodded, then flipped down my night vision goggles.

When the vehicle came to a stop, Mr. E came over our radio, which was connected to bone mic earbuds, and whispered, "Drone's showing two heat signatures on the roof of Yasin's location [*break*]. Heads on a swivel, boys. Dismount."

C-Lod and Eli departed the vehicle I was in while the rest of the ground team exited two other RGs. I looked at Raj and said, "Christian and the driver are going to stay in the truck with you and Abdullah. Lock the back door behind me."

Raj whispered back, "You got it, boss. Good luck."

As soon as I dismounted, I fell in with the patrol. Half of the ground force moved stealthily down one side of the street while my element was on the opposite side. Like ninjas, we crept our way through a sleeping city, halting and fading into dark corners anytime we heard a sound. During the entire deployment, we ran vampire hours, which meant that we went to bed around 5:00 a.m. and rose for our first brief at 5:30 p.m. My informant meetings were around 7:30 p.m., and if we had a mission, we were out the door between midnight and 2:00 a.m. By this point in the deployment, I had gotten so used to operating at night that it was like second nature. I could even identify each member of the team by his stride.

During our movement to Yasin's place, there was no talking or whispering. We communicated by hand signals only. Within fifteen minutes we were at the entrance of the two-story target house. When we got to the entrance, Eli, who was the point man, gave the hand signal for the breacher to move to the front; when he did, he worked his magic and got the locked door open without making any loud noises.

Like a river, we flowed into the house, filling the north end of the first floor. The last man in closed the entry door behind us, and, for the moment, the streets had their territory back.

Though several operators were clearing rooms on the first floor, there was a dead silence throughout the house. It was like we were ghosts—there but not there.

With my M4 and IR laser up, I bent down into a deep squatting position and peered into a room. I could tell it was a kid's room because there was a small bed and toys everywhere. *How can someone with kids be associated with a person who's killed kids?* I thought. I didn't see anyone from my vantage point, so I crept in slowly with my finger on the trigger. Another SEAL followed. It was empty, no one in or under the bed or in the closet. I whispered over my bone mic, "Northeast corner one clear."

Seconds later I heard other operators whisper over the bone mics the status of other parts of the first floor.

"Northwest corner one clear."

"Southeast corner one clear."

"Center one clear."

Hooty whispered over comms, "One clear. Move to two."

I crept up to Eli, who had his gun pointed up the stairs. Once I looked back and saw that four guys were lined up behind me, I placed my hand on Eli's shoulder and gave it a squeeze. He quietly began to move up the stairs while we followed with our guns pointed at different parts of the upper floor.

Many people have asked me, "What is it like sneaking into the house of a terrorist? Was there any fear? What were you thinking?" For me, there wasn't any fear at all. I knew I had received the best training in the world; that always gave me a sense of peace and confidence. More important, I knew I was rolling with the baddest dudes on the face of the planet. So whether it was sixteen of us sneaking into a complex where thirty known terrorists lived (which happened) or whether it was sixteen of us sneaking into a house of six, I was calm, cool, and collected. And as for what I was thinking? *Don't do anything or* not *do anything that will get the guy to your right or left killed. Your boys are more important than you.*

After the second floor was clear, operators whispered over the bone mics, "Southeast corner two clear." "Northwest corner two clear." "Southwest corner two clear."

Hoot gave the command, "Two clear. Move to roof."

In the country where we were, it got so hot during the spring and summer months that the locals would sleep on the roofs. From our ISR feed,[3] we knew there were two bodies up there. The question was, was Yasin one of them?

I was the first person at the short staircase that led to the roof, so I kept my gun pointed at the door of the roof, just waiting for someone with an AK-47 to slide it open—and secretly hoping that someone would be Umar.

After two minutes of holding on the door, the team lined up behind me, and I felt a squeeze on my shoulder. I slowly moved up the steps. When I got to the entrance of the roof, I saw the door was cracked open. I took my left hand off my M4 and pushed the door open just enough for my team and me to make entry. When the door didn't squeak, I moved onto the roof.

I immediately saw two bodies forty feet from my position. The roof entrance was at the center of the north end of the roof. The men were sleeping at the south end of the roof. They were lying about seven feet apart from one another. There was an AK-47 to the right of the guy on the right, which led me to believe he may have been Yasin's bodyguard. I kept the scope of my M4 pointed at the bodyguard's head while the team entered around me.

With their guns trained on the body to the left, three SEALs led by C-Lod moved diagonally south toward the east wall. We set up a half-cross ambush with the sleepers at the center point of the cross. Upon initiation C-Lod's element would move west to the center point while Eli and I moved south to the same point. Eli lined up behind me, and Hooty stayed at the door to monitor the takedown.

After Eli gave me the squeeze, everybody moved swiftly as one. We met at the center point at the exact same time. Without stopping I kicked the AK away from the bodyguard, then bent down and grabbed his ankle. C-Lod's element was already on top of the second sleeper. I dragged the bodyguard like a rag doll to the south wall away from him while Eli followed me with his gun pointed at the man's head.

After arriving at the south wall, Eli and I flipped the bodyguard over to examine his face. The look that he gave us was priceless. He was in a frozen state with his eyes and mouth wide open; he couldn't move. I probably wouldn't either if a six-foot-two, 210-pound black guy with a black ski mask and silencer on his gun just dragged me out of my dream and into a nightmare.

I lived for that look. Why? Because in my opinion 100 percent of terrorists are cowards! They kill innocent people. The high-level terrorists send kids to blow themselves up but never volunteer to do it themselves; then they go make a video and talk all kinds of ish as to what they're about to do. So I loved being the one who wakened them from their dreams and said, "What you got to say now, homie?" The utter fear in their eyes nourished me.

Once both guys were zip-tied, we kept them separated, then snuck back into the house.

Ox, who was our ops interpreter, asked the bodyguard in Arabic, "Yasin Zahid? Is that him?"

The bodyguard said nothing. To me, that was a good sign because it pretty much meant that it was Yasin.

I walked down to the first floor, where the other man was being held, and asked, "Yasin Zahid?" As usual with terrorists we captured, he shook his head, looked around at us, and said in English, "No, no . . . American friend." I didn't even respond. I just pulled out my digital camera, put it up to his face, and snapped a picture.

"I got the picture, sir," I told Mr. E over the comm.

"Roger. The vehicles are pulling up in ten minutes. Hooty should be done with SSE by then." SSE (sensitive site exploitation) consisted of packing up every document, photo, hard drive, thumb drive, bomb-making material, weapon, and money from the house into duffel bags and bringing it back to Camp Mercury for processing.

When the trucks pulled up, Eli and I sprinted to the truck where Abdullah was.

I gave the digital camera to Abdullah and told Raj, "Tell him he has ten seconds. Is this Yasin Zahid?"

Abdullah nodded without hesitation, and said, "Yasin Zahid! Yes!"

I jumped in the truck, closed the door behind me, then said over comms the phrase we used every time we snagged our target: "Jackpot, jackpot,

jackpot." Upon that command the rest of the team poured out of the house with three duffel bags of bomb-making material, AKs, and computers. They threw Yasin and his bodyguard into the other two trucks, and we sped off into the blackness of night.

• • •

Just finished your sermon, Remi. God is great! I cried about three times. It was beautiful. The Holy Spirit really reached out to me through it. I have been battling with some things, and your sermon really helped me to once and for all put some of that garbage out for good. I am thankful to you for sharing your past battles regarding lust, as this is a challenging thing to face. It will be easier for me to obey God after reading this. Every single paragraph, I was like, "He hit the nail right on the head!" And it is all so true. I felt like you were telling my story through your story. And there were a few pieces of advice where God was like, "You see? How many times do I have to tell you this before you believe Me?" Thank you for sending this. It made more of an impact than I thought it would, and than you would imagine.—Nia

The sermon was awesome. It will touch many lives similarly to the way that God has touched mine. I will be here praying for your quick and safe return home. Thank you for sharing it with me, and may God continue to bless you.—Kiera

All I can say is WOW! That is a truly powerful message.—Gamble

I sat at my laptop in my trailer and read through my recent e-mails with a huge sense of gratitude, growth, and fulfillment. I was four months into deployment, and as my intel skills grew, my ministry also grew. Christian and I facilitated two weekly church services for SEALs and support staff who wanted them. Even our HUMINT senior chief, Joe Kuhns, got in on the action. During a three-week stay to monitor and inspect our intel-gathering practices, he volunteered as a deacon, mentoring Christian and me in the ways of expository preaching. So between leading a church, gaining hours of writing experience from intel reports, and learning from Joe, I figured out a way to write sermons for family and friends back home. I called the series of written sermons "Letters from the Wilderness."

After reading through my e-mails, I said to myself, *Well . . . it's time to start another one.* I sifted through my notes, organized them into an outline, and followed my typical writing pattern, which consisted of speaking what I wanted to write and then typing it into the computer.

I said aloud, "Before you get into a relationship with someone you've just met—really don't know—it's important that you know yourself. If you don't understand who you are, how can you truly understand someone else?"

Then as usual when I started writing, there was a knock on my trailer door!

"Remi!" I heard Bingo yell. He was a contractor from the Philippines who could barely speak English, but he was great at maintaining our generators and trailers. Funny guy too.

I replied, "Hold on!" Then I continued my thought: Knowing yourself will reveal your true limits, the depth of your individual love, your true likes and dislikes, and most important . . .

"Remi! You start chicken now!" Bingo yelled in his thick Filipino accent.

"Hold on, man! Let me finish my thought!" I returned to typing: . . . what you really deserve. A lot of us get into relationships with just anybody because we really don't know what we deserve.

"How long gonna be?" Bingo asked.

I replied, "I'll be five minutes, maaannn!"

Then I continued, We've been conditioned so much by friends, family, media, teachers, and what everyday life tells us is good or bad, beautiful or ugly, real or false, that we've lost ourselves in the midst of it all, and some of us really don't know who we are.

I stood up and said to myself, *Got it. . . . That's a good start,* then made my way outside.

As soon as I saw Bingo, I said, "Bingo! Come on, man! I told y'all I'd do the mango chicken!" (Oh yeah. I added another specialty while on deployment: platoon grill master.)

"We do now. Church in two hours!" Bingo said.

"What! Today's Sunday?" I asked, surprised.

"Yes! That's why I knock now. Can't be late to mass!"

That wasn't the first time the pastor forgot about church! We all worked so hard seven days a week that every day felt like Monday.

I couldn't help but smile and throw my arm around him. As we walked toward the kitchen, I said, "Thank you, Bingo. And I'm sorry for yelling at you."

Usually people run from the idea of church, but here this guy was banging on my door to ensure that I, the pastor, made it to the church on time. Christian, Joe, and I must have been doing something right.

"It's okay. God forgives," Bingo said.

"Yes, He does, Bingo. . . . Yes, He does."

CHAPTER TWENTY-SIX

NOW I CAN GO HOME

As George Orwell pointed out, people
sleep peacefully in their beds at night
only because rough men stand ready
to do violence on their behalf.
—RICHARD GRENIER[1]

One day toward the end of deployment, I was lying in bed when I was abruptly awakened by a *bang, bang, bang!*

"Who?" I whispered, as I lay half-asleep in my bed.

Bang, bang, bang!

It was around eleven in the morning, which for me—since we ran vampire hours—was the equivalent of two in the morning.

Raj cracked open my trailer door, letting in the bright summer sun. I groaned. "At least come in and close the door!" I mumbled as I pulled the sheets over my face. "This better be good, Raj."

"I'm on the phone with Abdullah! Umar is back!" he said.

With my head still under the covers and my eyes closed, I asked, "How does he know?"

Raj replied, "Because he was just sitting right behind him in the mosque! We should go get him right now!"

"We can't go in or around the mosque. Raj, you know that."

"But—"

"I'll deal with it when I wake up later," I said into my pillow. "Tell him I'll call back."

I had wanted to capture Umar ever since I arrived six months earlier, but the last two times we went after him, the ops produced nothing but dry holes. Those ops were at night, so I figured that if we tried to go after him in the daytime, while the city was alive and buzzing, the results could potentially lead to disaster.

I could tell by the way Raj closed my door he was frustrated. I tried to go back to sleep but couldn't. I felt this heavy conviction. *"Remi, what are you doing? You have a responsibility. Get up and do your job. Trust Me."*

"All right!" I finally said, full of frustration.

I got out of the bed, slipped on my flip-flops, threw on a shirt, and headed out of my trailer. Raj lived in a trailer on Camp Mercury that was separate from the teams and support staff. It was funny: he had a picket fence around his trailer, and he even had a local dog called Zingy that he and a female interpreter adopted. The dog was—in my opinion—demonic, so we made him stay on Raj's "property" all the time.

As the hot sun beat down on me, I placed my hand on the top of Raj's fence, raised up on my toes, and yelled, "Raj!" Zingy started barking at me. "Shut up, dog . . . Raj!"

When Raj stepped out of his trailer, I apologized, then asked him to call Abdullah back.

As Raj put the phone to his ear, he asked, "Okay. What do you want me to tell him?" Then he paused and spoke into the phone, "Abdullah!"

"Ask him if Umar is still at the mosque."

After delivering the translation, Raj replied, "He said yes. He came with one other man. He wants you to come to the mosque now. Umar doesn't bring much security to mosque."

"Tell him we can't do that, and ask him if he knows which vehicle Umar rode in."

"He said yes," Raj replied. "He knows which vehicle."

"Okay, keep him on the line. I'm going to inform Mr. E."

I ran back to the team trailers and knocked on Mr. E's door. Being the leader of the platoon, he was up and at the door immediately. "What you got, Remi?"

"Abdullah is outside a mosque right now. He says that he was sitting right behind Umar. He's back in town, sir. What do you want me to do?"

"Abdullah's your informant; what do you think?" Mr. E asked.

"He's been one of my top three informants. I mean . . . the majority of his information has checked out. If he's saying Umar is there, I have no reason not to believe him."

Mr. E said, "Okay."

Within an hour we had a drone locked onto Umar's car, which Abdullah had identified for us. That meant wherever the car went, we would be watching.

An hour later Umar arrived at one of his wives' houses. Only one other person exited the vehicle with him. This was a surprise because he never traveled that light. It probably meant he believed that we didn't know he was back. But we did know, and by this point our team was loaded into three trucks and eagerly watching his every move.

Before we drove off, Mr. E, who was in one of the trucks, said over the radio, "It looks like the target is sitting outside in a walled courtyard [*break*]. Let's move out." The drivers flipped on the IED jammers; then we made our way off Camp Mercury and sped through the city.

Mr. E continued, "No pauses, guys. As soon as we pull up, immediately exit. Make entry over the wall and wrap up Umar. As always, if there is a fight, we fight together."

I could hear the team say through our bone mics, "Check." "Roger." "Check."

"Two minutes," Snowman said as he gave the hand signal for two minutes.

As soon as we pulled up to the residence, Fireteams 1 and 2 jumped out of the trucks, sprinted to the wall, and climbed over. By the time my feet hit the courtyard, I could see Umar climbing over the opposite wall, which led to a massive field of tall grass. *Abdullah was right again*, I thought. *Umar is back.* The second guy ran into the house.

Our team AOIC commanded Fireteam 2 to capture Umar's associate; then he looked at me, C-Lod, and Eli, and said, "Let's get this savage!" He radioed Mr. E and said, "Fireteam 1 is commencing foot pursuit."

"Roger."

We sprinted to the wall Umar had jumped, made the climb, and started following the path Umar was making through the field. Now, keep in mind a few things: One, we were loaded down with body armor, ammo, grenades, miscellaneous gear, and I was also carrying my trauma backpack full of medical gear. Two, Umar was wearing a *thawb*, or what we called a "man dress," which was made of linen. And three, it was about 120 degrees outside.

The combination of the heat, gear, and Umar's speed didn't make the chase fun! I had a flashback to one of my BUD/S instructors who always said during painful evolutions, "You think this sucks? I've been on ops that sucked worse than a day in BUD/S! So if you can't make it through this, you won't make it out there!" (And yes, a *ding, ding, ding* almost always followed.)

Mr. E was in constant communication with the drone pilot, so he radioed in an update as we ran through the field. "We've followed Umar to a house half a mile northeast of your location."

"Roger," AOIC replied.

When I got to the house, I was soaked in sweat. It was like I had just climbed out of a pool. We lined up on the door, Eli in front, followed by C-Lod, myself, and AOIC in the back. C-Lod gave Eli the squeeze, and we moved in. We were immediately met with screams and—I don't know how this happened—flying chickens. One of the family members pointed to the opposite end of the house to let us know where Umar exited. We slowly crept out of the house, being careful about not rushing into a hail of bullets. His trail had gone cold. There was no visible path that we saw, so we took a knee and waited for an update from the drone.

After about ten minutes of waiting, we heard a rapid succession of gunfire. *Bang, bang, bang, bang!* Lying low, our fireteam looked around to try to determine the location of the shots. AOIC radioed, "Shots fired, shots fired. Fireteam 1 reporting zero casualties or wounded. What's your status, Mr. E?"

"All are accounted for and well [*break*]. Move back to the trucks. Umar exited a second house and jumped into the back of a garbage truck."

I later found out from Abdullah that the shots were fired from one of the only incorruptible police officers in the area. Umar ran into his house (the second house) and asked him to hide Umar. Knowing who Umar was, the bold police officer wouldn't do it and instead demanded that Umar leave. When Umar refused, the cop pulled out his gun and shot several rounds into the air to scare Umar off. That bold move later cost the police officer and his entire family their lives. A week later a suicide bomber drove a car bomb into his house, killing everyone inside, kids included. That was the kind of person we were dealing with; Umar Zahid was a monster!

We loaded back into the trucks and geared up for what would turn into a six-hour chase: from a vehicle pursuit to sliding in and out of a swamp; from searching a village full of people to another vehicle pursuit. Finally we pulled into a secluded location in the desert, and Mr. E said, "All right, boys. We're going to stop playing this game. The drone still has a lock on Umar. He's not going anywhere out of our reach. He has to fall asleep at some point, and when he does, that's when we'll get him. We'll bed down here until nightfall. Fifty-fifty security: half get rest, and the other half—guns up."

. . .

Around 1:00 a.m., Mr. E called us in for a brief.

"All right. At ten p.m. the drone followed Umar's last known vehicle to a farming area on the outskirts of town. One individual exited. We believe it's Umar. The drone has a large group of people sleeping at the front of the house, south side, and two individuals sleeping at the back of the house, north side. We're not taking any chances. We'll offload the assault team three miles east." The assault team consisted of AOIC, Eli, C-Lod, Christian, Ox, me, and a few other operators. Looking at us, Mr. E said, "You'll hike in, quietly take down the two individuals at the south end, then assess whether you have to conduct a second search among the north group."

"ROGER," we all said.

"Any questions?" Mr. E asked. We shook our heads, then Mr. E finished with, "Mount up!"

As planned, we loaded the vehicles and with lights off, slowly drove to the insert point. When we got there, the assault force off-loaded, then started the hike. We crept through the large flat farmland. There was a full moon, so we made sure to spread out, and anytime we thought we heard or saw something that would give us away, we melted to the ground in the prone position.

At about 3:00 a.m. we finally arrived at the house. There was a large row of bushes running north to south that lined the east side of the property. Eli slowly peered through the bush and was able to see the two individuals who were fast asleep. "Two men, no weapons visible, no suicide vest visible," he whispered over our bone mics.

AOIC commanded in a low tone, "Remi, C-Lod . . . move through the bush onto the property and line up on the east wall, facing the two sleepers."

We nodded, then found a small opening in the bush to creep through without making noise. Our fireteam was essentially setting up an ambush similar to the one we'd used when we captured Umar's brother. Upon initiation, C-Lod and I were going to move north from the corner of the east wall and capture the sleeper on the right while the rest of the team was going quietly to take down the sleeper on the left.

Once I got in position and gave AOIC the nod, he whispered over our bone mic, "Initiate."

As I quietly crept north to the body on the right, Fireteam 2 moved in toward the second body. It was like a synchronized dance.

I moved in with my IR laser trained on the head of the sleeper. *I dare you to move*, I thought. Four steps, five steps, six. He was only about thirty feet from me, but the walk seemed to take forever. Sweat was dripping down my helmet, and my heart was racing in anticipation. I had set a goal to capture Umar Zahid at the beginning of the deployment, and in moments I might achieve it.

When I got to the man, he was still fast asleep. *It was Umar!* His face had been posted at my trailer desk for seven months, and now I had him in the flesh. Honestly, I wanted to put a bullet straight through his head—not for me but for the hundreds of innocent people he had killed and the family members who were left behind. I continued my scan to ensure he wasn't wearing a suicide vest or had a gun. All of this took place in seconds. Once I finished my scan, I kicked Umar over, which startled him from his sleep; then I knelt down on his back with my left hand pressed on the back of his neck.

"Don't move," I whispered.

I turned and looked at AOIC, who was in the process of zip-tying the second individual, and whispered, "Jackpot." And then I thought, *Now I can go home.*

CHAPTER TWENTY-SEVEN

SECOND CHANCE
AT LOVE

Go after what you want for all the right
reasons—and only the right reasons.

S orry," I said as I weaved in and out of lanes in my Infiniti G35. After I closely cut off another car, the driver held down his horn for a few seconds. I quickly gazed in my rearview mirror, where I could clearly see his middle finger. "I said I'm sorry, dude," I muttered as if he could hear me.

I was putting into action some driving techniques I had just learned. Three months after returning from deployment, I received an early promotion to SO1 and was sent to an advanced HUMINT school, where I learned surveillance and countersurveillance. I spent a month and a half in Washington, DC, training at an NSA interagency program; one week in San Diego, playing with surveillance gadgets (small cameras, small microphones, lock-picking kits, tracking devices, and so on); three weeks in the Los Angeles area, tracking notional bad guys; and two weeks in North Carolina, learning evasive and defensive driving techniques, as well as how to break into and hot-wire cars. Low-level UAV pilot school would come later.

"Yes! Shaved seven minutes off of my estimated arrival time," I said as

I looked at my GPS. I was on my way to a date and was projected to be late until now.

I pulled up to an apartment complex in the Hillcrest area of San Diego and waited.

Ten minutes later a beautiful five-foot-five Italian-looking girl with dark brown hair and tan skin made her way through the complex gate and headed toward my car. I thought, *Okay, unlike my last date, she looks exactly like she did on her Match.com profile.* I stepped out of the car and met her at the passenger door.

"Jessica?"

"Yes, and you must be Remi."

I was in the last week of my thirty-day match trial, which was exactly two years and eight months from my last relationship. After Cecilia, I felt led to stay single and celibate, so I did. It wasn't easy at first, but my no-quit attitude helped me maintain. However, in May 2011, I decided I was ready to find a wife (not a girlfriend, a *wife*), so I set up a profile and started to go on a few dates.

The funny thing was I found that dating as the new Remi was a lot different from the way I'd dated in the past, when looks and sex were most important to me. Now I wanted something deeper and lasting. Because of the shift, I felt like a foreigner in a new country, having to learn new customs and a new language. That said, my first words to Jessica were true, but probably too soon and too corny, "Yes, I . . . am Remi. . . . You are beautiful!"

"Thank you," she replied.

"Let me get the door for you." I opened the door, and once she was in, I closed it behind her.

As soon as I got in the car, she asked, "So where are we going?"

"Coronado Island. There's a beautiful restaurant that sits on the San Diego Bay, called Candelas. Do you like Mexican food?" I asked.

"Yeah, sure," she replied.

As I drove—safely now—I asked, "So I saw on your profile that you just moved down to San Diego for residency. What's your specialty?"

"Yeah, I'm from Tacoma, Washington. I just got here last week. I'm a family practice physician."

Family practice! What are the odds? I asked myself before continuing, "Wow! I started my Navy career in a family practice office."

"You did?" She seemed surprised.

"Yeah . . . you're going to laugh. . . . I assisted on pap smears."

"What? They let you do that?"

"Yup. And pregnancy tests, and Depo shots, and I checked in a lot of babies. Most of the doctors in the clinics were residents. Hey, maybe I can get a job at your hospital!" I joked.

She laughed and said, "I don't know if my patients would want you in the room for their pap smears."

I replied, "I wouldn't want to do that again either."

"So you're in the Navy?" she asked.

"Yup, nine years."

"Do you still work in a hospital?"

"No," I replied.

I knew what question was coming next, and a big part of me was hoping it wouldn't. I didn't like talking about my job, and at the time I really *couldn't* talk about my job.

"So what do you do in the Navy?"

Just tell the truth, Remi. It doesn't matter. "I'm . . . a SEAL."

"Huh?" she replied.

"I'm a SEAL in the Navy . . . a Navy SEAL."

She looked at me as if she was confused and asked, "What kind of job is that? You train with sea animals?" The girl was dead serious. And I kind of liked the idea that she didn't know what my job entailed. Kept me from answering more questions.

I chuckled and said, "No, it's just a specific job in the Navy."

She continued, "Cool. So you also listed you're a youth pastor. How did you get into that?"

"Yeah. Long story short, I started preaching on my last deployment, and when I got back, my pastor offered me the youth pastor position at our church, Dominion Center. It's cool. The kids are from the inner city, like me, so I see it as a great way to give back. Give some of the kids something I never really had."

"And that is?" Jessica asked.

I thought about it for a second, then said, "A consistent male role model."

"That's really a good thing, Remi."

"Thank you," I replied.

The first part of the date—which consisted of the drive—went well. We talked the entire ride, but when we got to the restaurant, something changed. The connection between us just dissipated. I felt it as clear as day, and by her demeanor I could tell that she felt it too. I remember both of us sitting at the table in silence, just trying to figure out what to say next. It was an awkward experience for both of us.

As I sat there, I thought, *Oh well, at least I tried. She's definitely not right for me, but . . . it is cool that she works in family practice.*

On our way back to her apartment, I felt kind of bad. A part of me wanted to try to make things right even though nothing wrong had happened. So when we pulled up at her apartment, though I had no intention of seeing her again, I said, "Hey, I know you're new to San Diego, so if you ever need anything, you got my number."

She said, "Thank you, Remi."

I felt even worse after saying that. I don't know, I felt like I had this obligation to offer her something else, so I added, "And . . . I make a great salmon dish . . . so . . . if you're ever hungry and want some good cooking, let me know."

She smiled as if to say, "Really? After how things went tonight?" Then she said, "Okay, thank you." The way she responded coupled with the way the dinner went, I figured she would never call again. But the even better news was I didn't feel bad anymore, because I completely left the ball in her court.

· · ·

Two weeks after our first date, I received a surprising call from Jessica. "Hey, Remi!"

Aw, man, I thought. For a second I regretted inviting her to call me. "Hey . . . how are you?"

"I'm doing good. I don't have any plans for tonight and was thinking . . . I might just take you up on that salmon dinner."

Dang it! I never should have offered. "Oh . . . um . . . yeah . . . I can . . . do that. Does six p.m. work?"

"Yes! That's great! I'll see you then," she replied.

After hanging up the phone, I said to myself, *How did that just happen? Why would she want to hang out again? Oh well, no excuses. I have to keep my word.*

I ran to the supermarket by my place to pick up the ingredients, drove back home, and started marinating the salmon.

Four hours later Jessica showed up. "Wow, Remi. This is a really nice house!" When I returned from deployment, I bought a 2,300-square-foot house in the suburbs of San Diego. The house was brand-new, so I was able to deck it out in a way that fit my personality. I saw it as a big achievement for me—coming from where I came from to purchasing a house on my own.

"Thank you. I've been here for six months. Have a seat. The salmon is almost ready."

She asked, "Jazz, huh?" referring to the music that played from the ceiling speakers.

"Yeah, I go back and forth between Miles and Coltrane."

"Who's that playing now?" she asked.

I replied, "Coltrane, 'My Favorite Things.' It's a classic."

As the night went on, our conversation continued easily; we weren't two people bashfully avoiding eye contact as on the first date. It was different. We stayed engaged the entire night. We even began to joke with each other.

"Your salmon wasn't as good as you *said* it would be!" Jessica said sarcastically.

"Um . . . well, your plate seems to be telling a different story." I stared closely at her plate and continued, "I can't seem to find a speck left, and what was that? Two . . . three helpings?"

"Okay, okay, you got me. It was good, and let's get it straight: I had two helpings, not three." She laughed and continued, "Okay! Since we're calling people out—"

"You started," I quickly said.

"I did. Oh, before I forget: I googled Navy SEAL."

"Did you?"

"Yes, that's a pretty impressive job you have."

"Well, what you do is impressive too," I said.

I expected her to continue with SEAL questions, but she just stayed on track with the jokes. "Back to calling people out . . . *what* is up with that obnoxious license plate? *SUPA DOC*, really? I was going to say something on our first date, but things were going so bad I figured I'd leave it alone. But now, since I think we're doing better, I want to know."

I replied sarcastically, "I *am* the Supa Doc, and I'm probably more qualified to treat a tension pneumothorax than you."

"What? Okay, I have to go," she said jokingly.

I replied, "Oh, you can dish it out but can't take it? I see!"

"Whatever," she said.

"Okay. I'll answer your *obnoxious* question. I used to be a medic with the Marines. In a platoon, marines refer to medics as Doc. I was bigger than most of my marines, and fit, so they called me Super Doc. Like Superman. Super Doc—get it?"

"I got it. And you decided to turn your nickname into a license plate?"

"That was the kind of stuff I used to do." My mood changed as I reflected on my past—and for some reason, specifically on how I used to treat women. "I . . . I was a very different person back then."

Her jokes stopped, and she said, "Tell me. I want to know."

I shared my entire story with her, starting with my childhood in Africa, the Nigerian government stripping my father's assets, the Bronx, hustling, my journey into the Navy, my conversion to Christianity, and the transformation that took place afterward. She listened intently, and then she went on to open up about her own miraculous story.

She shared with me how she was diagnosed with a rare autoimmune disease when she was nineteen and had a hole in her heart. The doctors had to put her on a specific type of steroid that would keep her condition under control and warned her that if she got off the medication, the results could be fatal.

"Along with all the other bad news, the doctors also told me I may never be able to have kids. That devastated me. I remember going through so much hopelessness. That's why I wanted to be a doctor. I want to be able to walk through the worst news of a patient's life and not only provide medical care but also provide comfort."

"So what happened?" I asked. "That was what . . . ten years ago? Are you still taking medication?"

"That's the crazy part of my story," she replied.

I said, "Oh, trust me. I can handle a crazy story."

"That's right," she continued with a smile. "I didn't go to church or read the Bible or do any of those things before the diagnosis. And then one day my college roommate invited me to a church service. I go to the service, which was all in Spanish, by the way, and as I'm sitting there, trying to keep up with the interpreter, the pastor suddenly comes up to me and says, 'You're sick. . . . God is telling me that you're very sick, but you're healed in the name of Jesus.' He then placed his hand on my shoulder, and I fell down. I don't know what happened—I literally collapsed. And in that moment I felt healed. I went back to the doctors and told them, 'I'm getting off of the medication; I'm healed.' They told me I was crazy and that my life would be in jeopardy.

"Well, I've been tested repeatedly for the last ten years, and there has been no trace of the disease. Even crazier, months after the church service I went for an echocardiogram on my heart, and the doctors discovered that the hole in my heart had disappeared! No medical explanation, right? And here I am ten years later, still no medication, still alive, and completely healthy. That's when I started to believe in God! I mean . . . how could I not?"

All I could say was, "Wow. That is a crazy story."

This may sound cornier than my first words to Jessica—*You are beautiful*—but that night I fell in love with her! Not because of her story per se or because of how she looked or because of the laughs. I fell in love with her because of her heart. That night we both let down the typical façade that those who have just met wear. We were both able to see past the looks, the makeup, the impressive backgrounds, the house and cars, and all the outward things of life and see each other's heart. And I felt like my heart lined up with hers and hers with mine. And for the first time in three years, I thought, *This is a woman I can marry. But before I do, I'm going to make sure I do everything right.*

• • •

As time passed, our relationship continued to grow but in a way that I never expected that a relationship could grow: through limitation. Jessica was in medical residency, so she worked twelve to fourteen hours a day, sometimes seven days a week. And I was out of town a lot for predeployment training. One week I'd be home; three weeks I'd be gone; two weeks I'd be home; five weeks I'd be gone. That pattern continued throughout our dating period.

At times I would land in San Diego, returning from training trips, speed to pick up dinner for both of us, then speed to the hospital to have dinner with her for however long she could get away, usually fifteen to twenty minutes. And on the blue moon when we both had a full day off, we would spend it together. I truly believe that because of how limited our time was, we had no choice but to ensure that time was of maximum quality. We didn't have time to fight or sit in a movie theater or hang out with other people. We had time only to genuinely invest in our relationship.

• • •

I yelled from the living room, "Jessie! Hurry up, babe! I need you to watch my devotional video so I can send it out before we go!"

I had started a small video ministry, where I would put together two-minute Bible studies and e-mail or text them to family and friends who wanted to receive them. Often, Jessica would screen them for me before I sent them out.

"Okay!" she yelled from the second floor. "I'm coming . . . I'm just cleaning up the room!" We were getting ready to fly to her family's house in Tacoma for Thanksgiving. Jessica had stayed the night so we could get up early and depart together. We had made sure to set strict boundaries early on in our relationship, so anytime she slept over, she stayed in the guest room while I stayed in the master bedroom. I hadn't seen her all morning, and as usual she was running late.

Five minutes later she came down with bags in hand. "Okay, where's your computer?"

"On the kitchen island," I said.

She replied, "Great," then gave me a kiss before walking to the computer. "So what's the devotional on this time?"

"Oh, Proverbs 31, the virtuous woman," I replied.

As the video played, she nodded along and said things like, "This is a good one, Remi. . . . Your videos are getting better and better. . . . I'm going to send this to my friend."

I crept over to the couch in the living room and thought, *Just keep watching; it gets better.*

In the video I got to a point where I said, "Proverbs 31 talks about a virtuous woman, and now I want to talk about my virtuous woman . . . Jessica."

She said in a sweet and humble way, "Remi. That's embarrassing."

"It's all good. You'll like the spin I put on it," I said.

In the video I continued, "Jessie is strong, full of integrity and compassion. She supports me through my hectic job without complaining one bit. She is my virtuous woman. And because of that . . . Jessica, will you marry me?"

By the time the video ended, I was on one knee behind her with the ring box opened. She slowly turned around in shock and tears, and said, "Yes, Remi! Yes!" And then she ran up to me to give me a hug, a kiss, and to get that ring.

Five months after we met, we had a secret shotgun wedding at the San Diego courthouse before my next deployment. It happened fast, but like they say, "When you know, you know!" I knew I was with Jessica for the right reasons: not for sex or money or looks but because I genuinely loved her and wanted to spend the rest of my life with her.

• • •

"What do you see?" Christian asked.

I kept gazing out of the small circular window of the C17 and said, "Nothing but desert, dude! Like they briefed, it looks like a no-man's-land."

Our small, nine-man SEAL Team was flying into a country that was partly controlled by a terrorist group. No American forces had been stationed on the ground there for a couple of years, and the US embassy had just recently reopened. We were all we had. As a matter of fact, our closest quick reaction force (QRF) was hundreds of miles away in another country.

"A lot different from our last one," Christian said.

"Yeah, I thought we were hanging it out last time; this is hanging it out on steroids," I replied.

Christian continued, "I heard Delta Platoon is in a similar situation in another part of the globe."

"Yeah, I miss them guys," I said as the plane prepared for landing. "And so it begins!"

Long story short: Christian and I had been pulled from Delta Platoon and placed in Alpha Platoon, which was set to augment a new mission. Christian was chosen because he was a stellar medic (better than me) and a sniper. I was pulled for my HUMINT qualifications. Whereas the focus of our last deployment was direct action (DA)—and in my case, DA and HUMINT—this deployment would revolve more around HUMINT, especially for me. We would be working with locals to prepare them to locate, gather intel, track, and capture HVTs.

Our C17 landed on a military airstrip that looked like it had been abandoned in the desert for decades. As we slowly taxied down the runway, our team got up from our seats and made our way toward the opening ramp doors in the back to assess our security situation. We were the only ones in sight. There were a few planes, but they definitely didn't look like they were in flyable condition.

"Chief!" one of the operators yelled. "We have a truck approaching with what looks like a mounted machine gun."

Okay, this is not a good start, I thought. We were wearing jeans, casual shirts, long beards, no body armor, and carrying only pistols. Our assault rifles and heavy weapons were on a pallet in the center of the plane.

Chief commanded, "Fireteam 1, hold security at the ramp. Fireteam 2, break out the M4s and heavy machine guns."

The truck stopped about two hundred feet from us with the gunner pointing his machine gun slightly high in our direction. The guys definitely weren't Americans. They looked like locals, each one with different tattered clothes. And to make matters worse, they weren't smiling about us being in their country. We didn't know if they were rebels, terrorists, or a group pissed off about being sent to pick up the neatly dressed Americans.

"Keep getting those weapons out!" Chief yelled.

Christian and I stood at the ramp with our pistols. We took a quick glance at each other as if to say, *Whatever happens, happens. I got your back, and I know you got mine.*

As he stared back at the vehicle, he asked, "Wasn't the embassy supposed to meet us here and make sure the local government had this area clear?"

With my eyes focused in the same direction, I said, "Yup!"

I squinted out and saw another vehicle quickly approaching, a second beat-up truck with a mounted machine gun. *Oh, the start of this deployment keeps getting better.*

"Hey, Chief!" an operator yelled.

"I see!" Chief replied.

Suddenly the second vehicle pulled sideways in front of the first vehicle.

A short guy in a local military uniform with medals down to his belly button jumped out of the just-arrived truck and loudly berated the occupants of the other vehicle in Arabic. He grabbed one guy by the shirt and shook him as he pointed at our plane. Then he turned, walked in our direction with his arms wide open, and said in broken English, "Americans! I apologize for my rude colleagues; they will be punished!" Then he placed his hand over his heart and yelled, "Welcome to our country!"

I guess I'll live to see another day, Jessie. I guess I'll live to see another day.

CHAPTER TWENTY-EIGHT

RESTORATION OF ADE (THE CROWN)

We must all come full circle.

B*ang, bang, bang, bang, bang!*
John, a machine gunner to my right, fired in rapid succession toward an enemy position. As I fired alongside him with my M4, I peered down a steep hill only to see bodies of soldiers sprawled out at the bottom. The mission started out with a three-hundred-member ground force, but now there were only about fifty of us left.

Our team leader looked at us and yelled, "We're sitting ducks! We have to get down that hill where there's more cover, or we won't last another minute!"

Right before our twelve-person team made the daring slide, another Osprey carrying a twenty-man QRF was shot down by enemy fighters, sending a great explosion into the air.

"Now!" our team leader yelled. Some slid; some rolled; others tried to traverse down on their feet.

I scuttled down the hill as fast as I could as debris rained down all around me. When I got to the bottom, I found what was left of a downed Osprey and knelt behind it. Moments later I was joined by two other SEALs,

John Divine and Perry Yee. While John and Perry reloaded, I popped up with my M4 and fired a burst of rounds at the enemy encampment, then yelled at John and Perry, "When you're done reloading, I'm going to prep the rocket launcher!"

"Roger!" they said.

Once they were both up and laying down cover fire, I dropped to my knee and started prepping the AT4 rocket launcher. *Boom! Boom!* Two more explosions went off a hundred feet in front of us, knocking all three of us off our feet.

"Damn, that was close!" Perry yelled.

"Yeah!" I said before creeping to my feet. I edged up past the smoldering debris to get the AT4 sight lined up with the enemy encampment. "Stand by, boys. . . . Rocket out!" I hit the trigger, but a rocket didn't come out.

"AND CUT!" the director, Michael Bay, yelled through a megaphone. And just like that, the chaos stopped.

Mark Wahlberg, our "Team Leader," Josh Duhamel, Laura Haddock, Santiago Cabrera, John, Perry, JP, Raul, and the rest of the actors walked off set in the direction of Michael Bay. We weren't on a literal battlefield. We were in Cardiff, Wales, on an enormous outdoor set of the film *Transformers: The Last Knight*. It was September 2016 (four years after the last deployment I mentioned), and I was in my fourth month of filming.

Holding his red camera, and full of excitement, Michael Bay approached us and said, "Good stuff, huh? That was a good cut!"

As I stood in his presence along with the other actors, I asked myself the question I'm sure you're asking: *How does this happen?*

A year after my first deployment as a married man, I received a phone call from a woman by the name of Megan Sanders. Megan and her husband (also a former Navy SEAL) provided on-set military consulting and military assets for Michael Bay's films. And get this: the couple started working with Bay in 1996 on a little film called *The Rock*.

During our initial call in 2013, she asked if I was available to film a scene on a TV show called *The Last Ship*. Acting was never anything I was interested in, so I was reluctant. But she was persuasive, and after some verbal arm-twisting, I capitulated.

The next day I showed up to set and just did what I was told to do when I was told to do it. Honestly, I hated the experience, and I decided then and there never to act again. But three weeks later a woman at my church approached me about another acting opportunity.

"Hey, Remi," she said.

"Hey, Sister Troy."

"I heard about your recent acting job. How did it go?" she asked.

I laughed and replied, "It was nothing. I sat in a boat and shot one scene. It's no big deal."

She continued, "Oh . . . well . . . there's a play called *Never Too Late* that's going into production at the Lyceum Theater. They're holding auditions, and there's a role I think you'd be a good fit for. I want you to audition."

One day of filming on *Last Ship*—okay. But standing onstage and having to recite memorized lines in front of a live audience? Absolutely not. "I'm sorry, Sister Troy. It's not my thing."

For three weeks Troy called, texted, and approached me in church about the play. And each time I respectfully declined. Then one Sunday she pulled me aside and said, "Look, Remi, this is a great opportunity. Just go audition, please." She was a sweet woman, and I knew she meant well, so I finally broke and said, "Okay, I'll go, Troy."

The following weekend I made my way to the audition. As I drove there, I decided that I was going to go in and intentionally bomb it. I wanted to ensure that nothing would come out of it. But when I arrived and saw the waiting room filled with nervous actors who were pacing and running what looked like acting drills, the military side of me kicked in. *Remi, you know that whatever you do you must do with excellence. I know this is not your thing, but go in and show these people that you can hang. It pays to be a winner! Roger that*, I said to myself.

After thirty minutes of waiting, the casting assistant walked in. "Remi Adeleke?"

"Yes, that's me," I replied.

"We're ready for you," she said. "Follow me."

I walked in and, as directed, made my way onto the stage. The casting director, casting assistant, director, and writer were in the front row.

"When you're ready," the casting director said.

I picked up my script and started, well, acting. I got through the first scene without being stopped; then the casting director asked me to turn to a second scene and act that out too. So I said, "Roger that," and continued. As I acted, I could see the writer and director taking notes, and that, coupled with their positive body language, led me to think, *I might be getting this role.*

The director finally stopped me. "All right, all right. At the end of the play, your character has to deliver a speech meant to bring a family and community together. We want you to improvise that scene. Act like . . . I don't know . . . we're the community, and you are . . . a reconciliatory agent. So just do what you would do in that situation."

It was like he threw a softball to an MLB player. I started rattling off a speech as if I had it prepared. The acting I had done while meeting with informants, coupled with the scores of sermons I had preached, all prepared me for that moment.

After I finished my improvisation, the director turned to look at the writer and casting director; they both nodded; then he looked at me and said, "What is your schedule like? Are you available for rehearsals?" That was his way of saying, "You got the part."

The play went well, but when it ended, I vowed once more that I would never act again. It wasn't me—it wasn't the future I had planned for myself. For a time I kept that vow, but in 2015, Megan reached out to me again for a national television commercial. I didn't have to audition at all; the part was just handed to me.

"No, I'm tied up," I told her.

Fast-forward to October 2015. I was at the end of my military contract. If I was to reenlist, I would have to deploy in 2016. By that time Jessica and I had two sons. Cayden was getting ready to turn two, and Caleb was four months old. Because my father died when Bayo and I were so young—I was only five—I wanted to be with my sons at home as much as I could; I needed to be in their lives to guide them down the right path. It would be hard for me, personally, to do that and continue my career as a SEAL. So when faced with the ultimatum to deploy for the fourth time or let my contract expire, I chose to let my contract expire.

This wasn't an easy decision. In fact, it was an extreme challenge for me because my initial plan after making it through BUD/S was to stay in the military for twenty years and then retire. I had been in the military my entire adult life and couldn't imagine life outside of the military. Honestly, there was a little bit of fear involved, but in the end I felt strongly that God had more in store for me outside the military. So I left. It was bittersweet.

During this discouraging time, I received a call from Megan Sanders.

"Remi! It's Megan!" she said over the phone.

"Oh hey, Megan! How's it going?" I said.

"It's going great. How about you? What are you up to nowadays?" she asked.

"Well, I have a year left of graduate school, and I'm doing speaking here and there."

She asked, "So is your schedule flexible?"

"Yeah, pretty much," I replied.

"Great! I have a project for you."

Oh gosh. Here we go with the acting thing again. I'm at the bottom, but I ain't that *desperate.* "What is it?" I asked.

"We're starting another *Transformers.* Bay wants SEALs again. It would only be one day's worth of work, but there may be an opportunity for additional filming."

I was shocked and excited. "Michael Bay?! I'm in! When?"

She said, "Tomorrow, San Bernardino. Here's what I need you to do— just e-mail me some pictures so I can show Bay. It doesn't have to be anything professional, but I do recommend something in your military gear."

"Roger that. I'll have them to you in ten minutes!" I replied.

"If he approves you, I'll have production e-mail you a call sheet."

"Great. Thank you so much, Megan."

"No problem! We look forward to having you!"

Bay approved the pictures, and the next day I was standing right in front of the man, with his handheld camera pointed right in my face.

One day in San Bernardino turned into three weeks in Arizona and Michigan. Then, during what was supposed to be my last week of filming, the extras casting director approached me and said, "Bay wants to keep you on until the film wraps. Are you available the next couple of months? You'll be upgraded to a principal, which means more money."

"Wow! Absolutely!" I replied. A week later, a new group of actors who were SEALs and former SEALs came on set: John, Perry, JP, Patrick, and Raul. We spent the next month and a half in Michigan, then made our way to London to continue filming.

And that, my friends, is how I ended up on a fictitious battleground in Wales.

As with many, many other times on set, I had to pinch myself as I stood in front of the same man whose first two films had inspired me to be a Navy SEAL! What were the odds? He played a role in my selection of my first career, and now, a potential second career.

• • •

"Hey, babe!" Jessica said on the other end of the phone. I was in London, and my family was in San Diego.

"Hey. How's it going? How are the boys?" I replied.

"Everything is going great. We love the new house. Your mom has been such a great help. But the boys miss you. Cayden's been crying for you every night."

"Aw, I'll talk to him after we finish."

"How's London?" she asked.

"It's great! We were in Wales all last week filming in a quarry, outside. It was *cold*! You know how I hate the cold!"

"Yes, you tell me all the time."

"Look, Jessie, I know this has been a tough stretch, but being gone most of the summer away from you and the boys has just validated that I made the right decision to get out. I really need to be home as much as I can."

"It's good that you see that, Remi. Wait; here's Cayden." I could hear her say, "It's Daddy . . . yeah." She turned her attention back to me and said, "He just smiled when I told him you're on the phone. Here he is."

Cayden, who was two and a half at the time, said, "Daddy!"

"Hey, bud. I miss you," I replied.

"I miss you," he repeated.

"I love you."

"I love you," he repeated again.

"I should be home next week, okay?"

"Okay, Daddy. Home, come home."

My heart melted when he said that. "I will, buddy . . . I will. Take care of Mommy and brother Caleb, okay?"

"Okay," he said.

"Bye-bye, buddy."

"Bye, Daddy."

Jessica took the phone back and said, "Hold on, Remi. Your mom wants to talk to you. And, hey, I have to go, so I'll talk to you the next time you get the chance. I love you."

"Okay. I love you, too, babe."

After a moment my mom's voice came over the line. "Remi . . . Remi."

"Hey, Ma."

"Remi! This . . . house . . . is *beautiful* . . . so beautiful!"

"Thank you, Mom. And thank you for helping Jessie and the boys move in."

"It's my pleasure; I love my grandbabies. You know, Remi . . . I can't help but praise God! From this house, to your family, to Bayo being an engineer and having his own family, to your careers . . . it's just amazing! Today I walked by the bird-of-paradise flowers that line your house. You may not remember this, but when we lived in Nigeria, I had bird-of-paradise all around our house. As I stared at the flowers today, I couldn't help but think about how everything has been restored to us! When your father died and we lost everything, I didn't know how I was going to make it. And at the time I didn't understand why we had to go through all that we went through, but look at us now! I'm so proud of you, Remi!"

"You're so right, Ma. I totally agree. I never knew years ago we'd have the life we could have now. Thank you, Ma. I'm proud of you too. I wouldn't be who I am without you."

"So tell me, how's it going out there?" Right when she asked, my phone started beeping.

"Hey, Ma . . . I'm sorry. Cody is calling me on the other line. I have to take this call."

"All right. I'll talk to you later. I love you," she said.

"I love you too," I said before clicking over. "Cody! What's up, man?"

A year and a half earlier, Cody Gifford and I were introduced through a ministry I had partnered with called I Am Second. We had become great friends—such good friends, in fact, that after I separated from the Navy, his mom, Kathie Lee Gifford, allowed me to attend an all-expenses-paid trip to Israel with her entire family and close friends.

"Hey, movie star. How's it going out there?" Cody asked.

I chuckled, then said, "Hey, man, great. Just been grinding it out."

He replied, "That's good. So we didn't get a chance to finish our last conversation."

"Yeah, about my future. I'm still holding the same mind-set. I'm thirty-three, I have a wife and kids, responsibilities . . . we just moved into a new house! I can't just drop everything and move to LA to pursue an acting career."

Cody replied, "I thought about that, but listen: you should at least give it a shot for a short period of time. If something comes out of it, good. If nothing . . . at least you tried. Do you know how hard it is for 99 percent of actors to be in your position?"

"No, not really."

"It's like a random guy being plucked off the street, with no qualifications to be a SEAL, and being told, 'You're officially a Navy SEAL.'"

"Yeah, that would never happen," I replied.

"Exactly! You got the break that most actors would sell their souls for. Here you are; it just falls into your lap. My advice . . . when you get back, pursue it. I can introduce you to some people. And like I said, if nothing happens, at least you gave it a shot."

Everything he said made sense, and, honestly, it was the extra push I needed. "Yeah, you're right. You're the third person in a month who's told me this. . . . I'd be a fool not to listen."

So I did listen. And that was the conversation that initiated my walk down a new path, the path of an actor.

I knew that if I was going to pursue acting, I couldn't wing it anymore. I needed to get the proper training. So when I got back from London, I started training at a local acting school called the Rehearsal Room. When I finished the program, I was requested for a national commercial, which I accepted. Three months later I was offered an endorsement deal with Jockey, which included another national commercial, which I also accepted. The offers didn't stop. I was offered a third commercial, as well as a minor consulting and acting gig on a national TV show. And it was at that point when I thought, *I'm starting to make a lot of money. I better get formal training in the event that bigger opportunities arise.*

At that point I applied to the prestigious Lee Strasberg Theatre and Film Institute, where great actors, such as Sally Field, Barbra Streisand, John Leguizamo, Christoph Waltz, Uma Thurman, Harvey Keitel, Scarlett

Johansson, and many others, have trained. I was accepted, and I immediately started training.

It was there at Strasberg that my disinclination for acting disappeared. Not only did I learn to respect the art, but I also I fell in love with it. I fell in love with being able to live in the skin of someone else for a moment, scene, or play. I enjoyed gaining lessons from that character's life, teaching lessons through that character's life, and experiencing life through that character's eyes. I loved—as therapy—being able to tap into the multitude of experiences I had in life (faith, hustling, womanizing, war, love, hate) and using those experiences to breathe life into a character. But the most important thing that Strasberg reinforced in me, and that I loved, was the fact that through acting and storytelling, I gained a new tool that I could utilize to potentially change lives or even save lives. I say that because it was through story (*Bad Boys* and *The Rock*) that a seed was planted in me that ultimately changed the trajectory of my life and, to this day, I believe played a role in saving my life. Now I could do the same for someone else out there in the world, perhaps many. It was as though everything in my life was not only being restored but also coming full circle.

. . .

One day I received a surprising e-mail:

> Hi, Romi,
>
> I have something of yours that I would like to return to you. It's your pin from your SQT graduation. I know that your graduation meant a lot, and I feel guilty for keeping it all these years. Can you shoot me your mailing address, and I'll have it mailed to you?
>
> Thanks so much, and I hope all is well!
>
> Cecilia

I sat at the computer, stunned. I say that because for almost a decade I had wanted to genuinely apologize to Cecilia for everything I put her through.

And I wanted her to know that the change she had helped bring about in my life wasn't just a fad, but it lasted. The fact that I couldn't do those things haunted me for a long time, but I had to keep my word and never contact her again; there was nothing I could do. Now, here she was, back in my life, giving me another opportunity for restoration.

Sitting at the computer, I decided, *I'm not sending her my address. I need to meet her in person.* But first I needed to honor my wife and get her blessing.

I got up from the computer and went into our bedroom. Jessica knew all about Cecilia, and how she played a major role in my conversion, but I wasn't quite sure how Jessica would respond.

She was sitting on the bed, reading a book. I walked over to her, put my arm around her, and said, "Jessie . . . you trust me, right?"

She replied, "Yes, Remi, I trust you. What's going on?"

I took a deep breath and said, "I just received an e-mail from Cecilia."

"Oh . . . really." She placed the book down and faced me.

"Yes, and I need to ask you something. I'm not telling you what I'm going to do; I'm asking your permission."

"O . . . kay . . . what is it?" she asked.

"I need to see her in person, Jessie. I need to look her in the eye and apologize to her without expecting anything in return. We never had closure, and I need that for me, and I'm sure she could use it herself."

Jessica took my hand and said, "Remi, you are the only man I've ever trusted. I know your heart. . . . I know who you are. . . . You're a good man. And I trust your judgment. So, yes, go do what you have to do and get the closure you need. All I ask as your wife is that you take someone with you."

"I'll take Michael. Thank you for this, Jessie. I love you." Then I leaned in to give her a kiss.

She kissed me back and said, "I love you too."

I went back to my computer and responded:

Cecilia,

Great hearing from you. This may sound crazy, but how about we meet up for a few minutes? I'd retrieve my pin, and then we can say what needs to be said and part ways positively. I totally understand

if you're uncomfortable with this. If you would be comfortable
bringing your significant other, that's cool too. What do you think?

An hour later she responded:

I am open to meeting with you. I'll be free next weekend; Saturday
works best. Just let me know when and where.

• • •

The following weekend, Michael, an ex-convict whom I mentored while he
was in prison, showed up at our house. I jumped in his car, and we made our
way to the local Starbucks.

"How you feeling, dog?" Mike asked.

"I'm good, brother. Thank you for doing this for me."

"Anything, man! Come on . . . you're my brother. Just . . . you know this,
but . . . just keep your wits." Like Jessie, Michael knew the story. He seemed
more nervous about me meeting with Cecilia than Jessica did!

"I will," I replied.

"What do you want me to do when we get there?" Michael asked.

"I'll grab a table, and you can sit at one in eye's view."

He said, "Okay."

We pulled up to the Starbucks, parked, and made our way to the outdoor
seating area. Cecilia hadn't arrived yet, so as planned, I grabbed a table, and
Michael grabbed one not too far from mine.

About ten minutes later Cecilia pulled up in her car. Even though I hadn't
seen her in years, I immediately recognized her. She looked exactly the same
as she had years before.

As Cecilia and her brother Marc made their way toward me, she smiled
and waved at me. I stood up and waved back. *I can't believe this is happening*, I
thought. *After all these years, I finally get to fix this.*

"Hi, Remi," Cecilia said as we both leaned in for a cordial hug.

"Hey, Cecilia," I replied. Then I looked at Marc and said, "Marc . . . good
seeing you."

Marc replied, "It's good seeing you too."

We sat down at the table and caught up on the last decade.

"How's what's-his-name . . . the baby-face guy?"

"She has kids now?"

"He's doing that? Wow!"

"How is your mom?"

I had forgotten how intertwined our friendships were.

After the smiles and laughs about the past and updates about the present, I said, "Listen, Cecilia, I am so sorry for absolutely everything I did to you . . . everything. There are no excuses for my behavior. You were such a good woman to me, and I did a lot of things that I regret. Now that I'm a father . . . I . . . I can't imagine someone doing to my kids what I did to you. So I also ask you to tell your mom and dad that I'm sorry for what I put you through."

"Thank you, Remi. I forgive you. I mean . . . I forgave you a long time ago. And I have to ask for your forgiveness too. I wasn't perfect in the end. I handled some things the wrong way as well. I should have let you be after we broke up, but I held on to you and to someone else. I was selfish. And I definitely shouldn't have spoken to you the way I did during our last call. I was just so angry."

I replied, "To me you were justified, but for whatever it's worth, I forgive you. It feels weird even saying that, because I feel so indebted to you. You led me to my faith in Christ in the darkest period of my life, and since then everything's changed. Can you believe I'm preaching now?"

She laughed and said, "It would be hard to believe if I hadn't watched one of your sermons."

"See? I don't feel like I should be saying I forgive you. If anything, I thank you."

"I changed, too, Remi. I was so bitter for such a long time, but I learned that being bitter doesn't make things better; it only makes things worse." She put her head down for a second, then looked back up at me and said, "I recently separated from someone. A lot has happened to me in the past couple of years. And I can't say that life is great at the moment, but I'm still trying to be strong . . . hold my head high. I'm working through my own personal issues, and my last relationship has brought me to a place where I need to really find the strength to get through the days. But every day gets better."

It was like a punch to my gut when I heard that. I had put her through so much hurt in the past, and to see her hurting again hurt me. That was not what I expected. I wished there was something I could do to fix it, but all I could do was what I had become good at doing: speak words of encouragement and wisdom.

"Cecilia, I'm sorry for what you're going through, but I want to tell you something. You are a beautiful, intelligent child of God. You deserve the best, and if a man can't see that, then it's his loss, not yours. You hear me?"

"Yes, Remi," she replied.

"Now, I want you to lift up your head. And when you look yourself in the mirror today or tonight or whenever you do it, tell yourself who you are. And you'd better not say you're a failure or anything else negative because you're not."

With tears rolling down her cheeks, she said, "You always knew the right things to say at the right time, Remi. Your words are helping me more than you know. Especially in a time when I'm filled with so much self-doubt, I appreciate it very much. And if you can, please convey my appreciation to your wife. Let her know that I am thankful she allowed us to meet up. It means a lot."

"I will, Cecilia."

We got up, she handed me the pin, and we hugged one last time and said our goodbyes.

When Michael and I got in the car, he asked, "How did it go?"

I said, "Honestly, it felt like a weight that I never knew was on my chest was lifted off. We both needed that . . . probably more than we thought."

Michael chuckled, shook his head, and said, "Jessica is a good woman! I don't know any other girlfriend or *wife* that would allow her man to do what she just let you do."

"Yeah . . . she's a warrior. . . . That's why I married her," I replied.

As soon as I got home, I ran into the house, found Jessica, and just hugged her. I wouldn't let go. "Thank you, Jessica, thank you. I love you," I whispered.

"I love you, too, Remi."

CHAPTER TWENTY-NINE

BACK TO THE BEGINNING

*Everything that happens in our lives
leads us to where we are today.*

So . . . you're American?" Oliver, a French national asked as we introduced ourselves on the plane.

"Well, yes, but I'm from Lagos. I lived there until I was five and haven't been back since."

"Lagosian! Wow. So this is a reunion trip?"

"Kind of . . . and business," I replied.

It was February 25, 2018, and for the first time in thirty years, I was on an Air France flight headed back to the land of my birth.

One of my older half brothers, Kevin, was an ER doctor. Through a series of events, Kevin was connected with one of our father's mentees, Obi Asaki, who was the founder of Lagos Social Media Week. Kevin had been requested to speak on a medical panel for the conference, and knowing my work, he figured that it would be good for me to come.

It was good timing. I was working on a project that was partly based on Nigeria, and I was in desperate need of a firsthand experience with the land.

"What do you do for a living?" Oliver asked.

I chuckled, then said, "A little bit of everything . . . writing, speaking, a little film and TV, and I own a consulting firm."

"Really? You are definitely a Nigerian!" he said.

"Why do you say that?" I asked.

He replied, "Before I finally settled in France, I lived and worked in Nigeria for twenty years. I even married a Nigerian. One thing I learned about your people is that you are *go-getters*. Is that a phrase you're familiar with?"

"Yes, we use that in the States," I replied.

Oliver continued enthusiastically, "Good! Well . . . go-getters . . . you people work extremely hard—brilliant people too!"

"Hmm . . . thank you." I couldn't help but reflect on my life: record label at nineteen, SEAL training twice, honor grad for both my bachelor's and master's programs, and multiple business ventures. What he said made sense; striving for greatness was interwoven in my DNA.

"So what is it that *you* do?" I asked.

"Well, I'm semiretired. I co-own a cocoa manufacturing plant in Nigeria. That's why I'm . . . well, on this plane. I'm heading down to check on my business. Before that, I owned a few companies that catered to infrastructure development in Nigeria."

"Oh, so you're an engineer?" I asked.

"No, no, no. I was always a businessman. I was the one who hired the engineers to do the work."

"My father was an engineer in Nigeria. John Adebayo Adeleke. Did you ever hear the name?"

Oliver stopped and looked up to search his mind. I was hoping that he knew of my father, even in a small way. After seconds of searching, Oliver said, "John Adebayo . . . hmm . . . no, I've never heard of him."

Honestly, his response was quite painful for me to hear. My father achieved one of the greatest engineering feats on the continent of Africa, and no one seemed to know his name, not even a person who worked in my father's field around the time of his death. It was as though his life had been wiped off the face of the earth, only to be remembered by a handful of people who were close to him.

I couldn't let my father's memory lie dead in the grave with him. "He was the engineer responsible for the Lagoon Development Project. I mean . . . that's what it used to be called. Now it's called Banana Island."

After my father's death the Lagos State Government went against his original design of multiple linked islands, and the rest of the land was filled in to create a banana-shaped island. My father had never intended his project to be a residential area to fan the pride of the rich but, instead, a commercial powerhouse that would make Nigeria proud.

I could tell by the way Oliver looked at me that he didn't fully believe what I had just said. "Your dad created Banana Island?"

"Well, yes . . . before the Lagos State Government took it from him."

The way he responded next was a bit ambiguous to me. Either he believed me or was acting like he did to make me feel good.

"Wow! Billions, man! That's what that land is worth now. You know, it's the country's most expensive residential estate. Some of the richest Africans on the continent live there!" Oliver sat back toward the window of the plane to get a better look at me and said, "Hmm, your father must have been a chief!"

Finally here's something, someone knows about my father without me having to tell them. I replied proudly, "Yes, he was a chief." Then I asked jokingly, "What do you think the chances are that our family will get the land back?"

He let out a loud laugh and then said, "In Nigeria? Slim to none, my friend, slim to none!"

. . .

"Do you have a gift for me?" a female customs agent asked.

"Excuse me?" I replied.

She continued, "A gift! What do you have for me to make me happy?"

Fighting back my anger, I lifted up my luggage sticker on the back of my boarding pass and placed it next to the sticker on my checked bag.

I had been in the country for only forty-five minutes, and I was already on my third bribe.

She took a long look at my stickers to make sure they matched. In a normal circumstance I would have been allowed to pass, but she wanted money.

You have no idea who you're dealing with, lady, I thought. Before I could say anything to escalate the situation, my military training kicked in. I pacified my thoughts and respectfully played her game. "I'm sorry . . . I have nothing for you." She stared at me for a second, smiled, then waved Kevin and me through.

When we exited into the moist evening air, I took in a deep breath of home. I never thought I'd return under my own will, but there I was, and despite my first encounters, it felt good to be back. The city was bustling and loud; people talking on their phones walked back and forth from the airport to the parking structures, motorcycles weaved through the gridlocked traffic, and Nigerian hip-hop—which reminded me so much of reggae—blasted out of cars. Being a city boy, I loved it!

I was in such a daze that I didn't realize Kevin had taken off ahead of me. "Remi! This way!" Kevin said as he pointed to a large parking structure about a quarter of a mile from where I stood. As Kevin waved me over, he continued, "The driver is waiting for us at the parking lot."

America is such a massive melting pot of cultures, ethnic groups, and backgrounds that it's hard for many people to pinpoint exactly where they came from. Even among the African American community, not many can trace their roots back to, say, Benin or Sierra Leone or Ghana or Congo. But as we walked to the parking lot, I couldn't help but stare at the people in awe. Why? Because though my last name and birthplace *told* me who I was, this was the first time I was able to clearly *see* who I was in everyone who walked by. Their skin tone, their features, their demeanor, and their mannerisms said it all: *You are me, and I am you.* It was a serene feeling of belonging, something that can only be experienced and not learned. And with that feeling of belonging came an intense love for Nigeria that I thought I could never have.

I have to be honest: after living through the aftermath of what the Nigerian government did to my father, especially after he sacrificed everything for the country, including his family's well-being, I had a love/hate relationship with Nigeria for a long time—and more hate than love. I was proud to be Nigerian, a descendant of Yoruba royalty, but I hated what the country did to my father. The good news was that my walk to the parking structure, coupled with my new sense of belonging, was rekindling my love for the land.

When we got to the parking lot, we quickly found our driver, loaded up the car, and began our hour-long drive to the hotel. I stared out the window to study the land that evening darkness covered. My hope was to see a place, or street, or building that would draw up a memory from thirty years earlier.

"Yo, Kev. How far is our hotel from the old house?" I asked as I kept staring out the window.

"No traffic, maybe fifteen minutes. Our hotel is just on the other end of V.I.," Kevin replied.

"That's not bad. So before we leave, I need to see the old house, Nike's Art Gallery, and Banana Island."

"Okay. The gallery and old house we can do for sure," he replied. "But Banana Island . . . that's going to be hard. The security is tight; it's like a fortress. And anyone who doesn't have a temporary or permanent residence card can't get in."

"I'm not leaving until we get on Dad's property. I'll figure out a way."

• • •

Unaffected by the massive time-zone jump, the next morning I was quickly up and ready to see Lagos! I walked to the window of my hotel room and pulled open the blackout blinds, exposing the city to my eyes. "I can't believe I'm here," I whispered. An awe came over me. My evening arrival had hidden the city from view, so now I was getting my first clear glimpse of Lagos in thirty years.

From my sixth-floor room, I could see part of the 1.6 million-square-meter Banana Island. *How many people on the planet can say that their father built an island?* I thought. *I have to get there!*

In the midst of my introspection, there was a knock at my door. "Remi! It's Kev!"

"Coming!" I said. I quickly ushered Kevin in and pointed him to the window to see the view. "Real quick, bro. I need you to take a picture of this."

"What?" he asked.

"Let's see . . . just of me staring out at all of this," I said, gesturing to the beautiful view of Lagos. "This is history right here! I feel like Killmonger from *Black Panther* . . . former Navy SEAL, dad was African royalty and died when he was young, mom was American, grew up in the inner city, went back to his homeland to reclaim his crown! I'm back in Wakanda, baby, minus the reclaiming-of-the-crown thing!"

Kevin laughed and said, "Yeah, this is dope! And real talk—I thought about you when I watched that movie! I told you it would be good for you to be here."

It had taken a lot of convincing on Kevin's part to get me to come. I almost backed out a couple of times.

"Thank you, Kev! Yeah, you were right, man," I replied.

After we took a few pictures, Kevin said, "Imma get ready to head to the conference. You want to go now?"

"Nah, I'll meet you there later. I was able to find a lap pool on the other end of the island at Eko Hotels and Suites. Imma head there for a swim."

"Oh, that's by Eko Atlantic!" Kevin replied.

Eko Atlantic is a project identical to the vision of the Lagoon Development Project. It involves the use of dredging and rock walls to reclaim 3.9 square miles of land from the Atlantic Ocean. Once complete, the ten-district city will boast a residential complex, mall, international hospital, and school, and, just as my father desired for the Lagoon development, a center of commerce, business, and finance that will stand as a beacon of success for all of Africa. However, one of the key differences between Eko and Chief's project is the partnership. Instead of one man working with *permission* from Lagos State, Eko Atlantic is a collaboration between the Lagos State Government, the federal government, and private investors from inside and outside of Nigeria. Some would say that the idea came from Chief. I believe wholeheartedly that it did.

Referring to Eko, I replied, "Yeah, the hotel is right next to it. I'll meet you at the conference after my swim. And if you can, please ask Obi if I can have some time with him. I'd like to discuss some topics related to our father."

"Yeah, I'll set it up," Kevin said.

After Kevin left, I pulled my swim fins out of my bag, headed down to the lobby, and jumped in a cab.

"Hey, brother, I'm going to Eko Hotel," I told the driver.

"Okay. Do you need a driver for the day or just a onetime drop-off?" he asked.

"Yeah, I can pay you for the day. What's your name?"

"Adefila."

"Yoruba, I take it?" I asked.

"Yes . . . you're American?"

Instead of answering, I just said my name, "Aderemi Adeleke."

He laughed and started speaking to me in Yoruba.

I stopped him. "Sorry, brother. I lost my native tongue a looooong time ago."

He sucked his teeth, then looked back in the rearview mirror and said, "You have to learn your native tongue."

"I know, I know. Maybe one day."

"Music?" Adefila asked.

"Yeah."

Like the airport the night before, the island was bustling. There were vehicles and people everywhere; old men conversed in circles of plastic chairs, scores of street vendors sold their goods, panhandlers and fruit stands lined the route, and taxi tricycles maneuvered dangerously around speeding cars. I soaked it all in as I videotaped my ride while nodding my head to Nigerian hip-hop.

The one thing that was eye-opening to me was the mixture of rich and poor. The poor were many, and the rich were few. But unlike most places in the States, they all operated and moved in the same space. I saw luxury high-rises and multimillion-dollar houses right next to shacks. I drove by my old private school, the British International School, which was walled off to keep out the solicitors that lined up along the outside walls.

The most common vehicles I saw throughout my trip were Range Rovers and Mercedes G trucks. Because of the condition of the roads, it made sense for the rich to drive those types of vehicles. The poor, on the other hand, had to make do with what they had. On multiple occasions during my ride, I watched as both kids and adults ran up to the windows of expensive vehicles and begged for money. It was a sight I had never seen before. Growing up in New York I saw panhandlers, but I had never witnessed groups of people—some kids, some adults with babies in their arms—who seemed so desperate that they would run out in the middle of traffic and plead for naira.

Another sad sight were kids who should have been in school but who were, instead, selling fruit on corners because their families needed them to work. *This is unacceptable!* I said to myself. My trip that started out with anger had shifted to joy and excitement and now to heartbreak. And keep in mind, I was in Lagos, the Nigerian city with the highest cost of living, so I could only imagine the plight of the rest of the country.

As I absorbed everything, I couldn't help but whisper to myself, "How the hell does this happen? Where is all the money from oil and cocoa and natural gas going?" Over the decades Mom had told me about the disparity between the poor and the rich, but I couldn't fully understand it until now.

Nigeria is not a poor African country by any means, but income inequality is one of the country's most serious problems. From oil alone the country generates more than $80 billion in revenue each year; yet according to an article written by Emmanuel Akinwotu and Sam Olukoya and published in the *Guardian*, 86 million Nigerians live in extreme poverty.[1] That's almost half of the population. In 2010, the number of Nigerian millionaires increased by 44 percent. The richest African on the continent is Nigerian tycoon Aliko Dangote, who has a net worth of $12.2 billion and, by the way, owns a mansion on Banana Island. However, the antipoverty organization Oxfam characterizes Nigeria's social spending (on health, education, and social protection) as "shamefully low" and "reflected in very poor social outcomes for its citizens." More than 4.7 million people in the region face food insecurity, and 49 percent of young people are either unemployed or underemployed in insufficient or part-time work. Oxfam put Nigeria dead last on a list of 152 countries committed to reducing inequality.[2]

"Adefila, can I ask you a question?" I said as I continued to stare out the car window.

"No problem, sir."

"With all due respect, and please forgive my ignorance, but what is going on with all this poverty? Help this ignorant American understand why I'm looking at all of *this* in such a rich country."

He laughed and said, "Corruption! Most people in government and social services *steal!*"

"That still goes on?" I asked.

He couldn't stop laughing. "Twenty billion dollars . . . GONE!"

"Excuse me?" I replied.

Adefila continued, "Yeah . . . under the last petroleum minister, twenty billion dollars went missing.[3] Do you know what could have been done with that money? The people it could have fed?"

"I'm sure a lot! Did anyone get arrested?"

As though I had said a joke, he laughed again. "No one ever gets arrested. And if they do, they just bribe the jailer or judge and get released. The people have gotten used to this. No one stands up. Oh, oh, oh, no—I'm wrong.

Those who are supposed to stand up, the politicians, only stand up when election time comes around. They hand out food to hungry people and make promises. The people vote them into office, then never see them stand up again until the next election year. But it is normal. And the rich . . . they like it the way it is."

"Why do you say that?" I asked.

"Because it's true. If there was equality, who would clean the toilet for a thousand naira a day? Who will drive? Who will nanny the kids for two meals a day . . . not pay, but meals?"

I couldn't help but ask, "What could be done, Ade?"

There was no laughter this time. He replied despondently, "Unless we get a benevolent dictator . . . there is nothing that can be done. Nothing will change."

The rest of the car ride was silent. When we pulled up to Eko, I gave Adefila a nice tip, exchanged WhatsApp numbers, and made my way to the pool.

My heart was broken because thirty years earlier corruption reigned and led to the seizing of my father's assets and our instant poverty. Today corruption still reigned. As I walked into the luxury hotel, I was greeted by the doorman, the custodian mopping the floor, and other service personnel. By my swimming at the luxury pool, I felt I was somehow in the wrong. Was I contributing to the problem? But what was I to do—turn around and say I wouldn't swim or stay in my luxury hotel or eat well because others couldn't? I didn't know. I was in a state of ambivalence.

Being a person who is wired to see an issue and deal with it, I let the wheels in my head turn as I got closer to the pool. *I'm going to swim, but after that I need to figure out a way to help fix this.* I thought and thought and thought.

I jumped into the pool and ran through the same hour-long swim routine I created before my second run at BUD/S. And as I swam, I tried to think of a solution to fix the corruption, but I couldn't come up with one. *There's nothing you can do. You're just one man, and you haven't even been here in thirty years! No one will respond to you. You'll be viewed as an arrogant American who thinks he knows it all. Just keep your mouth shut, go back to America, keep living your good life, and forget about what's going on here. That's the way it's been, and that's the way it will always be. Not even your father could change that. Roger that.* I continued swimming.

During the first thirty minutes of my swim, I was the only one in the pool; I had it all to myself. But halfway through, I saw a local kid who had to be about ten years old walk toward the pool in his swim trunks with his mother. Periodically, as I stroked, I would look up to see the kid watching me swim. When I finished one of my laps, his mom—who was in working clothes—sat down, and the kid jumped in and tried swimming diagonally in the shallow end from the east wall to the north wall. I say *tried* because, like my first swim session at the Camp Pendleton pool, he swung his arms like a windmill and kicked his legs violently, but despite all his effort, he barely moved.

Even though I didn't know the kid, I was so proud of him for getting in the water and at least trying. To encourage him, I waited for him to turn back in my direction, and when he did, I gave him a thumbs-up and said, "Good job." He didn't say anything; he just nervously nodded, and I went back to swimming.

After I was done, I changed and got ready to make my way out, but I felt this urging to go back to the boy. *Aw, man, this dude's mom is going to think I'm a pedophile. Please. I don't think it's a good idea to go up to him.*

I clenched my teeth, and instead of walking the short way back to the hotel exit, I walked the long way around so I could pass the kid. My timing was perfect. When I got to him, he had just finished a short fight to the side of the pool. He was huffing and puffing as though he were breathing through a straw.

"Hey . . . hey," I said as I quickly glanced up at his mom to make sure she didn't think I was doing anything inappropriate. He didn't say anything again; he just turned, faced me, and quickly wiped the water off of his face.

"I've done a lot of swimming in the past; can I help you?" I said.

Again, the kid didn't say anything; he just nervously nodded. I started to think he was a mute.

"Okay, so when you stroke like that [I made the motion he was making and continued] you're only fighting against the water. You don't want to fight the water, okay?"

He nodded again, so I continued, "You want to be smooth." I demonstrated smooth strokes with my arms. "Like this. Slow is smooth, smooth is fast. Don't fight the water; be one with the water. If you fight it, it will fight you. Do you understand me?"

He nodded. At this point I needed to find out if my new student was a mute or if he was really as nervous as he looked, so I asked him, "Okay, tell me what you're going to do."

His speech was like innocent beauty. I had always heard that when some Nigerians speak, it can sound like they're singing, but on that day I finally heard it firsthand. "I will do what you have said. . . . I will do what you have said."

I smiled and asked, "And what is that?"

He mimicked the motion I showed him and said, "I will not fight the water. . . . I will be smooth, and that will make me go faster."

I instantly felt like my whole life had prepared me for that moment. Without going through all that I had gone through, I wouldn't have been there to give that kid what he needed and to receive this priceless gift of hope from him. I wouldn't have been there if Lagos weren't the home I had to leave when everything was stolen; I wouldn't have been there if two movies by Michael Bay hadn't inspired my future; I wouldn't have been there if Petty Officer Reyes hadn't snuck me into the Navy; I wouldn't have been there if I hadn't learned how to swim at Camp Pendleton and gone through all I went through to become a SEAL; I wouldn't have been there if I hadn't transformed from darkness into light; and I wouldn't have been there if the project that took me there wasn't this book you're reading. Everything worked together to lead me to that moment with that boy.

Later I would meet with Obi and hear all about my father, things I never knew. Later I would sneak past the heavily guarded Banana Island gate with my brothers so I could stand on the land my father created. Later I would go on national Nigerian TV and radio and share my odds-defying story. But the highlight of my trip back to the beginning was my encounter with that young man by the pool. That moment reinforced the revelation that through my life, I may not be able to transform the land of my birth, and I definitely won't be able to transform the whole world, but I can influence those God places in front of me. And any little seed I can plant may be the one that generates the necessary transformation.

Seeing so much of myself in the kid, I gave him a huge smile and said, "That's right. Be smooth, my friend."

"Thank you, sir," the kid replied.

"You're welcome, buddy." *Now go off and do great things*, I thought, *and I'll be right beside you.*

AUTHOR'S NOTE

My Navy recruiter, Tiana Nadine Reyes, played a pivotal role in getting me into the Navy despite my background. If she hadn't taken the risk that she took, only God knows where I would be. With that said, I'd like to share an inspirational story about how I reconnected with her after *Transformed* was written.

About a year after my initial military enlistment, I lost contact with Tiana, and as the years passed, I completely forgot her name. When I wrote the early drafts of *Transformed*, I used a fictitious name for her, Petty Officer Mercado.

A week before my deadline I finished the last chapter of the book. My mom took the weekend to read it while I made last-minute edits.

After my mom read the chapter that describes Tiana sneaking me into the Navy, she said to me, "Remi, you know what's going to happen? This book is going to come out, and you're going to be somewhere doing a book signing, and Petty Officer Mercado is going to walk in and say, 'Remember me?' You're definitely going to see her again."

I looked at my mother and said, "I hope so, but I don't even remember her name. And it's been sixteen years. I may not even recognize her now." Just as I was finishing my statement, a thought popped into my head. *Remi, you received your military record when you separated from the Navy. It's sitting in your cabinet. You should be able to find her name in there.*

I yelled, "Mom! I think I know where to find her name." I got up and ran into my hallway. I threw open the cabinet, sifted through some papers, and within five minutes I found a recruiting page that she and I had signed. And below that, her signature was printed: Tiana N. Reyes.

"Ma, I found her name!" I said, full of excitement. "I'm going to google her. I'm sure she's on Facebook. And when I find her, I'm going to share how what she did wasn't in vain. I can't wait!"

With my heart racing I unlocked my phone, then typed in her full name and "Navy" into the search engine. Within seconds my excitement turned into sadness. I saw a link that read, "Tiana Forever in Our Hearts, Memory Of." I knew what that meant; she was no longer with us.

"What happened?" I said, full of anger and sadness.

I clicked on the link and discovered that on December 26, 2006—four and a half years after we met—she succumbed to a rare disease called myositis. She was only thirty years old.

As I scrolled through Tiana's memorial page, I saw that she was survived by her daughter, Ciara; her parents, Julie and Mario; and her brother, Anthony. With tears filling my eyes, I vowed that I would find her family, and whatever I could do to be as much of a blessing to them as Tiana was to me, I would do it. My emotions derived from the realization that she saved my life, and I couldn't hug her, thank her, or let her see the fruits of her decision.

On March 15, 2018, four days after discovering the bad news, I was on my way to Atlanta to help rectify a casting issue on a film I was helping out with. As I sat at the airport gate, a thought popped into my mind: *Why don't you start googling the names of her family members to try and find a way to contact them?* I followed the thought and started looking but quickly found that because of how common their names were, it was like finding a needle in a haystack. There were thousands of Mario, Anthony, and Julie Reyeses.

After further searching, I found an endowment page with a list of Tiana's family, friends, and coworkers who donated to her endowment. So I started googling the most uncommon names in hopes that I would be led to a social media page where I could send a direct message.

Right when I boarded the plane, I struck gold. I googled a woman by the name of Yvette. A phone number popped up for an event business that she ran. I stowed my bag, buckled my seat belt, and quickly dialed the number.

"Hello," a woman said.

"Hello, is this Yvette?" I replied.

She responded curiously in a thick New York accent, "Yesss. And who are you?"

"I know this sounds crazy, but . . ." I went on to explain what Tiana had done for me and how I was trying to get in contact with her family.

Amazed by what I shared, she said, "I'm Tiana's cousin. You have to talk to her brother, Anthony. I'm going to call him right now and give him your number. I'll tell him to call you right now, okay?"

"Okay, but hold on. My flight is about to take off, so tell him that if he calls and I don't pick up . . . just leave his number on my voicemail, and I'll call him back when I land."

"Where are you going?" Yvette asked.

"I'm flying to Atlanta."

"Atlanta! That's where he lives."

Wow! What are the odds? I thought. "Okay, okay, I'm going to try to connect with him in person when I land. I have to get off the phone. Thank you so much, Yvette."

By the time my flight landed, I had received a voicemail from Anthony. I immediately called him back, and we made arrangements to meet at his house. Within an hour of my landing, we were sitting on his back porch, talking about Tiana.

"Over the years," he said, "we've been contacted by other people who've said she did the same thing for them. Tiana would drive around the Bronx, find people she grew up with, pull them aside, and say, 'I see where your life is going. Come with me, and I'll get you into the military. Trust me: it will be good for you.' She knew that no one would give people like us a chance, so she went out and created the chances. Real talk, Remi: when I landed a few misdemeanors, she came home, gave me a stern talk, and the next thing I knew, I was in the Air Force. She loved people, and from the time she was small, all she wanted to do was help people."

We talked for two hours. As we reminisced about how Tiana got both of us into the military, it was further confirmed in my heart that it was God who guided me to the recruiting office that summer day in 2002, and right into Tiana's path. If any other recruiter would have run my background and found what she found, not only would I have been turned away, but my name would've been flagged, and I wouldn't have been able to join any branch of the service at any time. Tiana completely changed the trajectory of my story.

Now, here's the full-circle moment. After I left Anthony's house, I went to Alabama. The next morning I stood in an Alabama courtroom right next to a young African American man who was facing a twelve-year prison sentence. He was requested to be cast in a documentary I was helping out with, and there was a small chance that if the right people spoke on his behalf, he could be released into our custody, not only to be a part of the documentary but also to be rehabilitated by the mentors behind the project. As I stood in that courtroom and advocated on behalf of the young man, just as Tiana had done for me, I couldn't help but think about Tiana, her family, and the providential night of reminiscing. I know she was in heaven, smiling down on that courtroom because three weeks later the young man was released from jail and into our custody.

I've been asked by people who've heard Tiana's story, "How can I honor Tiana and her family?" My answer is to please consider donating to the Johns Hopkins Myositis Center at https://www.hopkinsmyositis.org/gift/. And please add to the donation memo, "Tiana Reyes Endowment." Due to the rare nature of this disease, the hospital doesn't often receive funds for myositis research. Through the Tiana Reyes Endowment the research team can allocate the monies at their discretion. To date, the investment has assisted the center's diagnostics and helped reduced the mortality rate by more than 40 percent since the time Tiana was initially misdiagnosed.

I want to thank Julie and Mario for raising such a giving, loving, and graceful woman. She was truly a gift to the world. I want to thank Ciara and Anthony for allowing me to share what Tiana did for me with the world. My hope is that her name will be known by many for as long as this earth is spinning.

ACKNOWLEDGMENTS

I have to be honest with you all. *Transformed* almost didn't happen. But it finally did, and I give credit to the following people for their support and, in some cases, constant push throughout the publishing process:

Jessica, I'm not the easiest man to be married to, but day after day you keep showing up. I'm always in awe of your strength, love, and grace. As you know, writing this book has been a roller-coaster ride, but you were right there with me every loop of the way. Thank you for your input; thank you for giving up the things that you wanted to do so I could do what I needed to do; thank you for allowing me to be transparent with my life before we met; and thank you for comforting the boys when they couldn't understand why Daddy had to stay in his office and write instead of helping put them to sleep. You are my warrior princess, and there is no way I could have written this book without your support. I love you.

Ma, thank you for giving me life. And thank you for never giving up, especially when we lost everything. People ask me all the time, "Remi, where do you get your perseverance and resilience from?" My answer will always be the same: "Throughout my entire life I've been blessed with the opportunity to witness a living example of perseverance and resilience." And that example has been you, Ma. Without you being who you are, I could never be who I am, and therefore this book would not be what it is. I love you, Ma.

Bayo, it's an honor to call you my brother. We've been through bad times and good times together. We've hated each other, and we've loved each other. We've called each other names, and we've prayed for each other. And now look at us: two successful men with families. Thank you for being by my side, and thank you for refreshing my memory as I wrote *Transformed*. I love you, bro.

Aunt Dokey, *wow*! You are a major catalyst in my life being what it is now. Without you withdrawing the money from your savings to help me get out of the mess I got myself into, who knows where I would be. Look at what that little $800 seed has grown into today. Your servant heart always inspires me. You will be my hero forever. I love you, Aunt Dokey. And happy one hundredth birthday!!!!!

Uncle Mike, you're the man! I'm sorry I couldn't squeeze any of our stories into the book. But I want you and the world to know that you've been an instrumental part of my life. You know this, but you were the very first person to recognize my potential and say, "Remi, you have a gift to inspire people. I'm proud of you." I will never forget that, and those words helped push me as I wrote this book. Thank you, Mr. Maxwell. I love you, Lauren and Jordan, always.

Uncle Carl, Aunt Des, and Xavier, when I first moved from Navy boot camp to San Diego, you were the only family I had in SOCAL. Thank you for taking me in and for always being there for me through the good times and bad. I love you.

Pastor Cedric Baltrip (Dominion Center Church) and Pastor Miles McPherson (The Rock Church), when I first came to faith in Christ, you both welcomed me into your churches and clearly instructed me. The foundation of my walk was built under your leadership, and, for that, I am eternally grateful. I hope that through the pages of this book, you are able to see the spiritual wisdom that you both imparted to me over the years.

Kathie Lee Gifford, I'm sorry, but I have to tell the world, YOU played the biggest role in the formation of this book. For years people told me, "Remi, your story is too inspiring for you not to write a book." Due to fear of what others might think of me if I wrote one, I said, "No, no, and no." And then I met you, Kathie. And not only did you verbally slap me upside my head for my hesitation and fear, but you walked me right to HarperCollins and told them, "You'd better sign this guy to a book deal now!" Thank you, Kathie. Thank you for helping me understand that it's more important to inspire many than to worry about the negative comments of the few. I am forever grateful.

Cody Gifford, ever since we met back in 2015, you've been a TRUE friend.

Thank you for being a sounding board anytime I ran into conflict. Thank you for always thinking of me every time you run into a person who makes you say, "I've got a guy you need to meet." And thank you for your prayers and guidance throughout the writing process. I'm looking forward to our decades of friendship.

Jon Land and Lindsay Preston: Jon, as you know, halfway through writing *Transformed* I didn't think I had it in me to finish. I hired you and Lindsay to take over, only to get the ball handed quickly back to me. Thank you for first showing, then telling, me that I was the only one who could write this book. You helped instill the confidence to keep writing, not give up, and not pass the responsibility off to another writer. Not many writers are willing to be so honest that their transparency costs them a job. So thank you, Jon.

Lindsay, thank you for your support and encouragement throughout the second half of writing the book. Your cheerleader-like e-mails motivated me to keep on going to and through the end. I already look forward to working with you on the prequel to *Transformed* (my mom's story).

Erin Healy, YOU ARE THE WOOO-MAN! I must be honest with you: before working with you, I had heard horror stories about the editing process. But you put all my fears to rest. I learned so much more about writing, storytelling, and even speaking through our editing meetings. Not only were you my editor, but you also became my teacher. Thank you for protecting my voice, and thank you for your constant grace and understanding. I greatly appreciate you, and I look forward to working with you on many more books in the future.

Reader, if you ever write a book and need an editor, HIRE ERIN HEALY!

Brad, I tell you, brother, you came on board at just the right time. Thank you for your selfless service to me and the company during the writing process. You helped manage my speaking engagements, acting opportunities, and even grabbed lunch *every day* so I could keep writing. I appreciate you, and I want you to know that what you think may have been a small role in the formation of this book was actually a *big* role. Thank you for your dedication to AE. I appreciate you, brother.

Michael Bay, I read somewhere that you "make movies to inspire the fifteen-year-old" (forgive me if I'm wrong or misquoted). Well, I was thirteen when *Bad Boys* came out and fourteen, almost fifteen, when *The Rock* was released. As a minister, I always try to relay to the congregants I speak to that sometimes it's not always about reaching the masses; sometimes it's about reaching that one person who will not only reach the masses but also affect generations. Your films have indeed fulfilled their mission in my life; they inspired a kid from the Bronx to achieve heights that I never could have imagined, and hopefully through my changed life and SEAL career, the effects of your inspiration in my life will inspire generations.

I also want to thank you for casting me in your films and subsequently carving out a second career path for me. And thank you for your continuing support of the military.

Naval Special Warfare, thank you for giving me the opportunity to serve among the greatest men and women on the face of this planet. Serving within your ranks not only equipped me for war but also for life. The skills you taught me have translated into my parenting, marriage, business, and writing. I would not be where I am today without the lessons you beat into me and also the warriors you allowed me to stand alongside.

I know a SEAL writing a book nowadays is considered the unpardonable sin within our community. But I hope that if you've read this book, you've seen my heart. And that it's not to get rich off the Trident but to inspire others, show young men and women in inner cities around the country that regardless of where they come from, it is possible to enter the ranks of SOF.

W Publishing, I would be lying if I didn't say we bumped heads *a lot*. But at the end of the day, your commitment made it possible to work through our issues, and now we have what we have—a *great* book. I know that the language and rawness in my story could turn off the majority of your market, so I thank you for supporting the way I needed to tell it. Daisy Hutton, Megan Dobson, and Paula Major, thank you for signing me, and thank you for your patience with me.

Readers, without you buying this book, all this would just be a diary. Thank you for being open to hearing my story. I hope you enjoyed the book, and, even more, I hope it inspires you to reach for dreams that you've thought might be impossible. God bless and much love.

NOTES

Chapter 3: Throne Overthrown

1. Transparency International, "Corruption Perceptions Index 2017," February 21, 2018, https://www.transparency.org/news/feature/corruption_perceptions_index_2017.

2. NDTV Offbeat Desk, "Millions Stolen in Nigeria. Accused: A Snake and Gang of Monkeys," NDTV, March 3, 2018, https://www.ndtv.com/offbeat/millions-stolen-in-nigeria-accused-a-snake-and-gang-of-monkeys-1819212; Adenike Akindude, "'Mysterious Fish' Swallows 52 Million Naira Government Fund in Abia," *Daily Family*, February 27, 2018, https://dailyfamily.ng/mysterious-fish-swallows-52-million-naira-government-fund-in-abia/.

Chapter 4: Coming to America

1. Food Research & Action Center, "Map: Poverty Rates by Congressional District," FRAC, accessed March 5, 2019, http://www.frac.org/research/resource-library/map-poverty-rates-congressional-district.

Chapter 5: Bad Times

1. Charles Hanson Towne, *The Rise and Fall of Prohibition: The Human Side of What the Eighteenth Amendment and the Volstead Act Have Done to the United States* (New York: Macmillan, 1923), 159–62.

2. Sean Gardiner, "Heroin: From the Civil War to the 1970s, and Beyond," CityLimits.org, July 5, 2009, https://citylimits.org/2009/07/05/heroin-from-the-civil-war-to-the-70s-and-beyond/.

3. US Drug Enforcement Administration, "1985–1990," https://www.dea.gov /sites/default/files/2018-07/1985-1990%20p%2058-67custom2.pdf, 58.

4. George James, "New York Killings Set a Record, While Other Crimes Fell in 1990," *New York Times*, April 23, 1991, https://www.nytimes.com/1991/04/23 /nyregion/new-york-killings-set-a-record-while-other-crimes-fell-in-1990.html.

5. Alvin Chang, "The Data Proves That School Segregation Is Getting Worse," Vox, March 5, 2018, https://www.vox.com/2018/3/5/17080218/school -segregation-getting-worse-data.

6. Joy Resmovits, "The Nation's Most Segregated Schools Aren't Where You'd Think They'd Be," *Huffington Post*, March 26, 2014, https://www .huffingtonpost.com/2014/03/26/new-york-schools-segregated_n_5034455 .html.

7. Ariel Jao, "Segregation, School Funding Inequalities Still Punishing Black, Latino Students," NBC News, January 12, 2018, https://www.nbcnews.com /news/latino/segregation-school-funding-inequalities-still-punishing-black -latino-students-n837186.

8. Janie Boschma and Ronald Brownstein, "The Concentration of Poverty in American Schools," *Atlantic*, February 29, 2016, https://www.theatlantic.com /education/archive/2016/02/concentration-poverty-american-schools/471414/.

9. Holly Yettick, "School Spending Increases Linked to Better Outcomes for Poor Students," *Education Week*, May 29, 2014, https://www.edweek.org/ew /articles/2014/05/29/33finance.h33.html.

10. Matt Barnum, "Less Money for Schools After the Recession Meant Lower Test Scores and Graduation Rates, Study Finds," *Chalkbeat*, January 12, 2018, https://www.chalkbeat.org/posts/us/2018/01/12/less-money-for-schools-after -the-recession-meant-lower-test-scores-and-graduation-rates-study-finds/.

Chapter 6: All I Ever Wanted

1. National Center for Fathering, "The Consequences of Fatherlessness," NCF, accessed May 19, 2018, http://www.fathers.com/statistics-and-research /the-consequences-of-fatherlessness/.

2. "Warning," words and music by Christopher Wallace, Osten Harvey, Hal David, and Burt Bacharach. © 1994 EMI April Music Inc., Justin Combs Publishing Company, Inc., Big Poppa Music, Bee Mo Easy Music, BMG Rights Management (UK) Ltd. and New Hidden Valley Music. All rights for Justin Combs Publishing Company, Inc., Big Poppa Music and Bee Mo Easy Music administered by Sony/ATV Music Publishing LLC, 424 Church Street,

Suite 1200, Nashville, TN 37219. All rights for BMG Rights Management (UK) Ltd. and New Hidden Valley Music Co. administered by BMG Rights Management (US) LLC. International copyright secured. All rights reserved—contains elements of "Walk On By" by Burt Bacharach and Hal David. *Reprinted by permission of Hal Leonard LLC.*

3. "Juicy" by Christopher Wallace, Jean-Claude Olivier, Sean Combs, and James Mtume. © 1994 EMI April Music Inc., Big Poppa Music, and Justin Combs Publishing Company Inc., & Publishers Unknown. All rights on behalf of EMI April Music Inc., Big Poppa Music, and Justin Combs Publishing Company Inc. administered by Sony/ATV Music Publishing LLC, 424 Church Street, Suite 1200, Nashville, TN 37219. All rights reserved. Used by permission. "Juicy" by Christopher Wallace, Jean-Claude Olivier, Sean Combs, and James Mtume. © 1994 Jumping Bean Songs & Publishers Unknown. All rights on behalf of Jumping Bean Songs administered by Sony/ATV Music Publishing LLC, 424 Church Street, Suite 1200, Nashville, TN 37219. All rights reserved. Used by permission.

4. "Ol' Man River," from *Show Boat*, lyrics by Oscar Hammerstein II, music by Jerome Kern. © 1927 Universal-Polygram International Publishing, Inc. Copyright renewed. All rights reserved. Used by permission. *Reprinted by permission of Hal Leonard LLC.*

Chapter 15: Affirmation

1. Paraphrase of remarks made by Hunter S. Thompson: "The Edge . . . There is no honest way to explain it because the only people who really know where it is are the ones who have gone over." *Hells Angels: A Strange and Terrible Saga* (New York: Ballantine, 1966), 271.

Chapter 17: Exactly Where I Needed to Be

1. Matthew 23:12 NIV.

Chapter 18: Everything Works Out

1. Matthew 23:12 NIV.

Chapter 22: The Wilderness

1. Romans 1:20 NLT.

2. "Next Lifetime," words and music by Erica Wright and Anthony Scott. © 1997 by Universal Music-MGB Songs, Divine Pimp Publishing and The

Little Fat Boy Done Good! Publishing. All rights for Divine Pimp Publishing administered by Universal Music-MGB Songs. International copyright secured. All rights reserved. *Reprinted by permission of Hal Leonard LLC.* "Next Lifetime," words and music by Anthony Scott [and other writers]. Published by Little Fat Boy Done Good / Reach Global (UK) Ltd. All print rights in the U.S. administered by Reach Music Publishing, Inc. All rights reserved.

Chapter 23: The Ultimate Transformation

1. John 9:25 NIV.
2. 2 Corinthians 5:17 NKJV.

Chapter 24: The Chameleon

1. Advance Liaison Team (ADVON).

Chapter 25: Warrior Prince

1. John Hurt as the War Doctor, "The Day of the Doctor," *Dr. Who*, BBC, November 23, 2013.
2. Modular lightweight load-carrying equipment (MOLLE).
3. Intelligence, surveillance, reconnaissance (ISR).

Chapter 26: Now I Can Go Home

1. Richard Grenier, "Perils of Passive Sex," *Washington Times*, April 6, 1993, F3. See also https://quoteinvestigator.com/2011/11/07/rough-men/.

Chapter 29: Back to the Beginning

1. Emmanuel Akinwotu and Sam Olukoya, "'Shameful' Nigeria: A Country That Doesn't Care About Inequality," *Guardian*, July 18, 2017, https://www.theguardian.com/inequality/2017/jul/18/shameful-nigeria-doesnt-care-about-inequality-corruption.
2. Oxfam International, "Welcome to Our 'Commitment to Reducing Inequality Index,'" Oxfam, accessed August 9, 2018, https://actions.oxfam.org/international/inequality-index/petition/.
3. See PBS NewsHour, "How a Cancer of Corruption Steals Nigerian Oil, Weapons and Lives," YouTube video, 4:00, https://www.youtube.com/watch?v=_r5PWtPB_og.

ABOUT THE AUTHOR

R emi Adeleke was born in western Africa, but following his father's death, he and his mother and brother relocated permanently to the Bronx in New York City. After years of making regrettable decisions, Remi joined the Navy in 2002 and later became a Navy SEAL. Ending his successful naval career in 2016, he was led to pursue a career in writing, speaking, and acting. Remi holds a bachelor's degree in organizational leadership and a master's degree in strategic leadership, both from the University of Charleston. He resides in Southern California with his wife, Jessica, and their three sons, Cayden, Caleb, and Carter, and daughter, Ciana.

Follow Remi on Instagram @remiadeleke